GLOBAL
MARKETING
PERSPECTIVES

Jagdish N. Sheth
Brooker Professor of Research
Graduate School of Business
University of Southern California

Abdolreza Eshghi
Associate Professor of Marketing
Bentley College

Published by

SOUTH-WESTERN PUBLISHING CO.

GN63AA

CINCINNATI   WEST CHICAGO, IL   CARROLLTON, TX   LIVERMORE, CA

PREFACE

As more and more industries begin to operate in a global economy, international marketing has become increasingly important in ensuring corporate profits and growth. Indeed, excess capacity, intense competition, and saturated domestic markets often require a corporation to think internationally on a proactive basis. Market leaders in each industry often discover that a significant share of their sales and revenues come from nondomestic markets.

At the same time, companies can experience significant difficulties and encounter numerous marketing failures as they expand from domestic to international markets. Extending a successful marketing program to international markets often does not guarantee success. Just as we need to understand the domestic environment and develop marketing programs that are compatible with it, we need to understand and appreciate the international context of marketing.

This volume is designed to supplement standard textbooks on marketing management for the MBA program, as well as for the advanced undergraduate level. It is intended to fulfill the accreditation requirements of internationalizing the required courses in business schools.

The volume is prepared to serve the following educational needs in marketing.

- It details the complexity of international environment, especially as it relates to global competition, government rules and regulations, public opinion, and cross cultural differences among markets.
- It provides a strategic and managerial perspective on international marketing.
- It spells out when—and whether—to extend or adjust the marketing mix (product, price, distribution, promotion, and customer service) in the international context.
- It includes an annotated bibliography, which will facilitate self-study or special projects related to international marketing.

A number of criteria were utilized in selecting the papers for this volume.

- They must have a managerial orientation.
- They must be practical and relevant to marketing practice as illustrated by case histories and real world examples.
- The papers must be well recognized for their contribution to the field.
- The authors must represent a perspective that is worldwide rather than limited to just the U.S.

Although the volume is designed to supplement the required marketing courses at the MBA and the advanced undergraduate levels, it also can satisfy the needs of Executive M.B.A. programs, as well as corporate executive seminars on international marketing.

We are grateful to Ramona Newman, now a Ph.D. student at the University of Illinois, Urbana, for her invaluable assistance in searching for articles and references included in this volume.

The editors and the Publisher are also grateful to the authors and publishers who granted permission to reprint articles included in this volume.

Jagdish N. Sheth
Abdolreza Eshghi

CONTENTS

INTRODUCTION

Why Companies Go International

There are several reasons why companies consider going international. The first, and probably most common, reason is lack of growth in the domestic market. This is especially true among companies that market mature products or services in a mature economy. In the U.S., for example, processed foods, appliances, industrial raw materials, public education, and public services all fall into this category. A corporation's growth objectives make many foreign markets very attractive, especially those of the newly emerging industrial countries such as Korea, Italy, Brazil, India, and China.

A second major reason for entering international markets is the existence of sharp experience curves and economies of scale in certain technologies and products. For example, electronics and biogenetic technologies are presumed to have significant economies of scale. Therefore, the marginal cost is low enough to consider going global and creating markets for products through a low-price, high-quality strategy. This strategy has been clearly demonstrated in the semiconductors industry, consumer electronics, and telecommunications.

A third major reason for going global is competition. Often an offshore manufacturer enters the domestic market with a successful marketing strategy. This encourages the domestic market leader to enter foreign markets, partly to retaliate against the new entrant and partly to position itself strategically to protect its domestic market. Clearly, this has been the response by several U.S. automobile companies as the Japanese and the Koreans successfully entered the U.S. automobile market. Several computer and telecommunications companies seem to have reacted similarly as foreign competitors enter the U.S. market upon the deregulation of the industry and the break-up of the Bell System's vertical integration.

Finally, some companies position themselves as niche marketers. Therefore, their unique position in a given product or market niche can be easily extended all over the world. For example, BMW and Porsche have become worldwide niche car marketers. The same is true of fashion houses, cosmetics, and pharmaceutical companies.

We summarize the diverse reasons for going international in Figure I.1.

It is unfortunate that most U.S. companies do not think of global markets and worldwide marketing orientation on a proactive basis. Instead, as discussed above, it is often a reaction to some external factor that motivates them to think international. This often results in developing crash international marketing programs that are based upon undergraduate market research. Such strategies consist of poor planning, wrong alignments with distributors or manufacturers, and, in general, implementation problems. Therefore, there are far more international marketing blunders than necessary or desirable, not because the foreign markets are unattractive or the product is inappropriate. Blunders and failures result from a reactive rather than a proactive process of going international.

Figure I.1

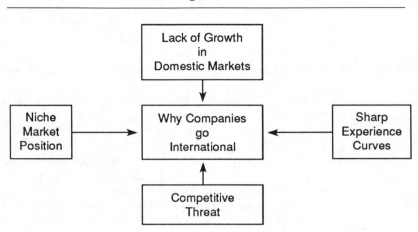

One of the key decisions a company has to make in international marketing is whether to extend its already existing, successful marketing programs (product, price, promotion, distribution, and service) or to customize them for each foreign market. There are strong advocates on either side of the issue. For example, Theodore Levitt argues that we must move away from customized products in each country and move toward standardized products that are advanced, functional, reliable—and low priced. Levitt strongly believes that the extraordinary worldwide success of Japanese companies across such industries as consumer electronics, watches, and automobiles is due to their ability to produce and market standardized, high quality but low priced products.

On the other hand, several scholars, including John Queleh and Richard Hoff, argue that international marketing is not simple. The real issue is not whether to go global but how to tailor the global marketing concept to fit each business and how to make it work. They provide a framework based on several factors: Products that enjoy economics of scale and are not grounded culturally tend to get global standardization. Good marketing ideas built around core products tend to become global. Examples are Marlboro's cowboy image, Walt Disney's amusement parks, and IBM computers. Finally, smaller and/or poor performing foreign markets are excellent targets for standardization.

The controversy over globalization vs. customization is not likely to be resolved soon. There are too many exceptions to each position. In our opinion, *within-country differences* in customers needs (biogenic and psychosenic) and customer resources (money, time, and expertise) often are larger than *between-country differences*. Therefore, the best marketing strategy may be to (1) segment the total world market on a set of common demographic or psychographic criteria and (2) examine the size of each segment across national boundaries. This strategy may make it possible to develop a global marketing strategy for a segment across all relevant country markets. In other words, there are no global markets but only global segments of a market. Figure I.2 illustrates this perspective.

Figure I.2

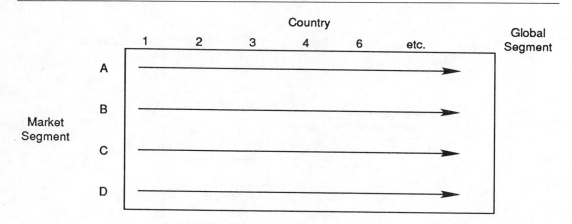

For example, a teenager segment for beverages, rock concerts, and fashion is likely to be global, whether the teenagers are living in the U.S., Europe, Japan, the USSR, and even China and India. The size of the teenage market, however, is likely to be different, depending on total population and age distribution in each country.

What Determines Within-Country vs. Between-Country Differences? _____

The way to assess within-country vs. between-country differences in market needs/wants and market resources depends on a number of environmental factors that have an impact on international marketing practices. We have developed the following framework, which attempts to consolidate the vast number of ad-hoc country specific differences (Figure I.3).

Perhaps the single most relevant dimension for global marketing is a country's level of economic development. The more economically developed a nation, the greater the degree of modernization and standardization of its markets, especially its industrial and commercial markets. Even consumer markets become more standardized as people's work, leisure, and life-styles become more homogenized by economic development and utilization of technology, especially the infrastructure technologies.

Of course, standardization through modernization can be mitigated by strong cultural differences between countries, especially if social institutions vary significantly both within and between countries. For example, as a social institution, religion has a great deal of control over people's values and behavior. A single-religion country such as Pakistan or Israel is, therefore, likely to have less within-country differences than a multi-religion society such as India or the United States. Similarly, a country with a homogeneous family structure is less likely to have within-country differences than a country with multiple family structures. In this regard, Japan is culturally more homogeneous than either the United States or many of the African countries, which have diverse tribes and family structures.

Figure I.3

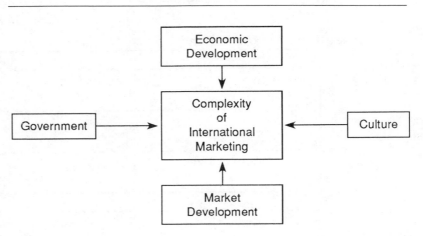

A third major environmental force is the government and its economic policy. This is especially critical in less developed countries that are committed to industrialization. It is also very important in many of the advanced countries, such as Germany and Japan, whose governments have traditionally tended to work together with their industries toward a common national industrial policy. The role of the government is also critical at the tactical level as well as the policy level. At the tactical level, the government determines tax structure, tariffs, product safety rules and regulations, promotion, and, in general, marketing practices. Furthermore, a host government often imposes special rules and regulations on foreign multinationals and their marketing practices.

Finally, the marketing environment varies significantly across countries because of differences in market development. In some countries, markets are highly mature and competitive, with a handful of large companies dominating the market. In other countries, markets are highly fragmented and emerging, having numerous local competitors, each of which controls a very small share of the market. It is obvious that competitive marketing strategies, including the marketing mix, will vary significantly between these environments.

The environment of global marketing tends to be more emotional than manufacturing or finance for a number of reasons. First, marketing practices carry a number of socially negative taboos in many countries and cultures because of its association with trading and selling. Second, the impact of marketing on people's values and behaviors is more tangible, visible, and often dramatic. It clearly reflects changes in people's cultural traditions and, therefore, is subject to social criticism. For example, the use of infant milk formula in many less developed countries has brought about a significant shift in breast feeding practices and hence has been subject to suspicion, mistrust, and accusations.

Finally, marketing utilizes public resources, such as mass media, and attempts to use both politics and public relations. Such strategies are often regarded as intrusive, insensitive, morally offensive, and even nondemocratic. In other words, marketing is presumed to be a powerful tool for making people do things contrary to their beliefs and values. It is, therefore, watched more carefully by social critics and government representatives than many other business activities.

Framework for Strategy Decisions _____

Developing an international marketing strategy is a complex task. So many factors are likely to play a significant role in shaping the strategy. This requires a framework that can capture the differences and summarize them into one or two underlying dimensions. The framework in Figure I.4 seems especially useful for making global marketing strategy decisions.

Clearly, in businesses where the advantages of standardized marketing (economies of scale, ease of operation, and/or organization structure) are enormous and the need for localized marketing is absent (lack of cultural, government, or competitive differences), global marketing practices will be very relevant. This is generally true for industrial machinery, computer, automotive, and commercial aircraft industries.

On the other hand, if businesses that have no scale advantages or in which standardization is likely to be very difficult must localize due to social, government or competitive reasons, it is much better for them to use a customized or localized marketing strategy. This is very true of processed foods, steel, cement, and retail trade.

If businesses gain low advantages from standardized marketing and they do not need to localize, it is better for them to adopt a multinational marketing strategy. In this instance, regional marketing is practiced by grouping countries that are physically proximate to one another. In other words, North America, Asia, Europe, Latin America, etc., may become separate multinational markets. This is generally found to be true for medical equipment, synthetic fibers, and cash dispensers.

Figure I.4

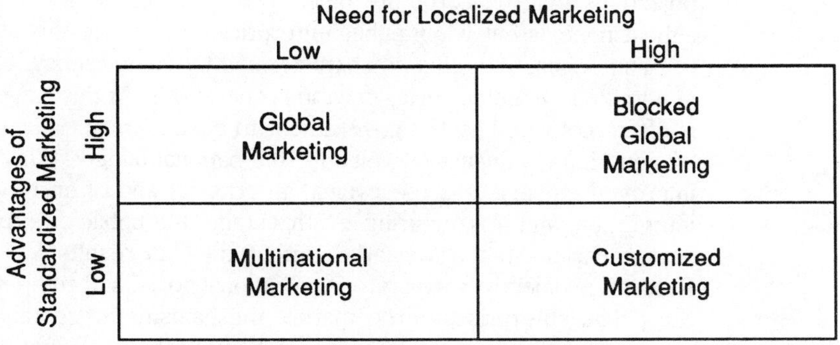

	Need for Localized Marketing	
	Low	High
High	Global Marketing	Blocked Global Marketing
Low	Multinational Marketing	Customized Marketing

Advantages of Standardized Marketing

Finally, some businesses gain significant economic advantages from standardized marketing practices but at the same time feel they are under a significant necessity to localize marketing practices. We find in these situations a true tradeofff, referred to as blocked global marketing strategy. Such businesses should use public opinion and politics to remove the need for localized marketing. For example, telecommunications and airline industries clearly can benefit from global marketing practices, but social and political reasons force them to be localized. It is possible to leverage government-to-government relationships to remove the need for localized marketing practices.

We hope this framework will be useful to students and instructors when they conduct field studies or examine case histories.

Marketing for Public Enterprises

The relevance of the marketing concept to public enterprises becomes very important in international marketing for several reasons. First, in most other countries, public-sector enterprises participate more actively in market processes through government ownership and management of businesses. For example, in most countries, railroads, telephones, military, public utilities, airlines, banking, and mass media are government owned and controlled. Such countries include Western Europe, Canada, Japan, and other advanced countries. Second, in many third world countries, the public sector often contributes a significant part of the total GNP. For example, in countries like India and China, the public sector is a very significant factor of the economy. Finally, in many advanced but smaller countries such as Singapore, Israel, Norway, and Denmark, government trade boards regulate private sector businesses.

Is it possible to extend marketing concepts to the economic and marketing practices of the public enterprises, in view of the fact that the traditional concepts of self-interest, profit motive, and markets as regulators are often not present?

In a very unique paper, Rao and Tagat suggest that public enterprises become more marketing driven as they evolve from the sheltered phase to the supportive phase and finally to the self-propelling phase of development. The sheltered phase consists of domination of national goals over corporate goals, rigid accountability for corporate policy and operations, and performance evaluation based more on national objectives than on corporate objectives. The marketing concepts are, therefore, almost nonexistent when public enterprises are still at this stage of development.

The supportive stage is characterized by complacency, excess capacity, and in general, micro-inefficiencies in various operations. At this stage, the public enterprise is often motivated by the government to become financially and fiscally responsible by generating a financial surplus for the national budget. This is achieved by setting improved efficiency as the evaluation criteria, and often results in reorganization, integration, and restructuring. At this stage, the public enterprise not only becomes cost conscious but also market oriented. This results in a number of changes. Enterprise objectives separate from national goals, and competition is created among the public enterprises. Free market mechanisms are established for products or services. High degree of autonomy is given to the public enterprise. Finally, product differentiation, market segmentation, and price changes become the operating norms for the marketing function.

The final stage is self-propelling. The public enterprise now begins to become fully market driven by focusing on its effectiveness as a business enterprise and adapting to changing socioeconomic, technological, and political dimensions. At this stage, corporate policy becomes distinctly separate from national goals. The corporate image becomes crystallized. Strategic planning of the public enterprise's activities becomes prevalent. Marketing activities become well delineated laterally and become interwoven vertically with corporate strategy. The marketing orientation looks beyond the traditional product-market matrix and begins to become a multi-technology, multi-product, and multi-market firm through diversification strategies.

Rao and Tagat also provide the traditional product portfolio analysis, with the hypothesis that at the sheltered stage, the public enterprise primarily possesses dogs and question mark businesses; at the supportive stage it shifts toward question marks and stars; and finally, at the self-propelling stage, it is dominated by stars and cash cow businesses.

There are a number of reasons why marketing orientation is likely to emerge in public enterprises. First, most governments are spinning them off as separate business enterprises for reasons of efficiency or effectiveness. The privatization of British Telecom, British Petroleum, and London Heathrow Airport by the British government is a good indication of this trend. And the trend is not limited to advanced countries. Recently, many less developed nations, such as India, Philippines, Malaysia, and others, have announced their plans to privatize their telecommunications industries.

Second, public enterprises have come to recognize that excess capacity and public opinion are serious challenges to maintaining traditional practices and structures. They are beginning to recognize that a customer-driven, market-oriented corporate culture may be more appropriate to better capacity utilization and a better public image. For example, in many regulated but competitive industries, such as airlines, railroads, agriculture, and industrial materials, public enterprises are becoming more market-driven instead of remaining resource-driven.

Finally, public enterprises are becoming multinational and global in their market-product scope. Therefore, national monopolies and domestic government sheltering seem less and less relevant to their international operations. This is clearly experienced by many French, Italian, Brazilian and Indian multinationals, which have emerged from the public enterprise sector of their domestic markets.

The diagram in Figure I.5 summarizes the four major forces behind a worldwide trend toward the use of marketing practices among government owned and managed public enterprises.

Book Summary _____

This volume on international marketing consists of four parts. Part I focuses on the nature and scope of international marketing, discussing the trade-offs involved in choosing between global and customized marketing programs and practices across

Figure I.5

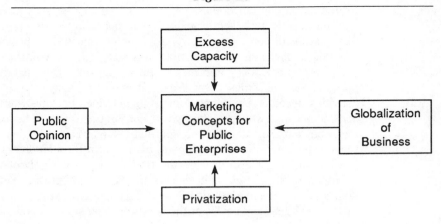

countries. Part II describes the international environment for marketing practice. The role of marketing as a social institution is likely to vary significantly from country to country. Therefore, certain marketing practices acceptable in one country may be irritating in others. These practices include haggling over prices, business negotiation tactics, bribery, and reciprocity business, as well as questionable selling and advertising practices. It is important to understand the public's social sensitivities with regard to marketing tools as well as to conduct market research that will be acceptable to each country.

Part III focuses on global competition and competitive strategies. For example, the recent successful marketing practices of the Japanese multinationals clearly point out the need for a long-term global perspective with respect to product design, cross subsidization, market prices designed to gain market share, and strong investment in R & D. It also requires a more fundamental decision with respect to international market expansion: should a company concentrate its marketing efforts on a few countries and a few segments of the market or should it diversify into multiple countries and multiple segments within each country?

Part IV discusses the special topic of the relevance of the marketing concept to public enterprises. We have chosen to focus on this special topic in this volume because a large part of world markets are managed by government enterprises.

I ——— THE NATURE AND SCOPE OF GLOBAL MARKETING ———

The Globalization of Markets
Theodore Levitt

Customizing Global Marketing
John A. Quelch and Richard J. Hoff.

1. The Globalization of Markets

THEODORE LEVITT

Mr. Levitt is Edward W. Carter Professor of Business Administration and head of the marketing area at the Harvard Business School. This is Mr. Levitt's twenty-third article for HBR; his classic "Marketing Myopia," first published in 1960, was reprinted in September-October 1975, and his last article was "Marketing Intangible Products and Product Intangibles" (May-June 1981).

Many companies have become disillusioned with sales in the international marketplace as old markets become saturated and new ones must be found. How can they customize products for the demands of new markets? Which items will consumers want? With wily international competitors breathing down their necks, many organizations think that the game just isn't worth the effort.

In this powerful essay, the author asserts that well-managed companies have moved from emphasis on customizing items to offering globally standardized products that are advanced, functional, reliable—and low priced. Multinational companies that concentrated on idiosyncratic consumer preferences have become befuddled and unable to take in the forest because of the trees. Only global companies will achieve long-term success by concentrating on what everyone wants rather than worrying about the details of what everyone *thinks* they might like.

A powerful force drives the world toward a converging commonality, and that force is technology. It has proletarianized communication, transport, and travel. It has made isolated places and impoverished people eager for modernity's allurements. Almost everyone everywhere wants all the things they have heard about, seen, or experienced via the new technologies.

The result is a new commercial reality—the emergence of global markets for standardized consumer products on a previously unimagined scale of magnitude. Corporations geared to this new reality benefit from enormous economies of scale in production, distribution, marketing, and management. By translating these benefits into reduced world prices, they can decimate competitors that still live in the disabling grip of old assumptions about how the world works.

Gone are accustomed differences in national or regional preference. Gone are the days when a company could sell last year's models—or lesser versions of advanced products—in the less-developed world. And gone are the days when prices, margins, and profits abroad were generally higher than at home.

The globalization of markets is at hand. With that, the multinational commercial world nears its end, and so does the multinational corporation.

The multinational and the global corporation are not the same thing. The multinational corporation operates in a number of countries, and adjusts its products and practices in each—at high relative costs. The global corporation operates with resolute constancy—at low relative cost—as if the entire world (or major regions of it) were a single entity; it sells the same things in the same way everywhere.

Which strategy is better is not a matter of opinion but of necessity. Worldwide communications carry everywhere the constant drumbeat of modern possibilities to lighten and enhance work, raise living standards, divert, and entertain. The same countries that ask the world to recognize and respect the individuality of their cultures insist on the wholesale transfer to them of modern goods, services, and technologies. Modernity is not just a wish but also a widespread practice among those who cling, with unyielding passion or religious fervor, to ancient attitudes and heritages.

Who can forget the televised scenes during the 1979 Iranian uprisings of young men in fashionable French-cut trousers and silky body shirts thirsting with raised modern weapons for blood in the name of Islamic fundamentalism?

In Brazil, thousands swarm daily from pre-industrial Bahian darkness into exploding coastal cities, there quickly to install television sets in crowded corrugated huts and, next to battered Volkswagens, make sacrificial offerings of fruit and fresh-killed chickens to Macumban spirits by candlelight.

During Biafra's fratricidal war against the Ibos, daily televised reports showed soldiers carrying bloodstained swords and listening to transistor radios while drinking Coca-Cola.

In the isolated Siberian city of Krasnoyarsk, with no paved streets and censored news, occasional Western travelers are stealthily propositioned for cigarettes, digital watches, and even the clothes off their backs.

The organized smuggling of electronic equipment, used automobiles, western clothing, cosmetics, and pirated movies into primitive places exceeds even the thriving underground trade in modern weapons and their military mercenaries.

A thousand suggestive ways attest to the ubiquity of the desire for the most advanced things that the world makes and sells—goods of the best quality and reliability at the lowest price. The world's needs and desires have been irrevocably homogenized. This makes the multinational corporation obsolete and the global corporation absolute.

Living in the Republic of Technology

Daniel J. Boorstin, author of the monumental trilogy *The Americans,* characterized our age as driven by "the Republic of Technology [whose] supreme law . . . is convergence, the tendency for everything to become more like everything else."

In business, this trend has pushed markets toward global commonality. Corporations sell standardized products in the same way everywhere—autos, steel, chemicals, petroleum, cement, agricultural commodities and equipment, industrial and commercial construction, banking and insurance services, computers, semiconductors, transport, electronic instruments, pharmaceuticals, and telecommunications, to mention some of the obvious.

Nor is the sweeping gale of globalization confined to these raw material or high-tech products, where the universal language of customers and users facilitates standardization. The transforming winds whipped up by the proletarianization of communication and travel enter every crevice of life.

Commercially, nothing confirms this as much as the success of McDonald's from the Champs Elysées to the Ginza, of Coca-Cola in Bahrain and Pepsi-Cola in Moscow, and of rock music, Greek salad, Hollywood movies, Revlon cosmetics, Sony televisions, and Levi jeans everywhere. "High-touch" products are as ubiquitous as high-tech.

Starting from opposing sides, the high-tech and the high-touch ends of the commercial spectrum gradually consume the undistributed middle in their cosmopolitan orbit. No one is exempt and nothing can stop the process. Everywhere everything gets more and more like everything else as the world's preference structure is relentlessly homogenized.

Consider the cases of Coca-Cola and Pepsi-Cola, which are globally standardized products sold everywhere and welcomed by everyone. Both successfully cross multitudes of national, regional, and ethnic taste buds trained to a variety of deeply ingrained local preferences of taste, flavor, consistency, effervescence, and after-taste. Everywhere both sell well. Cigarettes, too, especially American-made, make year-to-year global inroads on territories previously held in the firm grip of other, mostly local, blends.

These are not exceptional examples. (Indeed their global reach would be even greater were it not for artificial trade barriers.) They exemplify a general drift toward the homogenization of the world and how companies distribute, finance, and price products.[1] Nothing is exempt. The products and methods of the industrialized world play a single tune for all the world, and all the world eagerly dances to it.

Ancient differences in national tastes or modes of doing business disappear. The commonality of preference leads inescapably to the standardization of products, manufacturing, and the institutions of trade and commerce. Small nation-based markets transmogrify and expand. Success in world competition turns on efficiency in production, distribution, marketing, and management, and inevitably becomes focused on price.

The most effective world competitors incorporate superior quality and reliability into their cost structures. They sell in all national markets the same kind of products sold at home or in their largest export market. They compete on the basis of appropriate value—the best combinations of price, quality, reliability, and delivery for products that are globally identical with respect to design, function, and even fashion.

That, and little else, explains the surging success of Japanese companies dealing worldwide in a vast variety of products—both tangible products like steel, cars, motorcycles, hi-fi equipment, farm machinery, robots, microprocessors, carbon fibers, and now even textiles, and intangibles like banking, shipping, general contracting, and soon computer software. Nor are high-quality and low-cost operations incompatible, as a host of consulting organizations and data engineers argue with vigorous vacuity. The reported data are incomplete, wrongly analyzed, and contradictory. The truth is that low-cost operations are the hallmark of corporate cultures that require and produce quality in all that they do. High quality and low costs are not opposing postures. They are compatible, twin identities of superior practice.[2]

To say that Japan's companies are not global because they export cars with left-side drives to the United States and the European continent, while those in Japan have right-side drives, or because they sell office machines through distributors in the United States but directly at home, or speak Portuguese in Brazil is to mistake a difference for a distinction. The same is true of Safeway and Southland retail chains operating effectively in the Middle East, and to not only native but also imported populations from Korea, the Philippines, Pakistan, India, Thailand, Britain, and the United States. National rules of the road differ, and so do distribution channels and languages. Japan's distinction is its unrelenting push for economy and value enhancement. That translates into a drive for standardization at high quality levels.

Vindication of the Model T

If a company forces costs and prices down and pushes quality and reliability up— while maintaining reasonable concern for suitability—customers will prefer its world-standardized products. The theory holds, at this stage in the evolution of globalization, no matter what conventional market research and even common sense may suggest about different national and regional tastes, preferences, needs, and institutions. The Japanese have repeatedly vindicated this theory, as did Henry Ford with the Model T. Most important, so have their imitators including companies from South Korea (television sets and heavy construction), Malaysia (personal calculators and microcomputers), Brazil (auto parts and tools), Colombia (apparel), Singapore (optical equipment), and yes, even from the United States (office copiers, computers, bicycles, castings), Western Europe (automatic washing machines), Rumania (housewares), Hungary (apparel), Yugoslavia (furniture), and Israel (pagination equipment).

Of course, large companies operating in a single nation or even a single city don't standardize everything they make, sell, or do. They have product lines instead of a single product version, and multiple distribution channels. There are neighborhood, local, regional, ethnic, and institutional differences, even within metropolitan areas. But although companies customize products for particular market segments, they know that success in a world with homogenized demand requires a search for sales opportunities in similar segments across the globe in order to achieve the economies of scale necessary to compete.

Such a search works because a market segment in one country is seldom unique; it has close cousins everywhere precisely because technology has homogenized the globe. Even small local segments have their global equivalents everywhere and become subject to global competition, especially on price.

The global competitor will seek constantly to standardize his offering everywhere. He will digress from this standardization only after exhausting all possibilities to retain it, and he will push for reinstatement of standardization whenever digression and divergence have occured. He will never assume that the customer is a king who knows his own wishes.

Trouble increasingly stalks companies that lack clarified global focus and remain inattentive to the economics of simplicity and standardization. The most endangered companies in the rapidly evolving world tend to be those that dominate rather small domestic markets with high value-added products for which there are smaller markets elsewhere. With transportation costs proportionately low, distant competitors will enter the now-sheltered markets of those companies with goods produced more cheaply under scale-efficient conditions. Global competition spells the end of domestic territoriality, no matter how diminutive the territory may be.

ECONOMIES OF SCOPE

One argument that opposes globalization says that flexible factory automation will enable plants of massive size to change products and product features quickly, without stopping the manufacturing process. These factories of the future could thus produce broad lines of customized products without sacrificing the scale economies that come from long production runs of standardized items. Computer-aided design and manufacturing (CAD/CAM), combined with robotics, will create a new equipment and process technology (EPT) that will make small plants located close to their markets as efficient as large ones located distantly. Economies of scale will not dominate, but rather economies of scope—the ability of either large or small plants to produce great varieties of relatively customized products at remarkably low costs. If that happens, customers will have no need to abandon special preferences.

I will not deny the power of these possibilities. But possibilities do not make probabilities. There is no conceivable way in which flexible factory automation can achieve the scale economies of a modernized plant dedicated to mass production of standardized lines. The new digitized equipment and process technologies are available to all. Manufacturers with minimal customization and narrow product-line breadth will have costs far below those with more customization and wider lines.

When the global producer offers his lower costs internationally, his patronage expands exponentially. He not only reaches into distant markets, but also attracts customers who previously held to local preferences and now capitulate to the attractions of lesser prices. The strategy of standardization not only responds to worldwide homogenized markets but also expands those markets with aggresive low pricing. The new technological juggernaut taps an ancient motivation—to make one's money go as far as possible. This is universal—not simply a motivation but actually a need.

The Hedgehog Knows _____

The difference between the hedgehog and the fox, wrote Sir Isaiah Berlin in distinguishing between Dostoevski and Tolstoy, is that the fox knows a lot about a great many things, but the hedgehog knows everything about one great thing. The multinational corporation knows a lot about a great many countries and congenially adapts to supposed differences. It willingly accepts vestigial national differences, not questioning the possibility of their transformation, not recognizing how the world is ready and eager for the benefit of modernity, especially when the price is right. The multinational corporation's accommodating mode to visible national differences is medieval.

By contrast, the global corporation knows everything about one great thing. It knows about the absolute need to be competitive on a worldwide basis as well as nationally and seeks constantly to drive down prices by standardizing what it sells and how it operates. It treats the world as composed of few standardized markets rather than many customized markets. It actively seeks and vigorously works toward global convergence. Its mission is modernity and its mode, price competition, even when it sells top-of-the-line, high-end products. It knows about the one great thing all nations and people have in common: scarcity.

Nobody takes scarcity lying down; everyone wants more. This in part explains division of labor and specialization of production. They enable people and nations to optimize their conditions through trade. The median is usually money.

Experience teaches that money has three special qualities: scarcity, difficulty of acquisition, and transience. People understandably treat it with respect. Everyone in the increasingly homogenized world market wants products and features that everybody else wants. If the price is low enough, they will take highly standardized world products, even if these aren't exactly what mother said was suitable, what immemorial custom decreed was right, or what market-research fabulists asserted was preferred.

The implacable truth of all modern production—whether of tangible or intangible goods—is that large-scale production of standardized items is generally cheaper within a wide range of volume than small-scale production. Some argue that CAD/CAM will allow companies to manufacture customized products on a small scale—but cheaply. But the argument misses the point. (For a more detailed discussion, see insert, "Economies of scope.") If a company treats the world as one or two distinctive product markets, it can serve the world more economically than if it treats it as three, four, or five product markets.

Why Remaining Differences?

Different cultural preferences, national tastes and standards, and business institutions are vestiges of the past. Some inheritances die gradually; others prosper and expand into mainstream global preferences. So-called ethnic markets are a good example. Chinese food, pita bread, country and western music, pizza, and jazz are everywhere. They are market segments that exist in worldwide proportions. They don't deny or contradict global homogenization but confirm it.

Many of today's differences among nations as to products and their features actually reflect the respectful accommodation of multinational corporations to what they believe are fixed local preferences. They *believe* preferences are fixed, not because they are but because of rigid habits of thinking about what actually is. Most executives in multinational corporations are thoughtlessly accommodating. They falsely presume that marketing means giving the customer what he says he wants rather than trying to understand exactly what he'd like. So they persist with high-cost, customized multinational products and practices instead of pressing hard and pressing properly for global standardization.

I do not advocate the systematic disregard of local or national differences. But a company's sensitivity to such differences does not require that it ignore the possibilities of doing things differently or better.

There are, for example, enormous differences among Middle Eastern countries. Some are socialist, some monarchies, some republics. Some take their legal heritage from the Napoleonic Code, some from the Ottoman Empire, and some from the British common law; except for Israel, all are influenced by Islam. Doing business means personalizing the business relationship in an obsessively intimate fashion. During the month of Ramadan, business discussions can start only after 10 o'clock at night, when people are tired and full of food after a day of fasting. A company must almost certainly have a local partner; a local lawyer is required (as, say, in New York), and irrevocable letters of credit are essential. Yet, as Coca-Cola's Senior Vice President Sam Ayoub noted, "Arabs are much more capable of making distinctions between cultural and religious purposes on the one hand and economic realities on the other than is generally assumed. Islam is compatible with science and modern times."

Barriers to globalization are not confined to the Middle East. The free transfer of technology and data across the boundaries of European Common Market countries are hampered by legal and financial impediments. And there is resistence to radio and television interference ("pollution") among neighboring European countries.

But the past is a good guide to the future. With persistence and appropriate means, barriers against superior technologies and economics have always fallen. There is no recorded exception where reasonable effort has been made to overcome them. It is very much a matter of time and effort.

A Failure in Global Imagination

Many companies have tried to standardize world practice by exporting domestic products and processes without accommodation or change—and have failed miserably. Their deficiencies have been seized on as evidence of bovine stupidity in the face of abject impossibility. Advocates of global standardization see them as examples of failures in execution.

In fact, poor execution is often an important cause. More important, however, is failure of nerve—failure of imagination.

Consider the case for the introduction of fully automatic home laundry equipment in Western Europe at a time when few homes had even semiautomatic machines. Hoover, Ltd., whose parent company was headquartered in North Canton, Ohio had a prominent presence in Britain as a producer of vacuum cleaners and washing machines. Due to insufficient demand in the home market and low exports to the European continent, the large washing machine plant in England operated far below capacity. The company needed to sell more of its semiautomatic or automatic machines.

Because it had a "proper" marketing orientation; Hoover conducted consumer preference studies in Britain and each major continental country. The results showed feature preferences clearly enough among several countries (see the *Exhibit*).

The incremental unit variable costs (in pounds sterling) of customizing to meet just a few of the national preferences were:

	£	s.	d.
Stainless steel vs. enamel drum	1	0	0
Porthole window		10	0
Spin speed of 800 rpm vs. 700 rpm		15	0
Water heater	2	15	0
6 vs. 5 kilos capacity		10	0
	£6	10 s	0 d

$18.20 at the exchange rate of that time.

Considerable plant investment was needed to meet other preferences.

The lowest retail prices (in pounds sterling) of leading locally produced brands in the various countries were approximately:

U.K.	£110
France	114
West Germany	113
Sweden	134
Italy	57

Product customization in each country would have put Hoover in a poor competitive position on the basis of price, mostly due to the higher manufacturing costs incurred by short production runs for separate features. Because Common Market tariff reduction programs were then incomplete, Hoover also paid tariff duties in each continental country.

How to Make a Creative Analysis

In the Hoover case, an imaginative analysis of automatic washing machine sales in each country would have revealed that:

1. Italian automatics, small in capacity and size, low-powered, without built-in heaters, with porcelain enamel tubs, were priced aggressively low and were gaining large market shares in all countries, including West Germany.
2. The best-selling automatics in West Germany were heavily advertised (three times more than the next most promoted brand), were ideally suited to national tastes, and were also by far the highest priced machines available in that country.

3. Italy, with the lowest penetration of washing machines of any kind (manual, semiautomatic, or automatic) was rapidly going directly to automatics, skipping the pattern of first buying handwringer, manually assisted machines and then semiautomatics.
4. Detergent manufacturers were just beginning to promote the technique of cold-water and tepid-water laundering then used in the United States.

The growing success of small, low-powered, low-speed, low-capacity, low-priced Italian machines, even against the preferred but highly priced and highly promoted brand in West Germany, was significant. It contained a powerful message that was lost on managers confidently wedded to a distorted version of the marketing concept according to which you give the customer what he says he wants. In fact the customers *said* they wanted certain features, but their behavior demonstrated they'd take other features provided the price and the promotion were right.

In this case it was obvious that, under prevailing conditions, people preferred a low-priced automatic over any kind of manual or semiautomatic machine and certainly over higher priced automatics, even though the low-priced automatics failed to fulfill all their expressed preferences. The supposedly meticulous and demanding German consumers violated all expectations by buying the simple, low-priced Italian machines.

It was equally clear that people were profoundly influenced by promotions of automatic washers; in West Germany, the most heavily promoted ideal machine also had the largest market share despite its high price. Two things clearly influenced customers to buy: low price regardless of feature preferences and heavy promotion regardless of price. Both factors helped homemakers get what they most wanted—the superior benefits bestowed by fully automatic machines.

Hoover should have aggressively sold a simple, standardized high-quality machine at a low price (afforded by the 17% variable cost reduction that the elimination of £6-10-00 worth of extra features made possible). The suggested retail prices could have been somewhat less than £100. The extra funds "saved" by avoiding unnecessary plant modifications would have supported an extended service network and aggressive media promotions.

Hoover's media message should have been: *this* is the machine that you, the homemaker, *deserve* to have to reduce the repetitive heavy daily household burdens, so that *you* may have more constructive time to spend with your children and your husband. The promotion should also have targeted the husband to give him, preferably in the presence of his wife, a sense of obligation to provide an automatic washer for her even before he bought an automobile for himself. An aggressively low price, combined with heavy promotion of this kind, would have overcome previously expressed preferences for particular features.

The Hoover case illustrates how the perverse practice of the marketing concept and the absence of any kind of marketing imagination let multinational attitudes survive when customers actually want the benefits of global standardization. The whole project got off on the wrong foot. It asked people what features they wanted in a washing machine rather than what they wanted out of life. Selling a line of products individually tailored to each nation is thoughtless. Managers who took pride in practicing the marketing concept to the fullest did not, in fact, practice it at all.

Exhibit
CONSUMER PREFERENCES AS TO AUTOMATIC WASHING MACHINE FEATURES IN THE 1960s

Features	Great Britain	Italy	West Germany	France	Sweden
Shell dimensions*	34" and narrow	Low and narrow	34" and wide	34" and narrow	34" and wide
Drum material	Enamel	Enamel	Stainless steel	Enamel	Stainless steel
Loading	Top	Front	Front	Front	Front
Front porthole	Yes/no	Yes	Yes	Yes	Yes
Capacity	5 kilos	4 kilos	6 kilos	5 kilos	6 kilos
Spin Speed	700 rpm	400 rpm	850 rpm	600 rpm	800 rpm
Water-heating system	No†	Yes	Yes††	Yes	No†
Washing action	Agitator	Tumble	Tumble	Agitator	Tumble
Styling features	Inconspicuous appearance	Brightly colored	Indestructible appearance	Elegant appearance	Strong appearance

*34" height was (in the process of being adopted as) a standard work-surface height in Europe.
†Most British and Swedish homes had centrally heated hot water.
††West Germans preferred to launder at temperatures higher than generally provided centrally.

Hoover asked the wrong questions, then applied neither thought nor imagination to the answers. Such companies are like the ethnocentricists in the Middle Ages who saw with everyday clarity the sun revolving around the earth and offered it as Truth. With no additional data but a more searching mind, Copernicus, like the hedgehog, interpreted a more compelling and accurate reality. Data do not yield information except with the intervention of the mind. Information does not yield meaning except with the intervention of imagination.

Accepting the Inevitable _____

The global corporation accepts for better or for worse that technology drives consumers relentlessly toward the same common goals—alleviation of life's burdens and the expansion of discretionary time and spending power. Its role is profoundly different from what it has been for the ordinary corporation during its brief, turbulent, and remarkably protean history. It orchestrates the twin vectors of technology and globalization for the world's benefit. Neither fate, nor nature, nor God but rather the necessity of commerce created this role.

In the United States two industries became global long before they were consciously aware of it. After over a generation of persistent and acrimonious labor shutdowns, the United Steelworkers of America have not called an industrywide strike since 1959; the United Auto Workers have not shut down General Motors since 1970. Both unions realize that they have become global—shutting down all or most of U.S. manufacturing would not shut out U.S. customers. Overseas suppliers are there to supply the market.

Cracking the Code of Western Markets

Since the theory of the marketing concept emerged a quarter of a century ago, the more managerially advanced corporations have been eager to offer what customers clearly wanted rather than what was merely convenient. They have created marketing departments supported by professional market researchers of awesome and often costly proportions. And they have proliferated extraordinary numbers of operations and product lines—highly tailored products and delivery systems for many different markets, market segments, and nations.

Significantly, Japanese companies operate almost entirely without marketing departments or market research of the kind so prevalent in the West. Yet, in the colorful words of General Electric's chairman John F. Welch, Jr., the Japanese, coming from a small cluster of resource-poor islands, with an entirely alien culture and an almost impenetrably complex language, have cracked the code of Western markets. They have done it not by looking with mechanistic thoroughness at the way markets are different but rather by searching for meaning with a deeper wisdom. They have discovered the one great thing all markets have in common—an overwhelming desire for dependable, world-standard modernity in all things, at aggressively low prices. In response, they deliver irresistible value everywhere, attracting people with products that market-research technocrats described with superficial certainty as being unsuitable and uncompetitive.

The wider a company's global reach, the greater the number of regional and national preferences it will encounter for certain product features, distribution systems, or promotional media. There will always need to be some accommodation to differences. But the widely prevailing and often unthinking belief in the immutability of these differences is generally mistaken. Evidence of business failure because of lack of accommodation is often evidence of other shortcomings.

Take the case of Revlon in Japan. The company unnecessarily alienated retailers and confused customers by selling world-standardized cosmetics only in elite outlets; then it tried to recover with low-priced world-standardized products in broader distribution, followed by a change in the company president and cutbacks in distribution as costs rose faster than sales. The problem was not that Revlon didn't understand the Japanese market; it didn't do the job right, wavered in its programs, and was impatient to boot.

By contrast, the Outboard Marine Corporation, with imagination, push, and persistence, collapsed long-established three-tiered distribution channels in Europe into a more focused and controllable two-step system—and did so despite the vociferous warnings of local trade groups. It also reduced the number and types of retail outlets. The result was greater improvement in credit and product-installation service to customers, major cost reductions, and sales advances.

In its highly successful introduction of Contac 600 (the timed-release decongestant) into Japan, SmithKline Corporation used 35 wholesalers instead of the 1,000-

plus that established practice required. Daily contacts with the wholesalers and key retailers, also in violation of established practice, supplemented the plan, and it worked.

Denied access to established distribution institutions in the United States, Komatsu, the Japanese manufacturer of lightweight farm machinery, entered the market through over-the-road construction equipment dealers in rural areas of the Sunbelt, where farms are smaller, the soil sandier and easier to work. Here inexperienced distributors were able to attract customers on the basis of Komatsu's product and price appropriateness.

In cases of successful challenge to prevailing institutions and practices, a combination of product reliability and quality, strong and sustained support systems, aggressively low prices, and sales-compensation packages, as well as audacity and implacability, circumvented, shattered, and transformed very different distribution systems. Instead of resentment, there was admiration.

Still, some differences between nations are unyielding, even in a world of microprocessors. In the United States almost all manufacturers of microprocessors check them for reliability through a so-called parallel system of testing. Japan prefers the totally different sequential testing system. So Teradyne Corporation, the world's largest producer of microprocessor test equipment, makes one line for the United States and one for Japan. That's easy.

What's not so easy for Teradyne is to know how best to organize and manage, in this instance, its marketing effort. Companies can organize by product, region, function, or by using some combination of these. A company can have separate marketing organizations for Japan and for the United States, or it can have separate product groups, one working largely in Japan and the other in the United States. A single manufacturing facility or marketing operation might service both markets, or a company might use separate marketing operations for each.

Questions arise if the company organizes by product. In the case of Teradyne, should the group handling the parallel system, whose major market is the United States, sell in Japan and compete with the group focused on the Japanese market? If the company organizes regionally, how do regional groups divide their efforts between promoting the parallel vs. the sequential system? If the company organizes in terms of function, how does it get commitment in marketing, for example, for one line instead of the other?

There is no one reliably right answer—no one formula by which to get it. There isn't even a satisfactory contingent answer.[3] What works well for one company or one place may fail for another in precisely the same place, depending on the capabilities, histories, reputations, resources, and even the cultures of both.

The Earth is Flat _____

The differences that persist throughout the world despite its globalization affirm an ancient dictum of economics—that things are driven by what happens at the margin, not at the core. Thus, in ordinary competitive analysis, what's important is not the average price but the marginal price; what happens not in the usual case but at the interface of newly erupting conditions. What counts in commercial affairs is what happens at the cutting edge. What is most striking today is the underlying similarities of what is happening now to national preferences at the margin. These similarities at the cutting edge cumulatively form an overwhelming, predominant commonality everywhere.

The Shortening of Japanese Horizons

One of the most powerful yet least celebrated forces driving commerce toward global standardization is the monetary system, along with the international investment process.

Today money is simply electronic impulses. With the speed of light it moves effortlessly between distant centers (and even lesser places). A change of ten basis points in the price of a bond causes an instant and massive shift of money from London to Tokyo. The system has profound impact on the way companies operate throughout the world.

Take Japan, where high debt-to-equity balance sheets are "guaranteed" by various societal presumptions about the virtue of "a long view," or by government policy in other ways. Even here, upward shifts in interest rates in other parts of the world attract capital out of the country in powerful proportions. In recent years more and more Japanese global corporations have gone to the world's equity markets for funds. Debt is too remunerative in high-yielding countries to keep capital at home to feed the Japanese need. As interest rates rise, equity becomes a more attractive option for the issuer.

The long-term impact on Japanese enterprise will be transforming. As the equity proportion of Japanese corporate capitalization rises, companies will respond to the shorter-term investment horizons of the equity markets. Thus the much-vaunted Japanese corporate practice to taking the long view will gradually disappear.

To refer to the persistence of economic nationalism (protective and subsidized trade practices, special tax aids, or restrictions for home market producers) as a barrier to the globalization of markets is to make a valid point. Economic nationalism does have a powerful persistence. But, as with the present almost totally smooth internationalization of investment capital, the past alone does not shape or predict the future. (For reflections on the internationalization of capital, see the insert, "The shortening of Japanese horizons.")

Reality is not a fixed paradigm, dominated by immemorial customs and derived attitudes, heedless of powerful and abundant new forces. The world is becoming increasingly informed about the liberating and enhancing possibilities of modernity. The persistence of the inherited varieties of national preferences rests uneasily on increasing evidence of, and restlessness regarding, their inefficiency, costliness, and confinement. The historic past, and the national differences respecting commerce and industry it spawned and fostered everywhere, is now subject to relatively easy transformation.

Cosmopolitanism is no longer the monopoly of the intellectual and leisure classes; it is becoming the established property and defining characteristic of all sectors everywhere in the world. Gradually and irresistibly it breaks down the walls of economic insularity, nationalism, and chauvinism. What we see today as escalating commercial nationalism is simply the last violent death rattle of an obsolete institution.

Companies that adapt to and capitalize on economic convergence can still make distinctions and adjustments in different markets. Persistent differences in the world are consistent with fundamental underlying commonalities; they often complement rather than oppose each other—in business as they do in physics. There is, in physics, simultaneously matter and anti-matter working in symbiotic harmony.

The earth is round, but for most purposes it's sensible to treat it as flat. Space is curved, but not much for everyday life here on earth.

Divergence from established practice happens all the time. But the multinational mind, warped into circumspection and timidity by years of stumbles and transnational troubles, now rarely challenges existing overseas practices. More often it considers any departure from inherited domestic routines as mindless, disrespectful, or impossible. It is the mind of a bygone day.

The successful global corporation does not abjure customization or differentiation for the requirements of markets that differ in product preferences, spending patterns, shopping preferences, and institutional or legal arrangements. But the global corporation accepts and adjusts to these differences only reluctantly, only after relentlessly testing their immutability, after trying in various ways to circumvent and reshape them as we saw in the case of Outboard Marine in Europe, SmithKline in Japan, and Komatsu in the United States.

There is only one significant respect in which a company's activities around the world are important, and this is in what it produces and how it sells. Everything else derives from, and is subsidiary to, these activities.

The pupose of business is to get and keep a customer. Or, to use Peter Drucker's more refined construction, to *create* and keep a customer. A company must be wedded to the ideal of innovation—offering better or more preferred products in such combinations of ways, means, places, and at such prices that prospects *prefer* doing business with the company rather than with others.

Preferences are constantly shaped and reshaped. Within our global commonality enormous variety constantly asserts itself and thrives, as can be seen within the world's single largest domestic market, the United States. But in the process of world homogenization, modern markets expand to reach cost-reducing global proportions. With better and cheaper communication and transport, even small local market segments hitherto protected from distant competitors now feel the pressure of their presence. Nobody is safe from global reach and the irresistible economies of scale.

Two vectors shape the world—technology and globalization. The first helps determine human preferences; the second, economic realities. Regardless of how much preferences evolve and diverge, they also gradually converge and form markets where economies of scale lead to reduction of costs and prices.

The modern global corporation contrasts powerfully with the aging multinational corporation. Instead of adapting to superficial and even entrenched differences within and between nations, it will seek sensibly to force suitably standardized products and practices on the entire globe. They are exactly what the world will take, if they come also with low prices, high quality, and blessed reliability. The global company will operate, in this regard, precisely as Henry Kissinger wrote in *Years of Upheaval* about the continuing Japanese economic success—"voracious in its collection of information, impervious to pressure, and implacable in execution."

Given what is everywhere the purpose of commerce, the global company will shape the vectors of technology and globalization into its great strategic fecundity. It will systematically push these vectors toward their own convergence, offering everyone simultaneously high-quality, more or less standardized products at optimally low prices, thereby achieving for itself vastly expanded markets and profits. Companies that do not adapt to the new global realities will become victims of those that do.

Turtles All The Way Down

There is an Indian story—at least I heard it as an Indian story—about an Englishman who, having been told that the world rested on a platform which rested on the back of an elephant which rested in turn on the back of a turtle, asked (perhaps he was an ethnographer; it is the way they behave), what did the turtle rest on? Another turtle. And that turtle? "Ah, Sahib, after that it is turtles all the way down.". . .

The danger that cultural analysis, in search of all-too-deep-lying turtles, will lose touch with the hard surfaces of life—with the political, economic, stratificatory realities within which men are everywhere contained—and with the biological and physical necessities on which those surfaces rest, is an ever-present one. The only defense against it, and against, thus, turning cultural analysis into a kind of sociological aestheticism, is to train such analysis on such realities and such necessities in the first place.

From Clifford Geertz, *The Interpretation of Cultures* (New York: Basic Books 1973), With permission of the publisher

Notes

1. In a landmark article, Robert D. Buzzell pointed out the rapidity with which barriers to standardization were falling. In all cases they succumbed to more and cheaper advanced ways of doing things. See "Can You Standardize Multinational Marketing?" HBR November-December 1968, p. 102.
2. There is powerful new evidence for this, even though the opposite has been urged by analysts of PIMS data for nearly a decade. See "Product Quality: Cost Production and Business Performance—A Test of Some Key Hypotheses" by Lynn W. Phillips, Dae Chang, and Robert D. Buzzell, Harvard Business School Working Paper No. 83-13.
3. For a discussion of multinational reorganization, see Christopher A. Bartlett, "MNCs: Get Off the Reorganization Merry-Go-Round," HBR March–April 1983, p. 138.

2. CUSTOMIZING GLOBAL MARKETING

JOHN A. QUELCH

Mr. Quelch is an associate professor of business administration at the Harvard Business School, where he teaches in the new Multinational Marketing Management executive program. This is his sixth HBR article, the last being "How to Build a Product Licensing Program" (May–June 1985).

EDWARD J. HOFF

Mr. Hoff is a PhD candidate in business economics at Harvard University. He was an instructor in marketing at the Harvard Business School, which awarded him a Dean's Doctoral Fellowship to complete his PhD.

In the best of all possible worlds, marketers would only have to come up with a great product and a convincing marketing program and they would have a worldwide winner. But despite the obvious economies and efficiencies they could gain with a standard product and program, many managers fear that global marketing, as popularly defined, is too extreme to be practical. Because customers and competitive conditions differ across countries or because powerful local managers will not stand for centralized decision making, they argue, global marketing just won't work.

Of course, global marketing has its pitfalls, but it can also yield impressive advantages. Standardizing products can lower operating costs. Even more important, effective coordination can exploit a company's best product and marketing ideas.

Too often, executives view global marketing as an either/or proposition—either full standardization or local control. But when a global approach can fall anywhere on a spectrum from tight worldwide coordination on programming details to loose agreement on a product idea, why the extreme view? In applying the global marketing concept and making it work, flexibility is essential. Managers need to tailor the approach they use to each element of the business system and marketing program. For example, a manufacturer might market the same product under different brand names in different countries or market the same brands using different product formulas.

The big issue today is not whether to go global but how to tailor the global marketing concept to fit each business and how to make it work. In this article, we'll first provide a framework to help managers think about how they should structure the different areas of the marketing function as the business shifts to a global approach. We will then show how companies we have studied are tackling the implementation challenges of global marketing.

How Far to Go

How far a company can move toward global marketing depends a lot on its evolution and traditions. Consider these two examples:

■ Although the Coca-Cola Company had conducted some international business before 1940, it gained true global recognition during World War II, as Coke bottling plants followed the march of U.S. troops around the world. Management in Atlanta made all strategic decisions then—and still does now, as Coca-Cola applies global marketing principles, for example, to the worldwide introduction of Diet Coke. The brand name, concentrate formula, positioning, and advertising theme are virtually standard worldwide, but the artificial sweetener and packaging differ across countries. Local managers are responsible for sales and distribution programs, which they run in conjunction with local bottlers.

■ The Nestlé approach also has its roots in history. To avoid distribution disruptions caused by wars in Europe, to ease rapid worldwide expansion, and to respond to local consumer needs, Nestlé granted its local managers considerable autonomy from the outset. While the local managers still retain much of that decision-making power today, Nestlé headquarters at Vevey has grown in importance. Nestlé has transferred to its central marketing staff many former local managers who had succeeded in their local Nestlé businesses and who now influence country executives to accept standard new product and marketing ideas. The trend seems to be toward tighter marketing coordination.

To conclude that Coca-Cola is a global marketer and Nestlé is not would be simplistic. In *Exhibit I,* we assess program adaptation or standardization levels for each company's business functions, products, marketing mix elements, and countries. Each company has tailored its individual approach. Furthermore, as *Exhibit I* can't show, the situations aren't static. Readers can themselves evaluate their own *current* and *desired* levels of program adaptation or standardization on these four dimensions. The gap between the two levels is the implementation challenge. The size of the gap—and the urgency with which it must be closed—will depend on a company's strategy and financial performance, competitive pressures, technological change, and converging consumer values.

Four Dimensions of Global Marketing

Now let's look at the issues that arise when executives consider the four dimensions shown in *Exhibit I* in light of the degree of standardization or adaptation that is appropriate.

Business functions. A company's approach to global marketing depends, first, on its overall business strategy. In many multinationals, some functional areas have greater program standardization than others. Headquarters often controls manufacturing, finance, and R&D, while the local managers make the marketing decisions. Marketing is usually one of the last functions to be centrally directed. Partly because product quality and accounting data are easier to measure than marketing effectiveness, standardization can be greater in production and finance.

Products. Products that enjoy high scale economies or efficiencies and are not highly culture-bound are easier to market globally than others.

Exhibit I

19

GLOBAL MARKETING PLANNING MATRIX: HOW FAR TO GO

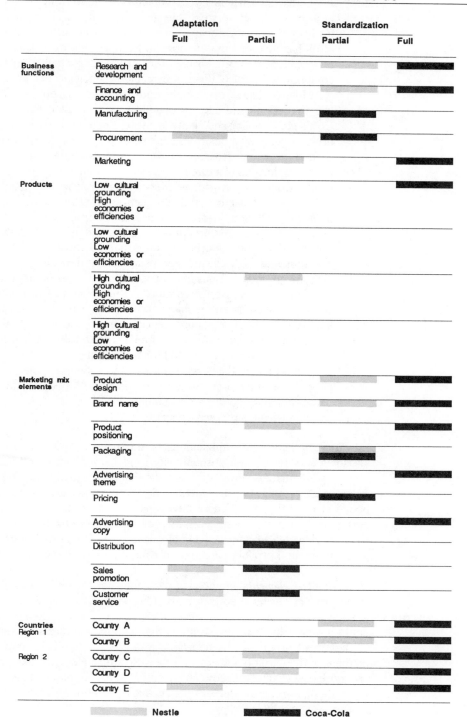

1. Economies or efficiencies. Manufacturing and R&D scale economies can result in a price spread between the global and the local product that is too great for even the most culture-bound consumer to resist. In addition, management often has neither the time nor the R&D resources to adapt products to each country. The markets for high-tech products like computers are not only very competitive but also affected by rapid technological change.

   Most packaged consumer goods are less susceptible than durable goods like televisions and cars to manufacturing or even R&D economies. Coca-Cola's global policy and Nestlé's interest in tighter marketing coordination are driven largely by a desire to capitalize on the marketing ideas their managers around the world generate rather than by potential scale economies. Nestlé, for example, manufactures its packaged soups in dozens of locally managed plants around the world, with some transference of engineering know-how through a headquarters staff. Products and marketing programs are also locally managed, but new ideas are aggressively transferred, with local managers encouraged—or even prodded—to adapt and use them in their own markets. For Nestlé, global marketing does not so much yield high manufacturing economies as high efficiency in using scarce new ideas.

2. Cultural grounding. Consumer products used in the home—like Nestlé's soups and frozen foods—are often more culture-bound than products used outside the home such as automobiles and credit cards, and industrial products are inherently less culture-bound than consumer products. (Products like personal computers, for example, are often marketed on the basis of performance benefits that share a common technical language worldwide.) Experience also suggests that products will be less culture-bound if they are used by young people whose cultural norms are not ingrained, people who travel in different countries, and ego-driven consumers who can be appealed to through myths and fantasies shared across cultures.

Exhibit I lists four combinations of the scale economy and cultural grounding variables in order of their susceptibility to global marketing. Managers shouldn't be bound by any matrix, however; they should find creative ways to prepare a product for global marketing. If a manufacturer develops a new version of a seemingly culture-bound product that is based on new capital-intensive technology and generates superior performance benefits, it may well be possible to introduce it on a standard basis worldwide. Procter & Gamble developed Pampers disposable diapers as a global brand in a product category that intuition would say was culture-bound.

Marketing mix elements. Few consumer goods companies go so far as to market the same products using the same marketing program worldwide. And those that do, like Lego, the Danish manufacturer of construction toys, often distribute their products through sales companies rather than full-fledged marketing subsidiaries.

For most products, the appropriate degree of standardization varies from one element of the marketing mix to another. Strategic elements like product positioning are more easily standardized than execution-sensitive elements like sales promotion. In addition, when headquarters believes it has identified a superior marketing idea, whether it be a package design, a brand name, or an advertising copy concept, the pressure to standardize increases.

Marketing can usually contribute to scale economies most significantly by creating a standard product design that will sell worldwide, permitting savings through globalized production. In addition, scale economies in marketing programming can be achieved through standard commercial executions and copy concepts. McCann-Erickson claims to have saved $90 million in production costs over 20 years by producing worldwide Coca-Cola commercials. To ensure that they have enough attention-getting power to overcome their foreign origins, however, marketers often have to make worldwide commercials expensive productions.

To compensate local management for having to accept a standard product and to fit the core product to each local market, some companies allow local managers to adapt those marketing mix elements that aren't subject to significant scale economies. On the other hand, local managers are more likely to accept a standard concept for those elements of the marketing mix that are less important and, ironically, often not susceptible to scale economies. Overall, then, the driving factor in moving toward global marketing should be the efficient worldwide use of good marketing ideas rather than any scale economies from standardization.

In judging how far to go in standardizing elements of the marketing mix, managers must also be mindful of the interactions among them. For example, when a product with the same brand name is sold in different countries, it can be difficult and sometimes impossible to sell them at different prices.

Countries. How far a decentralized multinational wishes to pursue global marketing will often vary from one country to another. Naturally, headquarters is likely to become more involved in marketing decisions in countries where performance is poor. But performance aside, small markets depend more on headquarters assistance than large markets. Because a standard marketing program is superior in quality to what local executives, even with the benefit of local market knowledge, could develop themselves, they may welcome it.

Large markets with strong local managements are less willing to accept global programs. Yet these are the markets that often account for most of the company's investment. To secure their acceptance, headquarters should make standard marketing programs reflect the needs of large rather than small markets. Small markets, being more tolerant of deviations from what would be locally appropriate, are less likely to resist a standard program.

As we've seen, Coca-Cola takes the same approach in all markets. Nestlé varies its approach in different countries depending on the strength of its market presence and each country's need for assistance. In completing the *Exhibit I* planning matrix, management may decide that it can sensibly group countries by region or by stage of market development.

Too Far too Fast _____

Once managers have decided how global they want their marketing program to be, they must make the transition. Debates over the size of the gap between present and desired positions and the speed with which it must be closed will often pit the field against headquarters. Such conflict is most likely to arise in companies where the reason for change is not apparent or the country managers have had a lot of autonomy. Casualties can occur on both sides:

- Because Black & Decker dominated the European consumer power tool market, many of the company's European managers could not see that a more centrally directed global marketing approach was needed as a defense against imminent Japanese competition. To make his point, the CEO had to replace several key European executives.

- In 1982, the Parker Pen Company, forced by competition and a weakening financial position to lower costs, more than halved its number of plants and pen styles worldwide. Parker's overseas subsidiary managers accepted these changes but, when pressed to implement standardized advertising and packaging, they dug in their heels. In 1985, Parker ended its much heralded global marketing campaign. Several senior headquarters managers left the company.

If management is not careful, moving too far too fast toward global marketing can trigger painful consequences. First, subsidiary managers who joined the company because of its apparent commitment to local autonomy and to adapting its products to the local environment may become disenchanted. When poorly implemented, global marketing can make the local country manager's job less strategic. Second, disenchantment may reinforce not-invented-here attitudes that lead to game playing. For instance, some local managers may try bargaining with headquarters, trading the speed with which they will accept and implement the standard programs for additional budget assistance. In addition, local managers competing for resources and autonomy may devote too much attention to second-guessing headquarters' "hot buttons." Eventually the good managers may leave, and less competent people who lack the initiative of their predecessors may replace them.

A vicious circle can develop. Feeling compelled to review local performance more closely, headquarters may tighten its controls and reduce resources without adjusting its expectations of local managers. Meanwhile, local managers trying to gain approval of applications for deviations from standard marketing programs are being frustrated. The expanding headquarters bureaucracy and associated overhead costs reduce the speed with which the locals can respond to local opportunities and competitive actions. Slow response time is an especially serious problem with products for which barriers to entry for local competitors are low.

In this kind of system, weak, insecure local managers can become dependent on headquarters for operational assistance. They'll want headquarters to assume the financial risks for new product launches and welcome the prepackaged marketing programs. If performance falls short of headquarters' expectations, the local management can always blame the failure on the quality of operational assistance or on the standard marketing program. The local manager who has clear autonomy and profit-and-loss responsibility cannot hide behind such excuses.

If headquarters or regions assume much of the strategic burden, managers in overseas subsidiaries may think only about short-term sales. This focus will diminish their ability to monitor and communicate to headquarters any changes in local competitors' strategic directions. When their responsibilities shift from strategy to execution, their ideas will become less exciting. If the field has traditionally been as important a source of new product ideas as the central R&D laboratory, the company may find itself short of the grassroots creative thinking and marketing research information that R&D needs. The fruitful dialogue that characterizes a relationship between equal partners will no longer flourish.

How to Get There _____

When thinking about closing the gap between present and desired positions, most executives of decentralized multinationals want to accommodate their current organizational structures. They rightly view their subsidiaries and the managers who run them as important competitive strengths. They generally do not wish to transform these organizations into mere sales and distribution agencies.

How then in moving toward global marketing can headquarters build rather than jeopardize relationships, stimulate rather than demoralize local managers? The answer is to focus on means as much as ends, to examine the relationship between the home office and the field, and to ask what level of headquarters intervention for each business function, product, marketing mix element, and country is necessary to close the gap in each.

As *Exhibit II* indicates, headquarters can intervene at five points, ranging from informing to directing. The five intervention levels are cumulative; for headquarters to direct, it must also inform, persuade, coordinate, and approve. *Exhibit II* shows the approaches Atlanta and Vevey have taken. Moving from left to right on *Exhibit II*, the reader can see that things are done increasingly by fiat rather than patient persuasion, through discipline rather than education. At the far right, local subsidiaries can't choose whether to opt in or out of a marketing program, and headquarters views its country managers as subordinates rather than customers.

When the local managers tightly control marketing efforts, multinational managers face three critical issues. In the sections that follow, we'll take a look at how decentralized multinationals are working to correct the three problems as they move along the spectrum from informing to directing.

Inconsistent Brand Identities. If headquarters gives country managers total control of their product lines, it cannot leverage the opportunities that multinational status gives it. The increasing degree to which consumers in one country are exposed to the company's products in another won't enhance the corporate image or brand development in the consumers' home country.

Limited Product Focus. In the decentralized multinational, the field line manager's ambition is to become a country manager, which means acquiring multiproduct and multifunction experience. Yet as the pace of technological innovation increases and the likelihood of global competition grows, multinationals need worldwide product specialists as well as executives willing to transfer to other countries. Nowhere is

Exhibit II

GLOBAL MARKETING PLANNING MATRIX: HOW TO GET THERE

		Informing	Persuading	Coordinating	Approving	Directing
Business functions	Research and development	■	■	■	■	■
	Finance and accounting	■	■	■	■	■
	Manufacturing	■	■	■	■	
	Procurement	■	■		■	
	Marketing	■	■	■	■	■
Products	Low cultural grounding / High economies or efficiencies	■	■			
	Low cultural grounding / Low economies or efficiencies					
	High cultural grounding / High economies or efficiencies	▨	▨	▨		
	High cultural grounding / Low economies or efficiencies					
Marketing mix elements	Product design	■		■		■
	Brand name	■	■	■		■
	Product positioning	■	■	■	■	■
	Packaging	■	■	■	■	
	Advertising theme	■	■	■	■	■
	Pricing	■	■		■	
	Advertising copy	■	■	■	■	■
	Distribution	■	■			
	Sales promotion	■	■			
	Customer service	■	■			
Countries Region 1	Country A				▨	■
	Country B			▨		■
Region 2	Country C			▨		■
	Country D		▨			■
	Country E	▨				■

▨ **Nestle**   ■ **Coca-Cola**

the need for headquarters guidance on innovative organizational approaches more evident than in the area of product policy.

Slow New Product Launches. As global competition grows, so does the need for rapid worldwide rollouts of new products. The decentralized multinational that permits country managers to proceed at their own pace on new product introductions may be at a competitive disadvantage in this new environment.

Word of Mouth

The least threatening, loosest, and therefore easiest approach to global marketing is for headquarters to encourage the transfer of information between it and its country managers. Since good ideas are often a company's scarcest resource, headquarters efforts to encourage and reward their generation, dissemination, and application in the field will build both relationships and profits. Here are two examples:

- Nestlé publishes quarterly marketing newsletters that report recent product introductions and programming innovations. In this way, each subsidiary can learn quickly about and assess the ideas of others. (The best newsletters are written as if country organizations were talking to each other rather than as if headquarters were talking down to the field.)

- Johnson Wax holds periodic meetings of all marketing directors at corporate headquarters twice a year to build global esprit de corps and to encourage the sharing of new ideas.

By making the transfer of information easy, a multinational leverages the ideas of its staff and spreads organizational values. Headquarters has to be careful, however, that the information it's passing on is useful. It may focus on updating local managers about new products, when what they mainly want is information on the most tactical and country-specific elements of the marketing mix. For example, the concentration of the grocery trade is much higher in the United Kingdom and Canada than it is in the United States. In this case, managers in the United States can learn from British and Canadian country managers about how to deal with the pressures for extra merchandising support that result when a few powerful retailers control a large percentage of sales. Likewise, marketers in countries with restrictions on mass media advertising have developed sophisticated point-of-purchase merchandising skills that could be useful to managers in other countries.

By itself, however, information sharing is often insufficient to help local executives meet the competitive challenges of global marketing.

Friendly Persuasion

Persuasion is a first step managers can take to deal with the three problems we've outlined. Any systematic headquarters effort to influence local managers to apply standardized approaches or introduce new global products while the latter retain their decision-making authority is a persuasion approach.

Unilever and CPC International, for example, employ world-class advertising and marketing research staff at headquarters. Not critics but coaches, these specialists review the subsidiaries' work and try to upgrade the technical skills of local marketing departments. They frequently visit the field to disseminate new concepts, frameworks, and techniques, and to respond to problems that local management raises. (It helps to build trust if headquarters can send out the same staff specialists for several years.)

Often, when the headquarters of a decentralized multinational identifies or develops a new product, it has to persuade the country manager in a so-called prime-mover market to invest in the launch. A successful launch in the prime-mover market will, in turn, persuade other country managers to introduce the product. The prime-mover market is usually selected according to criteria including the commitment of local management, the probabilities of success, the credibility with which a success would be regarded by managers in other countries, and its perceived transferability.

Persuasion, however, has its limitations. Two problems recur with the prime-mover approach. First, by adopting a wait-and-see attitude, country managers can easily turn down requests to be prime-mover markets on the grounds of insufficient resources. Since the country managers in the prime-mover markets have to risk their resources to launch the new products, they're likely to tailor the product and marketing programs to their own markets rather than to global markets. Second, if there are more new products waiting to be launched than there are prime-mover markets to launch them, headquarters product specialists are likely to give in to a country manager's demands for local tailoring. But because of the need for readaptation in each case, the tailoring may delay rollouts in other markets and allow competitors to preempt the product. In the end, management may sacrifice long-term worldwide profits to maximize short-term profits in a few countries.

Marketing to The Same Drummer

To overcome the limits of persuasion, many multinationals are coordinating their marketing programs, whereby headquarters has a structured role in both decision making and performance evaluation that is far more influential than person-to-person persuasion. Often using a matrix or team approach, headquarters shares with country managers the responsibility and authority for programming and personnel decisions.

Nestlé locates product directors as well as support groups at headquarters. Together they develop long-term strategies for each product category on a worldwide basis, coordinate worldwide market research, spot new product opportunities, spark the field launch of new products, advise the field on how headquarters will evaluate new product proposals, and spread the word on new products' performance so that other countries will be motivated to launch them. Even though the product directors are staff executives with no line authority, because they have all been successful line managers in the field, they have great credibility and influence.

Country managers who cooperate with a product director can quickly become heroes if they successfully implement a new idea. On the other hand, while a country manager can reject a product director's advice, headquarters will closely monitor his or her performance with an alternative program. In addition, within the product category in which they specialize, the directors have influence on line management appointments in the field. Local managers thus have to be concerned about their relationships with headquarters.

Some companies assign promising local managers to other countries and require would-be local managers to take a tour of duty at headquarters. But such personnel transfer programs may run into barriers. First, many capable local nationals may not be interested in working outside their countries of origin. Second, powerful local managers are often unwilling to give up their best people to other country assignments. Third, immigration regulations and foreign service relocation costs are burdensome. Fourth, if transferees from the field have to take a demotion to work at headquarters, the costs in ill will often exceed any gains in cross-fertilization of ideas. If management can resolve these problems, however, it will find that creating an international career path is one of the most effective ways to develop a global perspective in local managers.

To enable their regional general managers to work alongside the worldwide product directors, several companies have moved them from the field to the head office. More and more companies require regional managers to reach sales and profit targets for each product as well as for each country within their regions. In the field, regional managers often focus on representing the views of individual countries to headquarters, but at headquarters they become more concerned with ensuring that the country managers are correctly implementing corporatewide policies.

Recently, Fiat and Philips N. V., among others, consolidated their worldwide advertising into a single agency. Their objectives are to make each product's advertising more consistent around the world and to make it easier to transfer ideas and information among local agency offices, country organizations, and headquarters. Use of a single agency (especially one that bills all advertising expenditures worldwide) also symbolizes a commitment to global marketing and more centralized control. Multinationals shouldn't, however, use their agencies as Trojan horses for greater standardization. An undercover operation is likely to jeopardize agency-client relations at the country level.

While working to achieve global coordination, some companies are also trying to tighten coordination in particular regions:

■ Kodak recently experimented by consolidating 17 worldwide product line managers at corporate headquarters. In addition, the company made marketing directors in some countries responsible for a line of business in a region as well as for sales of all Kodak products in their own countries. Despite these new appointments, country managers still retain profit-and-loss responsibility for their own markets.

Whether a matrix approach such as this broadens perspectives rather than increases tension and confusion depends heavily on the corporation's cohesiveness. Such an organizational change can clearly communicate top management's strategic direction, but headquarters needs to do a persuasive selling job to the field if it is to succeed.

■ Proctor & Gamble has established so-called Euro Brand teams that analyze opportunities for greater product and marketing program standardization. Chaired by the brand manager from a "lead country," each team includes brand managers from other European subsidiaries that market the brand, managers from P&G's European technical center, and one of P&G's three European division managers, each of whom is responsible for a portfolio of brands as well as for a group of countries. Concerns that the larger subsidiaries would dominate the teams and that decision making would either be paralyzed or produce "lowest common denominator" results have proved groundless.

Stamped & Approved

By coordinating programs with the field, headquarters can balance the company's local and global perspectives. Even a decentralized multinational may decide, however, that to protect or exploit some corporate asset, the center of gravity for certain elements of the marketing program should be at headquarters. In such cases, management has two options: it can send clear directives to its local managers or permit them to develop their own programs within specified parameters and subject to headquarters approval. With a properly managed approval process, a multinational can exert effective control without unduly dampening the country manager's decision-making responsibility and creativity.

Proctor & Gamble recently developed a new sanitary napkin, and P&G International designated certain countries in different geographic regions as test markets. The product, brand name, positioning, and package design were standardized globally. P&G International did, however, invite local managers to suggest how the global program could be improved and how the nonglobal elements of the marketing program should be adapted in their markets. It approved changes in several markets. Moreover, local managers developed valuable ideas on such programming specifics as sampling and couponing techniques that were used in all other countries, including the United States.

Nestlé views its brand names as a major corporate asset. As a result, it requires all brands sold in all countries to be registered in the home country of Switzerland. While the ostensible reason for this requirement is legal protection, the effect is that any product developed in the field has to be approved by Vevey. The head office has also developed detailed guidelines that suggest rather than mandate how brand names and logos should appear on packaging and in advertising worldwide (with exceptions subject to its approval). Thus the country manager's control over the content of advertising is not compromised, and the company achieves a reasonably consistent presentation of its names ad logos worldwide.

Doing It The Headquarters Way

Multinationals that direct local managers' marketing programs usually do so out of a sense of urgency. The motive may be to ensure either that a new product is introduced rapidly around the world before the competition can respond or that every manager fully and faithfully exploits a valuable marketing idea. Sometimes direction is needed to prove that global marketing can work. Once management makes the point, a more participative approach is feasible.

In 1979, one of Henkel's worldwide marketing directors wanted to extend the successful Sista line of do-it-yourself sealants from Germany to other European countries where the markets were underdeveloped and disorganized as had once been the case in Germany. A European headquarters project team visited the markets and then developed a standard marketing program. The country managers, however, objected. Since the market potential in each country was small, they said, they did not have the time or resources to launch Sista.

The project team countered that by capitalizing on potential scale economies, its pan-European marketing and manufacturing programs would be superior to any programs the subsidiaries could develop by themselves. Furthermore, it maintained, the already developed pan-European program was available off the shelf. The European sales manager, who was a project team member, discovered that the salespeople as well as tradespeople in the target countries were much more enthusiastic about the proposed program than the field marketing managers. So management devised a special lure for the managers. The project team offered to subsidize the first-year advertising and promotion expenditures of countries launching Sista. Six countries agreed. To ensure their commitment now that their financial risk had been reduced, the sales manager invited each accepting country manager to nominate a member to the project team to develop the final program details.

By 1982, the Sista line was sold in 52 countries using a standard marketing program. The Sista launch was especially challenging because it involved the extension of a product and program already developed for a single market. The success of the Sista launch made Henkel's field managers much more receptive to global marketing programs for subsequent new products.

THE UNIVERSAL DRINK

In the postwar years, as Coca-Cola strove mightily to consolidate its territorial gains, its efforts were received with mixed feelings. When limited production for civilians got under way in the Philippines, armed guards had to be assigned to the trucks carting Coke from bottlers to dealers, to frustrate thirsty outlaws bent on hijacking it. In the Fiji Islands, on the other hand, Coca-Cola itself was outlawed, at the instigation of soft-drink purveyors whose business had been ruined by the Coke imported for the solace of G.I.s during the war. Most of the opposition to the beverage's tidal sweep, however, was centered in Europe, being provoked by the beer and wine interests, or by anti-American political interests, or by a powerful blend of oenology and ideology. Today, brewers in England, Spain, and Sweden are themselves bottling Coke, on the if-you-can't-lick-'em-join-'em principle. . . . In Western Europe, Coca-Cola has had to fight a whole series of battles, varying according to the terrain, not all of which have

yet been won, though victory seems to be in sight. Before Coca-Cola got rolling in West Germany, for instance, it had to go to court to halt the nagging operations of something called the Coördination Office for German Beverages, which was churning out defamatory pamphlets with titles like "Coca-Cola, Karl Marx, and the Imbecility of the Masses" and the more succinct "Coca-Cola? No!" In Denmark, lobbyists for the brewers chivied the Parliament into taxing cola-containing beverages so heavily that it would have been economically absurd to try to market Coke there. . . . At last word, the Danes were about to relent, though. But in Belgium the caps on bottles of Coke, including bottles sold at the Brussels Fair, have had to carry, in letters bigger than those used for "Coca-Cola," the forbidding legend *"Contient de la cafeine."*

From THE BIG DRINK (Random House)
©1959 by E. J. Kahn, Jr
Originally in The New Yorker

Motivating The Field ————————————————————————————————————

Taking into account the nature of their products and markets, their organizational structures, and their cultures and traditions, multinationals have to decide which approach or combination of approaches, from informing to directing, will best answer their strategic objectives. Multinational managers must realize, however, that local managers are likely to resist any precipitate move toward increased headquarters direction. A quick shift could lower their motivation and performance.

Any erosion in marketing decision making associated with global marketing will probably be less upsetting for country managers who have not risen through the line marketing function. For example, John Deere's European headquarters has developed advertising for its European country managers for more than a decade. The country managers have not objected. Most are not marketing specialists and do not see advertising as key to the success of their operations. But for country managers who view control of marketing decision making as central to their operational success, the transition will often be harder. Headquarters needs to give the field time to adjust to the new decision-making processes that multicountry brand teams and other new organizational structures require. Yet management must recognize that even with a one- or two-year transition period, some turnover among field personnel is inevitable. As one German headquarters executive commented, "Those managers in the field who can't adapt to a more global approach will have to leave and run local breweries."

Here are five suggestions on how to motivate and retain talented country managers when making the shift to global marketing:

1. Encourage field managers to generate ideas. This is especially important when R&D efforts are centrally directed. Use the best ideas from the field in global marketing programs (and give recognition to the local managers who came up with them). Unilever's South African subsidiary developed Impulse body spray, now a global brand. R. J. Reynolds revitalized Camel as a global brand after the German subsidiary came up with a successful and transferable positioning and copy strategy.
2. Ensure that the field participates in the development of the marketing strategies and programs for global brands. A bottom-up rather than top-down approach will foster greater commitment and produce superior program execution at the country level. As we've seen, when P&G International introduced its sanitary napkin as a global brand, it permitted local managers to make some adjustments in areas that were not seen as core to the program, such as couponing and sales promotion. More important, it encouraged them to suggest changes in features of the core global program.
3. Maintain a product portfolio that includes, where scale economies permit, local as well as regional and global brands. While Philip Morris's and Seagram's country managers and their local advertising agencies are required to implement standard programs for each company's global brands, the managers retain full responsibility for the marketing programs of their locally distributed brands. Seagram motivates its country managers to stay interested in the

global brands by allocating development funds to support local marketing efforts on these brands and by circulating monthly reports that summarize market performance data by brand and country.

4. Allow country managers continued control of their marketing budgets so they can respond to local consumer needs and counter local competition. When British Airways headquarters launched its £13 million global advertising campaign, it left intact the £18 million worth of tactical advertising budgets that country managers used to promote fares, destinations, and tour packages specific to their markets. Because most of the country managers had exhausted their previous year's tactical budgets and were anxious for further advertising support, they were receptive to the global campaign even though it was centrally directed.

5. Emphasize the general management responsibilities of country managers that extend beyond the marketing function. Country managers who have risen through the line marketing function often don't spend enough time on local manufacturing operations, industrial relations, and government affairs. Global marketing programs can free them to focus on and develop their skills in these other areas.

II _____ THE ENVIRONMENT OF GLOBAL MARKETING _____

A Cross-National Survey of Consumer Attitudes Towards Marketing Practices, Consumerism and Government Regulations
Hiram C. Barksdale, et. al.

Conducting and Co-ordinating Multicountry Quantitative Studies Across Europe
Philip Barnard

Public Consequences of Private Action
S. Prakash Sethi and James E. Post

3. A CROSS-NATIONAL SURVEY OF CONSUMER ATTITUDES TOWARDS MARKETING PRACTICES, CONSUMERISM AND GOVERNMENT REGULATIONS

HIRAM C. BARKSDALE, WILLIAM D. PERREAULT, JR., JOHAN ARNDT, J. A. BARNHILL, WARREN A. FRENCH, MICHAEL HALLIDAY, JEHIEL ZIF

The authors are, Professors: Hiram C. Barksdale at the University of Georgia, William D. Perreault at the University of North Carolina—Chapel Hill, Johan Arndt at the Norwegian School of Economics and Business Administration. J. A. Barnhill at Carleton University, Warren A. French at the University of Lancaster, Michael Halliday at the New South Wales Institute, and Jehiel Zif at Tel-Aviv University

Consumer attitudes on the national marketing systems of six countries were examined. The theory that opinions might follow a "life cycle pattern", reflecting the development of national consumer movements was found unsupported. Wide cross-national agreement was observed on many topics.

The Universal nature of consumer problems is demonstrated by the play "We Won't Pay! We Won't Pay!" which opened in New York City during December 1980. Written by a celebrated Italian playwright, and first performed in Milan, the play portrays an Italian family as it tries to cope with rising prices and other consumer problems. As the plot unfolds, frustration builds to a level where housewives stage an impromptu strike in a supermarket, and—when the manager ignores their protest—they walk out of the store with their arms full of merchandise, refusing to pay for it. At the same time, riders block the commuter train, and factory workers rebel against the food served in the plant cafeteria. The city of Milan grinds to a standstill. One critic wrote that the play depicts the same outrage expressed by Peter Finch, in the movie "Network", when he urges his viewers to open up the nearest window and shout "I'm mad as hell, and I'm not going to take this anymore."[1]

Over the past twenty years consumers in most industrialized nations have insisted that business organizations demonstrate greater responsibility in serving the needs of society. In more or less organized ways, articulate and energetic consumer groups have not only demanded safer products and more truthful advertising, they have also pressed for improvements in promotional activities, repair services, product warranties, and complaint handling procedures.

During this period, a number of special conferences have been held to discuss various facets of the consumer movement, and hundreds of articles, monographs, and books have been published on consumerism, consumer satisfaction, dissatisfac-

Reprinted from the *Columbia Journal of World Business 17*, No. 2 (Summer 1982), 71–85 by permission of Columbia University.

tion, and complaining behavior. Within this expanding body of literature, the majority of the empirical studies focus on individual products or services—examining consumer dissatisfaction with and complaints about specific products.[2] Only a few studies have been conducted at the macro or systems level—exploring consumer attitudes toward the operations of the overall marketing system.[3] All of these studies have consistently revealed that consumer discontent is high and that buyer dissatisfaction is widespread across product groups and consumer segments.

There have been no major cross-national studies of consumer attitudes toward marketing. Consequently, little is known about consumer perceptions of marketing and the operation of marketing systems in different countries of the world. The study described here is a response to this research need. It provides comparative data on consumer attitudes toward and perceptions of marketing in six countries: Australia, Canada, England, Israel, Norway, and the United States. Before describing the methodology and discussing the findings of the study, a brief review of consumer policy and protecton programs in the six research locations is presented.

Description of Research Locations

There are suggestions that the consumer movement, like most other innovations, follows a life cycle pattern of development.[4] Kaufman and Channon as well as Straver have identified four stages in the life cycle of consumerism: crusading, popular movement, organization/managerial, and bureaucracy. According to this concept, different countries of the world can be positioned along the cycle according to the quantity and quality of information supplied to consumers, the extent of protective legislation, the authority of government consumer agencies, and public funding of consumer education programs. Following this logic, the countries selected for this study occupy different positions in the life cycle of the consumer movement.

The countries studied are industrialized, affluent nations, and citizens of each country generally enjoy standards of living as high as the world affords. Yet there are important differences among the nations. There are variations in political and economic ideology as well as cultural conditions. Some of these differences are briefly outlined below.

Norway

Norway has a long history of involvement with consumer cooperatives and labor unions. Together with the state-funded Consumer Council, which publishes the *Consumer Report* and handles consumer complaints, the Consumer Ombudsman monitors marketing practices. Special laws empower regulators to intervene regarding products, prices, and promotion. For example, legislation prohibits advertising on the state monopoly television and radio broadcasting system. In addition, print advertising of alcoholic beverages and tobacco products is banned. A cradle-to-grave welfare system combined with high taxes has resulted in substantial equality of economic living conditions. During 1979–80, inflation in Norway rose to an annual rate of 14%.

Israel

In comparison with the other nations studied, the consumer movement in Israel is advanced in some respects, but lags far behind in others. Within the context of socialist ideology, the Israeli government and public institutions associated with the labor movement have assumed major responsibility for economic, cultural, and social life in Israel. The labor movement owns over 16% of the means of industrial production and about 90% of the medical facilities and services in the country. About 70% of all farm produce is distributed by the wholesale marketing association of the labor movement.

The government finances operations of the Israeli Consumer Council, and consumer representatives are expected to participate in various governmental committees and agricultural boards. One of the most popular programs on the state-owned television system is devoted to consumer issues. Yet, consumer organizations in Israel are relatively weak. Participation in organized consumer activities is limited and operating budgets are insignificant. For example, a publication similar to *Consumer Reports* is published bi-monthly by the Israeli Consumer Council, but it has only 6000 subscribers.

Efforts to create an industrial base, heavy dependence on imported goods, and large expenditures for military purposes have kept Israel's prices rising much faster than those of its trading partners. It has been estimated that inflation reached an annual rate of 134% in 1980.

United States

Resurgence of the consumer movement, during the 1960s, was instrumental in bringing about significant advances in consumer protection in the United States. The mechanisms for consumer protection in the United States are varied and include both public and private organizations. Federal government agencies and many large business organizations have appointed high-level personnel who work full-time on consumer matters. Many states and a few local government units have also established offices to improve consumer access to government agencies and provide advice to buyers with grievances. However, the authority of most of these offices is limited. Legislative efforts to establish a Federal Consumer Protection Agency over several years ended in failure.

There are numerous voluntary consumer groups operating at the national, state, and local levels. Many of these organizations are members of the Consumer Federation of America. There are also two well-known private organizations that conduct and report tests of consumer products: Consumer Research publishes *Consumers Bulletin* and Consumers Union publishes *Consumer Reports*. The latter publication has more than two million subscribers.

The annual inflation rate in the United States has been about 12% for the years 1979 and 1980.

Canada

While Canada and the United States are similar in many ways, Canada appears to have a more coherent and comprehensive consumer protection program than does the US. In 1967, Canada established a Federal Department of Consumer and Corporate Affairs. This Department gives consumers a voice within the highest councils of government. During its first decade, the Department played an aggressive role in shaping policy and programs to advance the interests of consumers.

Within the Department of Consumer and Corporate Affairs, the Bureau of Consumer Affairs is responsible for administering consumer protection and information programs. The Bureau has four branches: (1) the Consumer Research Branch conducts research and provides advice on new measures to promote consumers' interests; (2) the Standards Branch administers various acts concerned with consumer protection (e.g., Weights and Measures and Hazardous Products) and is responsible for developing new standards; (3) the Operations Branch provides a limited inspection service at the retail level to ensure compliance with consumer laws and regulations; and (4) the Consumer Services Branch handles consumer complaints and suggestions and helps to implement consumer education programs.

The act that set up the Department of Consumer and Corporate Affairs also established the Canadian Consumer Council to provide advice on consumer problems. Its members are drawn from private sectors of the economy.

The major private group serving the interests of Canadian consumers is the Consumers' Association of Canada. The Association publishes the *Canadian Consumer,* a bi-monthly magazine. The Canadian government provides an annual subsidy to help support the work of this Association.

The annual inflation rate in Canada was about 10% during 1979–1980.

England

In England consumerism is an important social force, rooted in a militant labor movement. Despite the strength of the Labor Party and the importance of consumer cooperatives, the consumer movement in England has not advanced as rapidly as it has in some other western countries.

England does not have a central Ministry of Consumer Affairs. Consequently, responsibility for consumer protection is scattered throughout various government agencies. As a general rule, the central government is not involved in handling individual complaints from consumers and educational efforts in the consumer field are limited. At the local level, there are several hundred Citizens' Advice Bureaus which provide information and handle complaints of individual consumers. These Bureaus receive limited financial support from local authorities.

In 1975, the National Consumer Council was established to present the views of consumers to government and to industry. The aim is to establish a better balance between the interests of consumers and industry in the country's decision-making process.

The most important private consumer organization is the Consumers' Association which publishes the monthly magazine, *Which,* as well as books on topics of interest to consumers.

The annual inflation rate in England was 18% in 1980.

Australia

Australia is one of the world's most unionized countries. Approximately 60% of the work force is organized—compared to about 20% in the United States. The posture that Australian labor takes is militant in the tradition of British unionism, from which it sprang.

Despite the strong labor movement, consumer policy has developed slowly in Australia. The Trade Practices Act passed in 1974, and amended in 1975, covers many consumer matters not previously handled at a national level. The Act established the Trade Practices Commission and assigned it responsibility to protect and promote the interest of consumers both in response to complaints and on its own initiative. In addition to its investigative power, the Commission also has the functions of research, public information, and consumer guidance.

The Trade Practice Act has two major thrusts: (1) to strengthen competition of private enterprise at all levels of the production-distribution process, and (2) to strengthen the position of consumers relative to producers and distributors.

The Australian Federation of Consumer Organizations is made up of private consumer organizations. Its objectives are to provide a forum for discussion of consumer affairs and to focus public attention on consumer problems.

During 1979–1980, the annual inflation rate in Australia was approximately 10%.

From this brief discussion, it is obvious that consumerism is a force in all of the countries included in the survey. It is also apparent that the consumer movement has not reached the same stage of development in each nation. Based on this review of consumer protection policies and programs, the six countries are positioned along the life cycle curve as shown in Chart 1.

Expected Results _____

The study was designed to provide cross-cultural comparisons of consumer attitudes toward marketing practices. The objective was not to test *a priori* hypotheses in a rigorous fashion. Nevertheless, there is a logical basis for developing some general expectations about the patterns of response.

In general, the attitudes expressed by consumers in each country should reflect the stage or position that the country occupies in the consumerism life cycle. Therefore, since it is thought that Norway has reached the mature, bureaucracy stage—the first expectation is that Norwegians will generally be more satisfied with the status quo and will be less likely to want additional government regulation.

In Israel, on the other hand, the situation is just the opposite. Because of conditions in Israel, consumers experience many unique problems. Hence, the second expectation is that Israelis will be less satisfied with the status quo and more likely to want government intervention on behalf of consumers.

The other four countries share a common heritage and are more or less homogeneous in terms of cultural attitudes, language, and political ideology. They also tend to cluster along the central section of the consumerism life cycle curve. Con-

Chart 1
THE LIFE CYCLE POSITION OF THE SIX COUNTRIES STUDIED

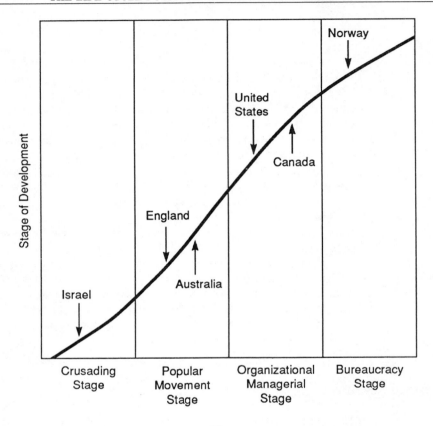

sequently, the third expectation is that consumer attitudes in Australia, Canada, England and the United States will fall somewhere between the opinions expressed by the Norwegians and Israelis.

Method

A basic problem in cross-national research is the isolation of true differences in the phenomena studied from variations caused by different methodology. The solution to the problem is to ensure equivalence in sampling procedure, stimulus material (questionnaire, test, or task), and mode of quantifying responses (scale used and procedure of scoring and coding). Borrowing from psycholinguistic terminology, sometimes a so-called *etic* (culturally universal) approach is feasible. This implies that behavior or mental states may be meaningfully described by formally equivalent measures or by universal categories having high reliability. In other cases, however, it is necessary to use *emic* (culturally specific) approaches. This means trading off formal equivalence for functional equivalence, that is, the procedures used in different cultures are intended to measure the same constructs.

Questionnaire

The measurement instrument was built on a questionnaire originally developed in the United States during the early 1970s.[5] In the first version, the questionnaire consisted of 40 Likert-type statements (chosen after a pretest of 67 items) and a number of questions about demographic charcteristics. For each statement, respondents were asked to indicate their level of agreement by checking one of five responses: strongly agree, agree, uncertain, disagree, and strongly disagree.

The original study (enlarged by six additional statements) was replicated in the United States in 1973, 1975, 1977, and 1979.[6] The high stability of responses in the five studies at an aggregate level suggests adequate instrument reliability.

In this study, particular care was taken to maintain equivalence of the questionnaire items. When the questionnaire was translated into another language, an iterative process was used. In Israel, Norway and Canada, translators converted the English version of the questionnaire into Hebrew, Norwegian, and French (for the French speaking section of Canada) and then another translator converted it back into English to isolate and correct problematic translations. In this fashion, the wording of the statements was made as similar as possible given language differences.

The United States version of the questionnaire contained a statement, concerning Ralph Nader, that was believed to be less meaningful in the other countries, so it was deleted. Hence, the number of statements was reduced from 46 to 45. Regarding the mode of quantifying responses, respondents in all six countries used the same five-point scale to indicate their level of agreement.

Data Collection

The method used to collect the data was essentially the same in all six countries. A questionnaire was mailed to a national sample of households in each country. The sample was drawn from telephone directories or national registration lists in the countries where such lists were available. With the exception of Canada and England, one follow-up was made. A summary of sample sizes and the response rates is given in Table 1.

Reservations

Similarity of the procedures used in the national studies should provide an acceptable level of equivalence and allow meaningful comparisons among the different countries. However, there are three points that should be mentioned. First, it should be noted that the relatively low level of telephone subscriptions in Norway (35 in Norway vs. 70 in the US per 100 inhabitants) may cause the Norwegian sample to be somewhat

Table 1
SAMPLING RESULTS AND SURVEY DATES

Sample Frame	Australia Federal Register	Canada Federal Election List	England Telephone Directories	Israel Register of Voters	Norway Telephone Directories	United States Telephone Directories
Number of Question-naires Mailed	1000	1500	1110	2000	500	1608
Number of Question-naires Delivered	980	1217	990	1655	484	1492
Number of Respondents Supplying Information	294	366	290	361	242	628
Follow-up	One	None	None	One (Subsample of non-respondents)	One	One
Response Rate	30%	30%	29%	22%	50%	42%
Survey Dates	Spring 1980	Fall 1979	Summer 1980	Fall 1979	Spring 1979	Spring 1979

less representative of the adult population than the United States counterpart. Second, although the response rates compare favorably with other mail surveys, the non-response must be considered in interpreting the results. Those returning the quesitonnaires may have stronger (and more positive or negative) opinions than those who did not respond. Third, the questionnaire was developed in the United States. While it is thought that the concepts included in the questionnaire have universal meaning, it is possible that the study contains some element of "methodological ethnocentrism."

Results

For purposes of discussion the 45 statements included in the questionnaire are grouped into the following categories: (1) philosophy of business, (2) product quality, (3) advertising, (4) other marketing activities, (5) consumer responsibilities, (6) consumerism, (7) government regulation, and (8) prices and price control.

Philosophy of Business

In all of the countries studied, there appears to be a high level of skepticism as well as considerable uncertainty about the operating philosophy of business (Table 2). Consumers in Australia, Canada, England, and the U.S. tend to hold similar views, while respondents in Israel were more negative and those in Norway were more positive in the opinions that they expressed.

In response to the statement, "Most manufacturers operate on the philosophy that the consumer is always right", one out of four Norwegians agreed, as contrasted to only one out of 11 Israelis. English and U.S. respondents were more negative on this issue (66% and 68%, respectively) and less uncertain than the remaining groups.

If manufacturers do not believe the consumer is always right, do they project an attitude of "Let the buyer beware"? Only 26% of Norwegians agreed, while 59% of Israeli respondents supported this notion. Respondents in the remaining four countries registered affirmative responses between the 40th and 50th percentiles.

About one-fourth of all respondents were uncertain whether manufacturers shirk their responsibilities to consumers. The preponderance of those expressing an opinion, however, held negative attitudes. Norwegians, who were evenly divided, were an exception to this pattern.

When put to a test of consumer opinion, the traditional "marketing concept" of business serving consumers is judged to be wanting; about 75% of respondents in five nations agreeing that profits were the stronger motivating force. Again, Norwegians were less critical of business with less than 50% holding negative views.

If consumers are skeptical about the intentions of business, they generally agree on the efficiency of the competitive system. Well over 50% of respondents in each country expressed the opinion that competition ensures fair prices. Yet, it may come as a surprise to North Americans to learn that both Canadian and U.S. respondents expressed less confidence in the effectiveness of the competitive system than other national groups.

Product Quality

Responses in Table 3 summarize attitudes toward product quality. In all six nations the majority of respondents (63%–84%) agree that manufacturers make an effort to design products to fit the needs of consumers. The level of agreement was lowest in Israel (63%), and the level of uncertainty (31%) there was highest. However, Israelis (43%) are the most positive in their attitude that the quality of products is improving. This is in contrast to other respondents; Britain, where 65% hold the opposite view, provides the sharpest contrast.

In line with their concerns about declining product quality, respondents in the English-speaking nations overwhelmingly believe that improvements in product quality are more desirable than style changes. In Britain, 86% of respondents expressed this view, while in Israel at the opposite extreme, only 51% held this opinion.

Pursuing the question of product quality, the data reveal high levels of uncertainty among most groups about manufacturers designing products to wear out as quickly as possible and manufacturers deliberately withholding product improvements to

Table 2
ATTITUDES TOWARD PHILOSOPHY OF BUSINESS

Statements	Country Surveyed	Percentage of Consumers				
		Strongly Agree	Agree	Uncertain	Disagree	Strongly Disagree
Most manufacturers operate on the philosophy that the consumer is always right.	Australia[1]	2	17	21	50	10
	Canada[2]	3	17	20	50	10
	England[3]	2	15	17	50	16
	Israel[4]	3	6	34	38	19
	Norway[5]	1	22	33	38	6
	United States[6]	1	15	16	55	13
Despite what is frequently said, "Let the buyer beware" is the guiding philosophy of most manufacturers.	Australia	9	34	30	26	1
	Canada	7	36	30	24	3
	England	7	41	27	24	1
	Israel	18	41	27	14	0
	Norway	5	21	35	33	6
	United States	8	33	28	29	2
Competition ensures that consumers pay fair prices for products.	Australia	17	55	7	17	4
	Cananda	14	42	13	25	6
	England	22	46	11	16	5
	Israel	28	41	18	11	2
	Norway	21	51	13	14	1
	United States	16	42	11	25	6
Manufacturers seldom shirk their responsibility to the consumer.	Australia	0	28	27	40	5
	Canada	3	29	23	40	5
	England	1	28	25	40	6
	Israel	6	22	24	38	10
	Norway	2	35	27	32	4
	United States	2	20	23	47	8
Most manufacturers are more interested in making profits than in serving consumers.	Australia	23	53	11	13	0
	Canada	21	53	11	13	2
	England	29	53	9	9	0
	Israel	33	45	17	5	0
	Norway	7	41	24	25	3
	United States	25	54	10	10	1

[1]Sample size 294   [4]Sample size 361
[2]Sample size 366   [5]Sample size 242
[3]Sample size 290   [6]Sample size 628

Table 3
43

ATTITUDES TOWARD PRODUCT QUALITY

Statements	Country Surveyed	Percentage of Consumers				
		Strongly Agree	Agree	Uncertain	Disagree	Strongly Disagree
In general, manufacturers make an effort to design products to fit the needs of consumers.	Australia	4	80	5	10	1
	Canada	6	75	6	12	1
	England	4	72	11	11	2
	Israel	5	58	31	5	1
	Norway	5	78	12	5	0
	United States	6	74	8	11	1
Over the past several years the quality of most products has not improved.	Australia	8	45	14	32	1
	Canada	10	37	19	32	2
	England	15	50	7	25	3
	Israel	6	27	24	38	5
	Norway	6	40	21	30	3
	United States	11	43	12	31	3
From the consumer's point of view, style changes are not as important as improvements in product quality.	Australia	27	57	8	7	1
	Canada	27	46	8	16	3
	England	28	58	5	8	1
	Israel	14	37	19	27	3
	Norway	8	52	17	21	2
	United States	29	51	7	12	1
Manufacturers do not deliberately design products which will wear out as quickly as possible.	Australia	1	30	22	34	13
	Canada	1	29	25	28	17
	England	4	31	26	29	10
	Isael	9	37	37	13	4
	Norway	2	25	37	25	11
	United States	3	32	28	24	13
Manufacturers often withhold important product improvements from the market in order to protect their own interests.	Australia	11	37	35	16	1
	Canada	15	37	31	15	2
	England	15	50	25	10	0
	Israel	22	43	24	11	0
	Norway	5	28	44	23	0
	United States	13	39	30	17	1
The wide variety of competing products makes intelligent buying decisions more difficult.	Australia	7	45	10	35	3
	Canada	7	54	6	30	3
	England	6	55	7	28	4
	Israel	10	36	22	27	5
	Norway	10	62	8	19	1
	United States	8	49	7	32	4
For most types of products, the differences among competing brands are insignificant and unimportant to consumers.	Australia	5	36	7	45	7
	Canada	4	33	7	50	6
	England	7	41	8	36	8
	Israel	14	41	25	17	3
	Norway	4	48	14	30	4
	United States	4	29	8	53	6

protect their own interests. Almost half of Canadian and Australian respondents find manufacturers suspect when it comes to designing products that will wear out quickly. Israelis (46%) disagree, but then another 37% of this same group is uncertain. The English and Israelis are in agreement (65%) that manufacturers withhold product improvement. Only 33% of Norwegians share this view, while 44% are uncertain.

The two statements concerning competing products drew interesting responses. While many consumers believe there is a significant difference among competing brands, most also believe that the existence of a variety of competing brands makes buying decisions more difficult.

In summary, Israeli and Norwegian attitudes are somewhat at odds with those of the four other national groups on issues of product quality. In general, however, consumer opinion suggests that product quality and product improvement are important areas of consumer concern. The notably harsh attitudes of Britons may well reflect declining standards of living as well as their response to manufacturers who have had to lower the quality of products in order to survive in a highly inflationary period.

Advertising

The similarities in respondent attitudes toward advertising are more conspicuous than the differences (Table 4). Despite wide variations in the volume of advertising and differences in levels of government regulation of advertising from one country to another, respondents in all six nations consistently expressed negative opinions about advertising.

At the outset, respondents (45–65%) do not think that most product advertising is believable. In five countries opinion is even more negative when manufacturers are linked to advertising. More specifically, in responding to the statement: "Manufacturers' advertisements are reliable sources of information about the quality and performance of products," consumers registered a negative (57–70%) response. Israelis are more negative (65%) on product advertising and less negative (57%) on reliability of manufacturers' advertisements than other groups.

When the statement about reliability of manufacturers' advertisements is couched in somewhat different terms, North Americans (63% Canada, 62% U.S.) are joined by Australians (61%) in their disbelief that manufacturers' advertisements usually present a true picture of the products advertised. Opinions in the three remaining nations (Israel, England, and Norway) are somewhat less negative (41%–50%). Consumers in Israel are the least positive (13%) and most uncertain (37%).
Attitudes about advertised products fall within the same negative range as opinion on advertising in general and advertising related to manufacturers. Regardless of nationality, most consumers (52–66%) simply do not believe that advertised products are more dependable than unadvertised ones. The highest positive rating of advertised, relative to unadvertised, products came from consumers in the US (22%).

Other Marketing Activities

While consumers were universally critical of advertising, they express somewhat more favorable opinions about some other marketing activities (Table 5). From a low of 85% of consumers in Israel to a high of 96% in Australia, Norway, and the

Table 4
ATTITUDES TOWARD ADVERTISING

Statements	Country Surveyed	Percentage of Consumers				
		Strongly Agree	Agree	Uncertain	Disagree	Strongly Disagree
Most product advertising is believable.	Australia	0	39	14	39	8
	Canada	1	32	14	41	12
	England	0	35	20	33	12
	Israel	2	5	28	44	21
	Norway	2	23	22	40	13
	United States	2	33	14	39	12
Manufacturers' advertisements are reliable sources of information about the quality and performance of products.	Australia	2	15	13	47	23
	Canada	1	16	13	44	26
	England	1	17	19	44	19
	Israel	3	11	29	34	23
	Norway	1	13	25	48	13
	United States	3	14	16	45	22
Generally, advertised products are more dependable than unadvertised ones.	Australia	2	16	16	57	9
	Canada	2	16	16	53	13
	England	0	20	18	45	17
	Israel	3	16	29	35	17
	Norway	2	13	22	51	12
	United States	3	19	18	49	11
Manufacturers' advertisements usually present a true picture of the products advertised.	Australia	1	22	16	51	10
	Canada	1	20	16	51	12
	England	1	28	22	38	11
	Israel	4	9	37	40	10
	Norway	0	28	31	38	3
	United States	1	20	17	49	13

U.S., consumers express faith in the distribution system, agreeing that the products required by the average family are easily available at convenient places. These high positive ratings suggest that most consumers are satisfied with product availability. In a similar vein, approximately two-thirds (or more) of the respondents in every country but Israel (41%) believe that product guarantees are backed up by the manufacturers who make them.

On the other hand, lack of improvement in the quality of repair and maintenance service was a matter of concern for consumers in all six nations. The proportion of respondents who thought that repair and maintenance service was improving was higher in Norway (29%) relative to other countries, but was still low overall.

Consumers everywhere expressed considerable skepticism about the honesty of games and contests sponsored by manufacturers. Israelis were the most skeptical and Australians the least.

Table 5
ATTITUDES TOWARD OTHER MARKETING ACTIVITIES

Statements	Country Surveyed	Percentage of Consumers				
		Strongly Agree	Agree	Uncertain	Disagree	Strongly Disagree
Generally speaking, the products required by the average family are easily available at convenient places.	Australia	19	77	1	3	0
	Canada	25	64	3	7	1
	England	13	78	3	5	1
	Israel	20	65	9	5	1
	Norway	26	70	2	2	0
	United States	30	66	1	3	0
In general, the quality of repair and maintenance service provided by manufacturers and dealers is getting better.	Australia	1	20	25	46	8
	Canada	3	23	25	39	10
	England	1	15	28	41	15
	Israel	1	15	41	33	10
	Norway	2	27	42	25	4
	United States	1	19	26	42	12
Generally, product guarantees are backed up by the manufacturers who make them.	Australia	4	75	10	9	2
	Canada	4	65	17	13	1
	England	3	67	18	10	2
	Israel	4	37	37	16	6
	Norway	2	64	24	9	1
	United States	3	68	16	12	1
The games and contests that manufacturers sponsor to encourage people to buy their products are usually dishonest.	Australia	4	15	36	42	3
	Canada	7	18	41	32	2
	England	4	16	43	34	3
	Israel	2	28	44	14	2
	Norway	4	20	46	28	2
	United States	6	14	44	33	3
The (name of country) marketing system operates more efficiently than those of other countries	Australia	0	7	77	13	3
	Canada	1	18	65	12	4
	England	3	14	65	14	4
	Israel	2	3	41	34	20
	Norway	3	8	79	9	1
	United States	16	39	39	5	1

Consumers were highly uncertain (as high as 79%) about the comparative efficiency of their own nation's marketing system. The most affirmative response came from US consumers, the majority of whom (55%) agreed that their marketing system operated most effectively, but even in the US, 39% were uncertain. The most negative response (54% disagreeing) came from Israeli consumers. From the answer patterns it is clear that most respondents do not feel confident in evaluating the relative efficiency of their nation's marketing system.

Consumer Responsibilities

Some of the most provocative findings of the study derive from Table 6, which deals with consumer responsibilities. Not only are there great differences in consumer opinion among the six countries studied, but in some cases opinion is sharply divided within nations.

Contemporary consumers may not feel that they are the first ones to face problems in the marketplace, but they do believe that their problems are as serious, if not more serious, than those faced by their predecessors. In reacting to the statement that consumers' problems are less serious now than in the past, only in Norway did more consumers agree (43%) than disagree (31%). Canadians held a position at the other extreme with 65% disagreeing and 19% agreeing that consumer problems are less serious now.

When asked to indicate whether or not their problems as consumers were relatively unimportant, compared with the other questions and issues faced by the average family, 63% of the US respondents and 60% of those in Canada disagreed. In contrast, 65% of the Norwegians agreed that consumer problems were less important than other questions.

Respondents universally recognized that not all consumer problems are the fault of business. More than 70% of the sample in each country agreed that many of the mistakes that consumers make in buying products are the result of their own carelessness or ignorance. In Israel, where the consumer movement is relatively weak, 91% of respondents thought that many mistakes in buying were due to carelessness or ignorance. Consistent with this response, only 19% of the Israelis believe that the information needed to become a well-informed consumer is readily available to most people.

Table 6
ATTITUDES TOWARD CONSUMER RESPONSIBILITIES

Statements	Country Surveyed	Percentage of Consumers				
		Strongly Agree	Agree	Uncertain	Disagree	Strongly Disagree
The problems of consumers are less serious now than in the past	Australia	2	26	23	44	5
	Canada	2	17	16	50	15
	England	2	27	18	42	11
	Israel	2	14	30	44	10
	Norway	2	41	26	28	3
	United States	3	19	22	45	11
The information needed to become a well-informed consumer is readily available to most people.	Australia	2	44	18	32	4
	Canada	7	53	12	23	5
	England	4	38	20	34	4
	Israel	3	16	22	42	17
	Norway	4	44	21	27	4
	United States	6	44	15	31	4

(continued)

Table 6 (continued)
ATTITUDES TOWARD CONSUMER RESPONSIBILITIES

Statements	Country Surveyed	Percentage of Consumers				
		Strongly Agree	Agree	Uncertain	Disagree	Strongly Disagree
The average consumer is willing to pay higher prices for product that will cause less environmental pollution.	Australia	4	20	21	48	7
	Canada	6	25	26	39	4
	England	5	19	24	44	8
	Israel	10	29	38	20	3
	Norway	10	35	30	22	3
	United States	4	27	28	36	5
The problems of the consumer are relatively unimportant when compared with the other questions and issues faced by the average family.	Australia	4	34	21	36	5
	Canada	3	20	17	52	8
	England	3	39	17	35	6
	Israel	5	17	26	42	10
	Norway	11	54	16	18	1
	United States	3	18	16	51	12
Many of the mistakes that consumers make in buying products are the result of their own carelessness or ignorance.	Australia	9	70	6	14	1
	Canada	12	62	9	16	1
	England	12	59	10	16	3
	Israel	34	57	6	3	0
	Norway	13	64	10	11	2
	United States	14	59	10	15	2
Consumers often try to take advantage of manufacturers and dealers by making claims that are not justified.	Australia	3	20	27	45	5
	Canada	5	29	26	34	6
	England	2	19	26	43	10
	Israel	3	10	24	49	14
	Norway	4	16	15	52	13
	United States	6	24	21	42	7
For most types of products consumers do not find it worthwhile to shop around to find the best buys.	Australia	4	42	5	41	8
	Canada	5	35	8	43	9
	England	7	32	7	40	14
	Israel	12	36	12	33	7
	Norway	8	42	10	36	4
	United States	4	32	7	47	10
Concern for the environment does not influence the product choices made by most consumers.	Australia	9	63	14	14	0
	Canada	7	57	14	20	2
	England	16	65	10	8	1
	Israel	13	52	21	11	3
	Norway	5	60	20	12	3
	United States	8	55	16	19	2

It might be assumed that inflation would encourage most consumers to shop around to find the best buys. However, consumer opinion is mixed on this issue in all six countries. US respondents led the English speaking nations in their belief that consumers find it worthwhile to shop around, while Norwegians and Israelis lean the other way. In Israel with triple-digit inflation, consumers apparently do not perceive any great price differential from one retail outlet to another. In the US, on the other hand, retailers compete by advertising "specials", and for some people shopping becomes a family pastime or entertainment. In addition, the mobility of consumers may encourage retailers to compete for business. Even though Israel is a modern nation in many respects, with only one automobile for every ten persons mobility is limited, and it is probably difficult for most consumers to engage in comparison shopping. In turn, there is probably little competition among retailers who are assured of captive customers.

Does concern for the environment influence the product choices made by consumers? Most respondents report that it does not. Pushed one step further on the environmental issue, a mixed pattern of opinion emerges on whether consumers are willing to pay more for products that will cause less environmental pollution. Britons and Australians appear the least concerned about the environment and the least agreeable to paying more to ensure its integrity. Respondents in the other four nations are more concerned, but views were mixed, as to whether consumers are willing to pay more for products that are environmentally safe. Given the above attitudes, it seems doubtful that manufacturers will be able to pass on successfully the additional expenses sometimes involved in making "socially responsible" decisions in product designs unless such designs are mandated by government.

Consumerism

Over the years the consumer movement in many countries has exerted considerable effort to make manufacturers more attuned to the complaints of consumers as well as to make consumers more aware of their rights and even more assertive in exercising these rights. Just how does the situation stand now? Are manufacturers more sensitive to consumer complaints than they were in the past? More than half of the respondents in four countries think they are, but only 43% of Britons and 44% of US consumers agree. (Table 7).

One measure of manufacturer sensitivity might be the ease with which consumers are able to get problems with products corrected. About one-third of Australians agree that it is usually easy to rectify problems with products. Agreement by respondents in the other countries is lower; only one in 11 Israeli consumers think it is easy to get problems with products corrected (as compared to about one in four remaining countries).

Given the above response, it is interesting to note that over one-half of the respondents in each nation but Israel believe that most business firms make a sincere effort to adjust consumer complaints fairly.

Well-intentioned as business might be, the majority of consumers in five nations do not believe the procedures followed by most manufacturers in handling complaints and settling grievances are satisfactory. In Norway, however, only 44% express

Table 7
ATTITUDES TOWARD CONSUMERISM

Statements	Country Surveyed	Percentage of Consumers				
		Strongly Agree	Agree	Uncertain	Disagree	Strongly Disagree
Manufacturers seem to be more sensitive to consumer complaints now than they were in the past.	Australia	5	49	18	22	6
	Canada	5	48	19	21	7
	England	3	40	20	30	7
	Israel	17	45	26	10	2
	Norway	2	56	27	13	2
	United States	4	40	22	27	7
When consumers have problems with products they have purchased, it is usually easy to get them corrected.	Australia	2	32	18	43	5
	Canada	2	26	15	48	9
	England	0	23	21	47	9
	Israel	2	7	33	45	13
	Norway	1	24	28	42	5
	United States	1	22	18	49	10
Most business firms make a sincere effort to adjust consumer complaints fairly.	Australia	1	54	23	21	1
	Canada	3	59	23	13	2
	England	2	53	26	18	1
	Israel	6	24	49	17	4
	Norway	2	51	31	15	1
	United States	3	54	22	19	2
From the consumer's viewpoint the procedures followed by most manufacturers in handling complaints and settling grievances of consumers are not satisfactory.	Australia	7	45	22	26	0
	Canada	12	43	21	23	1
	England	13	49	16	20	2
	Israel	20	54	19	7	0
	Norway	7	37	36	19	1
	United States	10	47	23	18	2
Consumerism or the consumer crusade has not been an important factor in changing business practices and procedures.	Australia	1	28	27	41	3
	Canada	3	16	23	51	7
	England	3	31	31	31	4
	Israel	5	28	28	33	6
	Norway	0	22	42	33	3
	United States	3	23	25	43	6
The exploitation of consumers by business firms deserves more attention than it receives.	Australia	21	55	13	10	1
	Canada	26	49	15	8	2
	England	23	50	13	12	2
	Israel	32	48	14	5	1
	Norway	10	51	25	13	1
	United States	20	53	19	6	2

dissatisfaction with the procedures for handling complaints. In essence, consumers appear to be indicating that business seems to be sincere and is making an effort to settle grievances, but there is just too much inconvenience and red tape in getting complaints adjusted.

If business practices have changed, do respondents think that the consumer movement has been an important factor in bringing about that change? Respondents in Canada (58%) and the U.S. (49%) think it has. Australians (44%) and Israelis (39%) are not too far behind US respondents in crediting the consumer movement with positive change on the part of business. English consumers, however, are evenly divided on this issue.

Even though consumers believe that business is improving in settling grievances and that the consumer movement has been an influence in bringing about change, about three-fourths of the respondents in five nations still think that exploitation of consumers deserves more attention than it receives. Even in Norway where business practices appear to be held in higher regard than elsewhere, 61% of the respondents believe that consumer exploitation deserves more attention, suggesting that business in all six nations cannot afford to relax on matters relating to customer relations.

In conclusion, the message that respondents convey in this section is threefold: (1) the intentions of business are good; (2) the performance of business still falls short of consumer expectations; and (3) the consumer movement is responsible for the positive change in the performance of business.

Government Regulation

The extent to which business activities are regulated by government varies from one nation to another. Consumers in countries with a strong socialist orientation are likely to take one attitude toward government regulation. Consumers in capitalist countries, on the other hand, are likely to see things differently. In addition to political orientation, other factors such as levels of inflation, standard of living, strength of the consumer movement, and attitudes toward business may influence opinions about government regulation of business. Differences and similarities of opinion concerning government regulation are summarized in Table 8.

In every nation studied, 60% or more of respondents agreed that government should test competing brands of products and make the results of these tests available to consumers. Israelis (91%) and Canadians (82%) are at one extreme in favoring this form of government regulation. US consumers (60%) are at the other.

Respondents everywhere favor government established quality standards for all consumer products. Israeli (95%) and US (58%) consumers are at the extremes on this issue. One might suppose that US consumers are least in favor of government setting quality standards because they view this as a monumental task that would disrupt the flow of goods. Moreoever, having watched government intervention in other areas, many US consumers may not be convinced on a cost-benefit basis that government can do a satisfactory job.

Consumers also believe that the government should exercise greater control over the advertising, sales, and marketing activities of manufacturers. More uncertain on this point than the two previous issues, consumers (48–85%) still give strong

Table 8
ATTITUDES TOWARD GOVERNMENT REGULATION

Statements	Country Surveyed	Percentage of Consumers				
		Strongly Agree	Agree	Uncertain	Disagree	Strongly Disagree
The government should test competing brands of products and make results of these tests available to consumers.	Australia	28	40	8	20	4
	Canada	42	40	5	9	4
	England	30	42	7	15	6
	Israel	64	27	4	4	1
	Norway	22	49	10	14	5
	United States	22	38	10	21	9
The government should set minimum standards of quality for all products sold to consumers.	Australia	35	49	4	10	2
	Canada	30	49	9	9	3
	England	33	46	6	12	3
	Israel	59	36	2	2	1
	Norway	18	47	15	17	3
	United States	15	43	12	21	9
The government should exercise more responsibility for regulating the advertising, sales, and marketing activities of manufacturers.	Australia	17	45	15	20	3
	Canada	20	47	14	15	4
	England	19	39	14	23	5
	Israel	42	43	8	6	1
	Norway	7	42	23	21	7
	United States	11	37	16	26	10
A Federal Department of Consumer Protection is not needed to protect and promote the interests of consumers.	Australia	2	10	8	45	35
	Canada	4	4	10	49	33
	England	7	13	6	44	30
	Israel	3	6	5	38	48
	Norway	6	18	11	41	24
	United States	6	13	7	45	29
In general, self-regulation by business itself is preferable to stricter control of business by the government.	Australia	12	47	12	22	7
	Canada	10	38	19	27	6
	England	16	48	15	17	4
	Israel	12	30	20	29	9
	Norway	12	35	18	29	6
	United States	22	43	17	15	3

support to a notion of "let government do it". US (48%) and Norwegian (49%) consumers were least in favor and Israelis (85%) were most.

Having expressed support for increased government control over product quality and marketing activities, it is not surprising that about three-fourths or more of the respondents in five nations favor a National Department of Consumer Protection to protect and promote the interest of consumers. Norwegians (65%) were least in favor of such an agency, an opinion which is consistent with the more favorable

Table 9
ATTITUDES TOWARD PRICES AND PRICE CONTROL

Statements	Country Surveyed	Percentage of Consumers				
		Strongly Agree	Agree	Uncertain	Disagree	Strongly Disagree
The most important problem facing conumers today is the high prices of consumer goods.	Australia	36	36	5	21	2
	Canada	40	35	7	16	2
	England	48	32	5	12	3
	Israel	50	37	7	5	1
	Norway	28	43	8	20	1
	United States	42	39	6	11	2
High prices of consumer goods are caused primarily by wholesale and retail middlemen taking excessive profits.	Australia	28	35	19	17	1
	Canada	23	37	16	18	6
	England	32	38	13	14	3
	Israel	46	34	13	5	2
	Norway	17	30	23	23	7
	United States	24	38	20	16	2
Considering wage rates and income levels today, most consumer products are priced fairly.	Australia	2	36	15	37	10
	Canada	4	29	13	43	11
	England	1	27	18	40	14
	Israel	1	8	17	52	22
	Norway	2	47	16	28	7
	United States	1	26	15	46	12
Refusal of consumers to buy expensive products is the most effective way of keeping prices of consumer goods at reasonable levels.	Australia	15	47	10	25	3
	Canada	22	44	14	16	4
	England	31	46	9	11	3
	Israel	50	34	11	4	1
	Norway	9	47	18	24	2
	United States	26	46	12	14	2
Government price control is the most effective way of keeping the prices of consumer products at reasonable levels.	Australia	10	37	16	31	6
	Canada	10	26	27	31	6
	England	17	32	13	30	8
	Israel	36	35	18	9	2
	Norway	16	55	12	12	5
	United States	9	22	20	32	17

attitudes they expressed toward business. US consumers (74%) appear to have shifted their attitudes on the matter of a Federal Department of Consumer Affairs, considering they were least in favor of government establishing quality standards or regulating marketing activities. However, they may be indicating an interest in a centalized "watchdog" agency to protect the interests of consumers rather than a number of different costly agencies employing many people to make minute inquiries and decisions regarding countless numbers of products and a variety of marketing practices.

Over one-half of the respondents in the US (65%), England (64%), and Australia (59%) think that self-regulation is preferable to stricter control of business by the government. Consumers in Canada (48%), Norway (47%), and Israel (42%) were also favorable, but to a lesser degree. The opposing viewpoint was supported at the 38% level in Israel.

Prices and Price Control

Although the rate varies from country to country, rising prices have been a fact of life in each of the six nations under study. Confronted with triple-digit inflation, it is not surprising that Israelis (87%) view high prices as the most important problem facing consumers (Table 9). Even with the indexing of wages, only 9% of the Israeli sample believes that most products are priced fairly. At the opposite extreme, almost 50% of the Norwegians think products are priced fairly considering wage rates and income levels.

Always the scapegoat, middlemen are seen as taking excessive profits and hence are blamed for high prices by 60% or more of respondents in five countries. Norwegians (47%) are somewhat less critical in this view.

If respondents are troubled by inflation and high prices, they still feel that consumers have some control and can exert some influence in keeping the prices of goods at reasonable levels. Over half of those responding in each nation, ranging from a low of 56% in Norway to a high of 84% in Israel, expressed agreement that refusal to buy expensive products is the most effective way of keeping prices of consumer goods at reasonable levels.

Consumers can delay discretionary purchases, but many items are necessities, and purchase of these products cannot be postponed. Government price control is viewed as the most effective means of keeping prices of consumer goods at reasonable levels by 71% of respondents in Israel and Norway. US respondents (31%), perhaps recalling ineffective efforts to control prices, are least favorable. Among the six national groups, only Norwegians believed that government price control would be more effective than refusal of consumers to buy as a means of keeping prices whithin reason.

Conclusions

It was anticipated that the opinions expressed by consumers in each nation would reflect, in a general way, the stage of development of the consumer movement within each country. However, the response patterns do not support this concept. While it appears that Norwegians are generally less critical of business than the Israelis, on some other issues they are in close agreement. Similarly, opinions of consumers in other nations do not follow any consistent pattern. In other words, no clear patterns of opinion emerge that would suggest that any particular nation would fit neatly into a particular stage of the consumer movement life cycle.

Consumers in all countries expresss similar opinions on many topics. While it was anticipated that there would be general agreement on some issues, the high level of agreement across all nations on particular statements was a surprising element in the study. For example, the majority of consumers in all six countries acknowledge that the products required by the average family are conveniently available. Also, consumers everywhere express concern about the high prices of goods and services, despite the wide variations in inflation rates and price levels. Consumers also concede that many of the mistakes they make in buying are the result of their own carelessness and ignorance. Product quality is another universal concern that is reflected in the response to a number of statements. Negative attitudes toward advertising are registered by consumers in all six nations. Respondents simply do not accept advertising at face value; nor do they believe that advertised products are superior in quality to unadvertised ones. Finally, there is strong feeling in all countries that government has a responsibility to safeguard the rights of consumers.

4. CONDUCTING AND CO-ORDINATING MULTI-COUNTRY QUANTITATIVE STUDIES ACROSS EUROPE

PHILIP BARNARD

This paper was presented at a joint seminar 'International research: a view from both sides of the Atlantic' held at the Waldorf Astoria, New York, sponsored by the International Research Committee of The Market Research Society and the New York Chapter of the American Marketing Association, October 1981.

Introduction

Nearly $3 billion of marketing research was *commissioned* worldwide in 1980, around 85% of it in the United States and Western Europe. Most of this expenditure was accounted for by multinational corporations and about one-third of it handled by a dozen or so multinational research suppliers (see page 64).

MARKETING RESEARCH EXPENDITURE WORLDWIDE, 1980*

	$ m
Total	2,750
North America	1,350
Europe	1,000
Asia/Oceania	270
Central/South America	70
Africa	40
Middle East	20

*Unless otherwise specified, all tables are based on Research International estimates.

Although most of the research spend is made by local (national) subsidiaries of multinationals, a significant proportion is commissioned internationally from corporate or regional head offices. Even locally generated work is often influenced by corporate policies, standardised procedures and central advice and recommendation.

Reprinted from the *Journal of Market Research Society 24*, No. 1 (January 1982) 46–64 by permission of the Journal of Research Society.

American corporations dominate the ranks of the multinationals and, hence, set the pattern for the ways in which international research is commissioned. Whereas, in the US domestic market, a client will normally use the services of an American research supplier, the range of commonly used options is much wider internationally. In the simplest case of a US client wishing to commission a survey in one foreign country, four commonly used approaches are illustrated:

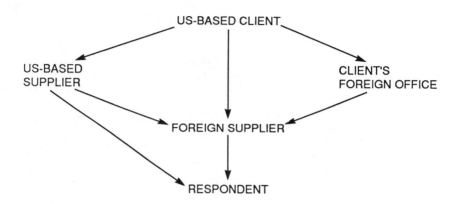

In reality, the picture is more complex in that, for example:

(i) the US and foreign research suppliers may be part of the same chain or group;
(ii) the client's local office may be involved in a (part) funding capacity as well as (possibly) local agency selection and control;
(iii) an advertising agency or consulting organisation may commission the study on the client's behalf.

Even in this simple one country case, a specialist international coordinating agency in a third country may be involved and this becomes particularly attractive when the research programme extends to several countries, either concurrently or sequentially.
Against this background, the principal suppliers of international research are:

- multinational research companies ⎫
- research chains ⎭ using one of their units as a co-ordinating agency— commissioned in the client's own country or elsewhere
- national (local) research suppliers, commissioned directly by the client or via a co-ordinating agency
- 'travellers' from research companies in the client's own country or elsewhere.

What Approach? ——

There are many influences determining what type of supplier might be most suitable and how a particular international research project might best be handled:

(i) The nature of the commissioning organisation and whether or not, it has offices or representation in the countries to be researched is a key factor:

Who commissions international research?
Multinational company
■ International Head Office
■ Regional (eg European) Head Office
■ National subsidiary
National company
Advertising agency
Consultant
■ Organisation
■ Individual
Market research supplier
Non-commercial organisation

Any of the types of organisation shown above may be the 'client' who actually commissions the international co-ordinating agency or local supplier. Most typically, it would be a multinational company and in this case it is particularly important for the research supplier to be aware of the corporate structure and which part of the organisation is (a) funding and (b) handling the project.

The operating procedures and communication channels for an international study will be more complex where the client's corporate HQ, European (or other) regional office and local (eg French, British and German) operations are all involved. The balance between the forces of decentralisation and head office or regional control can add a *political* dimension that suppliers ignore at their peril.

(ii) Companies also display different international marketing strategies and styles which, depending on the nature of the product/service and corporate philosophy, can generally be characterised as:
■ similar *brand* everywhere (eg ethical pharmaceuticals, office equipment, automobiles)
■ similar *product* but variation in the marketing mix (eg many packaged goods industries, including food and drink)
■ meeting similar *needs* with different products/mixes (eg financial services)

The greater the magnitude and time scale of pre-launch R & D investment, the greater the need for a rapid multi-country payback (with product/brand variation by market being less acceptable), which argues for marketing research to be conducted more or less simultaneously on a multi-country basis.

(iii) The number and homogeneity of the countries involved is of great importance and the opportunity to use a *lead country* in a rolling or sequential programme of research can often enhance the value of the whole project.

If one of the research purposes is to establish country priorities then comparability across countries becomes more important.

(iv) The nature of the market place information sought is the other main determinant of the research approach adopted. The more strategic issues tend to involve greater central (client HQ) interest whereas tactical concerns are often dealt with in a more decentralised fashion with much input from the client's local operating subsidiaries.

It is convenient to consider information needs in broad categories that can provide guidance in three main areas:

(a) *market orientation*—the basic data required prior to market entry and to establish between-country priorities is represented by (eg) market size and structure; companies/brands represented; prices; distribution channels and media availability/costs.

(b) *strategy orientation*—to help develop or modify marketing and promotional strategies requires more detailed and diagnostic information such as market shares; brand awareness/trial; product/brand imagery and competitive weaknesses; consumer motivations/attitudes and profiles.

(c) *problem orientation*—research designed specifically to help clients optimise product design/formulation; brand positioning/target group; advertising/promotion; pricing; packaging and distribution.

Some of the information requirements listed under *market* and *strategy* orientation can be satisfied by desk research and drawing on syndicated (sometimes continuous) research services. Specific *problem*-related information needs generally require fresh data collection and this leads to the more typical international research survey.

In summary, the main issues determining the overall approach to an international research project are:

1. The client company's international management structure and operating procedures;
2. The products and brands concerned—their 'internationalism', investment implications and 'sophistication';
3. Whether the purpose is primarily strategic or tactical;
4. The number and nature of the geographic markets of interest;
5. Funding—the size and source of budgets;
6. Time scale;
7. The expertise and knowledge required both for the co-ordination tasks and for understanding the product or business sector involved.

Local Factors

These broad influences on how international research may be approached must be seen against the background of considerable variation in the cultural, socio-political and industrial characteristics of European countries. Many such factors are relevant to the design and implementation of international research studies.

Language differences are so obvious that, paradoxically, they tend to be ignored except when questionnaire translation is being considered. However, the influence of language is far deeper (see page 61) and it is also important to remember that several European countries are multi-lingual or have significant linguistic minorities—with associated cost, and other, implications.

It is also easy to overlook the fact that each nation state in Europe has its own distinctive *'frame of reference'* defined by legislation; business practices; population size and structure; degree of urbanisation/industrialisation and shared cultural and historical experience.

The diversity produced by these general factors alone emphasises the need, in most marketing contexts, to treat 'Europe' as 20 different countries rather than 20 regions of one country.

However, the point is strongly reinforced by examination of particular business sectors and more specific aspects of the marketing infrastructure. For example, whilst television is virtually ubiquitous and there is relatively little variation in levels of car ownership, there are still marked differences in the household penetration of other consumer durables:

HOUSEHOLD PENETRATION OF CERTAIN CONSUMER DURABLES IN SELECTED EUROPEAN COUNTRIES

(% households owning, 1980)	Automobile	Telephone	Freezer	Dishwasher
Belgium	81	70	45	14
Finland	62	77	47	9
France	69	60	28	15
Germany	76	70	59	19
Italy	75	50	27	17
Spain	57	40	na	8
UK	68	69	50	3
USA	86	97	45	42

Perhaps of greater significance are the variations in such fundamental features of the marketing environment as money, the retail trade structure, the media and (for OTC and ethical pharmaceutical products) health care systems.

Just consider the various forms of money in Western Europe. Only in the UK do credit cards of the Visa and Mastercard type have any widespread penetration. The Post Office Giro dominates regular transactions in the Netherlands and several other countries. The use of current or checking bank accounts also varies greatly across countries and all this clearly affects the framework within which consumer purchasing behaviour occurs and may need to be taken into account in the design and interpretation of research studies.

Consider too the retail trade. We are so accustomed to thinking of increasing trade concentration that the very large differences still existing between countries can be overlooked. For example, about 80% of grocery sales in the US pass through supermarkets. In the UK it is around 50%, in Italy under 20% and in Spain about 5%. The *total* number of food outlets and the growth of hypermarkets both bear little relationship to total populations and more to national culture and a protective legal framework for small independent retailers in many countries.

Advertising expenditure as a proportion of GNP varies by a factor of at least four across Europe and the patterns of media expenditure show wide variation too. Television's share, for example, ranges from zero in Norway (Sweden, Denmark and Belgium also have no commercial television—except that beamed over the borders) and 9% in France to nearly 50% in Greece. This has obvious implications for advertising research and much wider effects too, especially in new product development and the launching/re-launching of brands:

PROFILES OF ADVERTISING EXPENDITURE

	Norway	France	Germany (BRD)	USA	UK	Japan	Brazil	Greece
Cinema	2	1	1	na	1	na	1	2
Radio	—	6	3	7	2	5	20	5
TV	—	9	11	20	24	35	40	47
Print	78	39	65	38	61	37	31	45
All others (outdoor, direct, etc.)	20	45	20	35	12	23	8	1

Source International Advertising Association.

The Local Market Research Scene

Some features of the market research environment are fairly consistent from country to country within Europe. Market measurement accounts for about half of each market and the research spend is generally split fairly evenly between three types of supplier:

- Audit and panel operators
- Large ad hoc research suppliers (with international links)
- Medium/small ad hoc suppliers

and *personal* interviewing still dominates the research scene in all European countries.

However, there are many aspects of the market research business that do vary by country, such as:

- size of market research market
- role of omnibuses
- degree of supplier specialisation
- 'original' v 'screening' research
- literacy level/postal efficiency/telephone penetration
- data bases/sampling frames

The very size of a country's market research market conditions the degree of specialisation the industry can support. The supplier resource you are looking for may not exist in that country. Whilst retail audits of food and drug stores exist throughout Europe as do consumer panels measuring general grocery markets, many other services have only partial coverage—distribution checks, audits of specialist outlets, industrial/agricultural audits/panels and mini-test markets.

In some of the smaller countries research can be dominated by the use of omnibuses and suppliers may have considerable experience in screening new products developed elsewhere but only limited knowledge of how to handle a new product development programme from scratch.

The application of common or similar techniques across European countries rarely in itself presents major problems. There are, however, some associated pitfalls. For example, socio-economic classifications vary by country and national occupation groupings are influenced considerably by the size of the rural/farming population.

Another example concerns the apparently straightforward area of focus groups and depth interviews. In some countries, most suppliers would automatically tape the groups (one-way mirrors are rarely used in Europe) or interviews and produce a full content analysis from the transcripts as a precursor to the final report. Many British suppliers adopt the more pragmatic line of tailoring the depth of analysis to the research objectives and, for example, using more limited analytical procedures for a study involving the evaluation of alternative pack or advertising stimulus material than would be the case in a more fundamental project designed to uncover buying motivations in an unfamiliar market. Either way, the client should be aware that such divergences of approach can exist and be prepared to define clearly what he requires.

Nevertheless, most of the techniques, scalar devices, visual aids and procedures commonly used in the USA *can* be applied in European countries. The problems arise mainly when local suppliers are asked to apply techniques or administer procedures that are unfamiliar or not commonly used by them—although intrinsically they might work well in that country. This is where the development of standard techniques and procedures by research groups or chains can be of benefit.

To an American research buyer, one of the most obvious differences between European countries is that of research prices. It is notoriously difficult to provide comparative data on this as price levels depend on such factors as:

- the nature of the study;
- whether local agencies are able to use their normal working practices and data collection methods or have to employ less familiar (and, hence, usually more expensive) approaches;

■ the mix of costs involved (eg is it mainly data collection or is there a significant executive component?).

Exchange rate fluctuation and rapid inflation in some countries adds to these difficulties. With these caveats, the table illustrates relative *cost* levels in Europe for fieldwork out-of-pockets in mid-1981:

EUROPEAN COSTS FIELDWORK OUT-OF-POCKETS

Sweden	2.9	Italy	1.5
Denmark	2.4	Netherlands	1.4
Germany	2.0	Belgium	1.3
France	1.9	Austria	1.3
Finland	1.7	UK	1.0
Spain	1.7	Greece	0.7

1981
Indexed to UK (= 1)

A major element in this league table is the role played by employer-funded social costs which can add up to half as much again to the basic interviewer fee. In France, for example, the figure is indeed 50% whereas it is zero in the UK, unless the interviewer earns more than about $200 in a month when a 9% levy becomes payable.

Executive costs show a different pattern and, although Britain remains the cheapest major European country, the differentials are narrower than for fieldwork.

Comparison with American cost levels is rendered difficult as the US market research supply industry differs substantially from the European pattern:

■ more research design and analysis is generally handled in the client company than is the case in Europe;

■ perhaps for that reason, US suppliers often recover executive costs through a gross margin or general mark-up whereas major European suppliers generally charge an hourly rate for the estimated/actual executive time involved;

■ unlike their European counterparts, most US suppliers do not operate their own fieldforce but sub-contract;

■ personal interviewing at home is still the most common form of data collection in Europe whereas mall intercept and telephone methods predominate in the USA;

■ a higher proportion of American ad hoc research is accounted for by regular or standardised services which offer the costs benefits of amortising setting-up expenses over many studies and permitting 'production line' efficiencies to develop.

All this not only has a number of general implications for the dialogue between American and British researchers but, more specifically, also makes it impossible to compare like with like where costs are concerned. However, it would seem that US interviewer and executive *costs* are closer to those of continental Europe and, perhaps, $1\frac{1}{2}$–2 times those obtaining in the UK although, for the reasons discussed, *prices* may show rather different patterns.

I have emphasised many of the national variations both in market research practices/ facilities and more general societal features because one of the keys to success in international research is a familiarity with, and ability to work within, these differing frameworks. In particular, the research supplier's local knowledge and 'feel' is critical to the smooth running of such studies.

Operating Mechanics of International Studies

The six main areas that, in my experience, buyers tend to cover when evaluating international research organisations are set out opposite.

Research supplier criteria

1. Resources
2. Management/geographical structure
3. Systems and procedures
4. Technical capability
5. Business sector knowledge
6. Experience

Let us assume that a concurrent multi-country study has been commissioned and a co-ordinating agency appointed which then uses local agencies (perhaps, but not necessarily, part of its own group or chain) to handle the data collection whilst centralising the co-ordination and other tasks. The flow of a typical international job using a co-ordinating agency in this way is shown on page 65.

In spite of the apparent complexity, the sequence is fairly straightforward. The scope for duplication (or triplication!) of effort and for mis-communication is, however, enormous. It is essential, therefore, to allocate the tasks clearly to the several parties concerned and above all to be systematic and unambiguous—using familiar, standard procedures whenever possible.

I would like to make some brief observations about the issues to be considered at the several stages of such a study.

Client Briefing

For the potential co-ordinating agency, the project really begins when the client first mentions the possibility of an international job. The spectrum of client *briefing* approaches is far wider than normally encountered with national studies. It can range from a request for a very general cost and timing estimate where even country selection is very uncertain, through to a formal brief incorporating a detailed job specification and questionnaire as already used elsewhere, typically in the United States.

The scope for creative proposal writing and for the research supplier's executives to add value through their problem interpretation and research design skills does,

SEQUENCE OF TASKS IN MULTI-COUNTRY STUDY

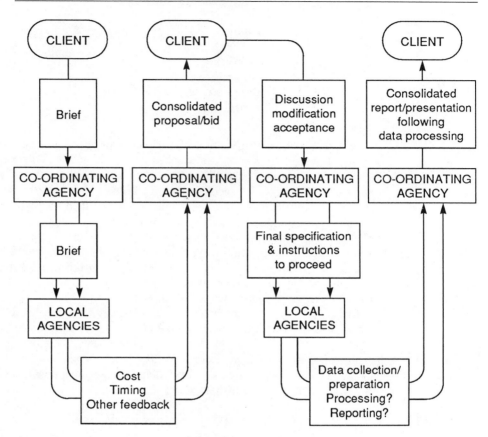

therefore, vary greatly. It can be of considerable benefit if the supplier has an American office to permit clarification of any uncertainties at the briefing stage and to ensure that the enquiry is a serious one which justifies the international communication costs in preparing a formal proposal.

Local Agency Briefing

Except for the simplest international studies, the co-ordinating agency will want to *communicate with the local agencies* before preparing its client proposal. The local agency should be briefed in writing—telex is usually the most efficient means initially—both to provide a record and to give an opportunity for the recipient to digest the requirements and discuss any issues with colleagues before responding.

As ambiguity is the enemy of international research, it is very helpful for the co-ordinating agency to use a standard form of checklist when briefing the agencies which will conduct the local fieldwork. For example, the checklist we use in Research International is designed to ensure that all relevant job details are given and all identifiable tasks are clearly allocated between co-ordinating and local agencies.

Apart from background information, the checklist covers a range of tasks categorised thus:

Function	Number of tasks
Executive	18
Production	11
Data collection	21
Data processing	13
Commercial	5
Timing	7

Of course, such a systematic and disciplined approach to local agency briefing is not always necessary at this pre-proposal stage especially if the job is simple and the client only requires an outline proposal or quotation initially. However, at *some* stage before finalising the specification for the local agencies, this *kind* of checklist can usefully be consulted. The more knowledge the fieldwork agencies have about the job they are required to do, the less risk there is of duplicating work and either under- or over-costing through misunderstandings or uncertainty.

When well briefed, the local agencies will be able to *feed back* not only a cost estimate and a time schedule but also comments on the proposed method and on cost sensitive aspects in relation to the country concerned and the local agency's own resources and planned work commitments.

If you work closely with particular agencies it can be very useful to keep details of their resources, facilities, experience, cost rates, standard services and so on.

Although the following list summarises the headings contained in the internal handbook covering my own organisation's agencies around the world, the contents may be helpful in suggesting the information *any* co-ordinating agency or client might wish to know about the suppliers to which it subcontracts.

LOCAL AGENCY DETAILS

Staff
numbers by type/function
cost rates by type/function
contact executives

Data Collection
field force
postal panel
other postal
test centres
telephone
street interviewing
hall/mall
workplace
specialist interviewers
cost rates

Production
equipment
cost rates

Standard Services
Data Processing
editing method
data transfer method
program/language
location of computer
cost rates

Qualitative Research
specialist executives
freelancers
recruitment procedures
video facilities
cost rates/standard costs

International Research
contact executives
experience
specialist expertise
translation facilities/cost

Special National Conditions
data law/export
limiting factors

Familiarity with foreign agencies' cost rates and operating procedures makes it possible for the co-ordinating agency (particularly if a member of the same group or chain) to give a preliminary ballpark quotation to the client without the need to contact the local agency at all. Often this is enough to frighten off a client who has unrealistically low expectations of international research costs or to help him eliminate low probability countries from the research programme. It is also essential for the co-ordinating agency to have a feel for international cost levels to permit any questioning of the estimates that must eventually be sought from local agencies to be directed most fruitfully.

Proposals

Coming now to *proposal preparation*, there are a number of aspects particularly relevant to the writing of international research proposals. These include:

- spelling out assumptions and definitions very very clearly;
- the necessity to explain the cost sensitive features of the research design to give the client an idea of what can and cannot be modified with little penalty;
- drawing attention to the nature, and physical resources, of the local fieldwork agencies being used by the co-ordinating agency;
- defining clearly the tasks to be undertaken; this is particularly important to counteract the problem of under-costing by competing suppliers that may be inexperienced in international work and have not fully identified the range of tasks required to get the job done well.

Data Collection

The *data collection* phase itself requires a series of control procedures agreed, and understood, by client, co-ordinating agency and local agencies. Some of the desired features of these procedures are summarised and expanded upon in the succeeding paragraphs:

  (i) develop a master questionnaire
  (ii) arrange local translation
  (iii) final central check of local questionnaires
  (iv) pilot/pre-test
  (v) agree respondent selection and interviewing procedures
- sampling frame
- sampling method
- contact procedure
- record keeping
  (vi) lead country
  (vii) quality control by co-ordinating agency
- validation
- minimum acceptable specification
- systematic monitoring
- on-site visits

It is even more important than with national work to observe the basic elements of good design in the co-ordinating agency's construction of the master questionnaire.

Master questionnaire design
1. Simple uncluttered format.
2. Logical/easy flow with clear routing.
3. Avoid complex grids.
4. Straightforward question wording.
5. Well-spaced DP codes.
6. Easily retrieved classification details.
7. Provide glossary of technical/brand terms.
8. Permit local agencies to lay out questionnaire in their normal style.
9. Put country specific questions at end.

It is advisable for translation of questionnaires and other materials to be the responsibility of the local fieldwork agency, although often the client's local office can play a valuable part in this. Independent back-translation is a useful extra precaution.

It is essential for each local agency to send copies of the *final* questionnaire to the co-ordinating agency for checking. Although budgets do not always permit this, it is desirable for all local agencies to conduct a pilot exercise (perhaps preceded by a pre-pilot in a lead country) following which they should each submit a written report to the co-ordinating agency before a final international briefing session. Again, budgets often preclude such international meetings but their value to complex studies can be considerable.

In agreeing how to select and interview respondents it must be borne in mind that sampling frame availability varies greatly by country—a point of more practical significance for industrial, than consumer, market research. Local agencies operating procedures vary greatly in sampling and contacting methods, although various forms of quota sampling and, to a lesser extent, random location approaches are commonly used in Europe.

The co-ordinating agency must take full responsibility for quality control of local fieldwork and should exercise this through a variety of agreed procedures such as:

- a pre-determined level of back-checking by each country agency;
- specification with the country agencies of a guaranteed minimum number of interviews and of minimum standards for each completed interview;
- monitoring of fieldwork progress at pre-arranged dates, ideally using a standardised, telexable reporting format;
- if possible, by using a 'lead country' in which fieldwork commences a few weeks earlier than elsewhere; this can help pre-empt problems that might occur in the other countries, provide a check on time schedules, aid the early preparation of specimen coding frames for open-ended questions and provide an advance data set for checking, editing and the primary analysis phase;
- if the budget permits, on-site visits during each country's main fieldwork phase can be valuable to check progress and procedures, to inspect questionnaires and discuss details of editing.

Data Processing

For the bigger surveys, centralised *data processing* is advisable with punch cards usually the preferred form of data transmission. Tapes can get wiped, cards only bent and occasionally dropped and it is also easier to change a card than alter data on tape—unless you have an interactive system. It is also essential to ensure that the formatting is agreed by all if tapes are used, but even with cards there are different conventions, particularly concerning the use of O, X and V codes and not all foreign suppliers even use 80 column × 12 row cards. The growing use of Optical Mark Reading can add another dimension to this phase of the study in some countries.

Data preparation and processing
1. Centralised DP advisable.
2. Punch cards, tape (or even questionnaires) from local agencies—copies retained.
3. Master code book and standard DP codes.
4. Ensure DP conventions understood.
5. Computer data editing?
6. Agree print-out language.
7. Data law—does it present any problems?

So, here again, in data preparation and processing take nothing for granted. The only assumption one should make is that anything that can go wrong, *will* go wrong.

Reporting

At the final *reporting* stage—assuming it is not just a 'field' or 'field and tab' study—it is necessary for the co-ordinating agency to accommodate a variety of client company preferred styles and conventions, particularly the relative roles to be played by reports and presentations, the balance of verbatims, tables and commentary and whether local reports, an international summary or both are required.

Some Guidelines and Hints _____

A number of themes recur in the management of successful international research studies and have been touched upon in this paper. Three warrant some additional emphasis—communication, language and 'commercial mechanics'.

Communication

The importance of all parties—client, co-ordinating agency and local agencies—being fully aware of what is going on is paramount. Preliminary discussions should lead to operating procedures being agreed and provision made for regular situation updates—preferably in telex or letter form.

A wide variety of communication mechanisms exist—telephone; mail; cable; telex; facsimile/telecopier; air freight; courier and travel itself! All can play a role but, at the present time, telex has the great advantages of widespread business establishment penetration, speed and provision of hard copy which give it a central role in international research—complemented by telephone and personal contact.

Language

Procedures for questionnaire and stimulus material translation have already been discussed but the problem of language goes deeper and has a number of dimensions:

- several European countries have more than one language;
- similar or apparently identical languages must be treated separately eg a French questionnaire requires local adaptation for the Quebecois as does a Dutch one for Flemish and Afrikaans respondents, a German one for the Schweizer Deutsch and certainly an English one for the United States (and vice versa).
- some linguistic concepts do not translate directly into other tongues and important nuances of meaning can be put at risk especially in the advertising area; 'equivalent' meanings are perhaps as much as one can hope for in many situations and this often requires the preliminary elicitation of relevant *consumer* language via qualitative research.
- communication between the central client and his local affiliate, co-ordinating agency and local supplier is very often possible in the business lingua franca, English. However, even where this is the case, a more subtle problem can arise with fluent English-speaking foreigners. Their very skill in English can suggest a complete understanding of all nuances of the discussion—which experience has shown is not always the case. Again, constant vigilance and checking is the only safeguard.

Commercial Mechanics and Research Business Conventions

A whole series of factors can make the commercial relationship between buyer and seller more complex than within a national market. These include:

1. Cost/price variation by country
2. Inflation/duration of bid validity
3. Stage payment conventions
4. Sales tax
5. Bid/payment currency
6. Exchange rates and cover
7. Contracts
8. Codes of practice
9. Plus or minus 10%?
10. Can funds be remitted?

Whatever precautions are taken, the conducting and co-ordination of multi-country studies is a complex management task and rarely will *everything* go according to plan. Some of the more commonly encountered problems are:

- local agency reports difficulty in meeting quota/dates/budget;

- client changes job specification immediately prior to/during fieldwork;
- someone's currency crashes (usually the client's!);
- unbudgeted meetings (abroad!) are necessary to resolve unexpected difficulties;
- long lead times before bid acceptance/rejection hinder forward planning;
- variation in vacation patterns across countries prevents simultaneous fieldwork.

Suppliers can reduce the risks inherent in international research and, hence, provide a better service to their clients, by following five ground rules: acquiring background knowledge; gaining exposure to the marketing problem; receiving and giving full briefings; piloting/pre-testing and communicating clearly and frequently.

The Benefits of International Co-ordination _____

International research co-ordination

- standardises
- centralises
- communications
- design/translation
- processing/analysis
- provides quality control
- contributes expertise/experience/advice
- minimises problems

It does not have to be rigid, mechanistic and *over*-standardising in its application and multi-country co-ordinated studies frequently show variation in data collection method, sample, questionnaire or timing without compromising the required level of inter-country comparability.

Britain has emerged as a major centre of international co-ordination for a variety of reasons associated with its international business and business service tradition. It is home to more corporate and regional head offices of multinational corporations than any other European country which provides a firm base from which to develop a strong international research business. The widespread use of English in international business and Britain's geographic position in the European time zones add to these advantages.

Specifically in the marketing research context, Britain is fortunate in having an extremely vigorous research industry with a very active Market Research Society (and other bodies) containing a lively International Research Committee. Together with Britain's spending a higher proportion of GNP on market research than any other country and having lower prices than most, this had led to international research becoming something of a speciality on the British research scene.

This is supported by the number of internationally orientated suppliers' found in the various European countries—based on research companies listed in the ESOMAR Handbook:

UK	91	Spain	20
Germany	76	Norway	15
France	58	Denmark	15
Netherlands	55	Finland	13
Italy	44	Austria	11
Switzerland	29	Greece	8
Sweden	23	Portugal	6
Belgium	22	Turkey	2

Britain is well represented too in the list of the world's major research organisations:

TOP 10 MARKET RESEARCH COMPANIES WORLDWIDE, 1980

	Research revenues ($m)	Countries with office	International head office
1 A C Nielsen	363	22	USA
2 IMS International	102	57	UK (USA parentage)
3 SAMI	63	2	USA
4 Arbitron	55	1	USA
5 Research International	51	29	UK
6 Infratest	49	6	Germany
7 AGB	46	9	UK
8 GfK	40	8	Germany
9 Burke Marketing Services	33	7	USA
10 Market Facts	26	2	USA

Source Advertising Age/Jack Honomichl, Company reports and Research International estimates.

especially when the other major *international* groups and chains are also considered:

INRA	62	31	–
Gallup	48	36	UK
MRBI	13	10	UK (USA parentage)

Conclusion

If there is a message in this review of 'Conducting and co-ordinating multi-country quantitative studies across Europe', it is that a disciplined and systematic approach to international research is necessary to cope with the inherent complexity of the tasks involved.

With the advent of satellite (TV) communication, it is likely that a new impetus will be given to international branding, and this in turn will increase the demand for co-ordinated international research.

5. PUBLIC CONSEQUENCES OF PRIVATE ACTION:
THE MARKETING OF INFANT FORMULA IN LESS DEVELOPED COUNTRIES

S. PRAKASH SETHI

S. Prakash Sethi is Professor of International Business and Business and Social Policy at the School of Management and Administration, University of Texas at Dallas, where he is also the Director of the Center for Research in Business and Social Policy. He is the author of numerous articles in various professional and academic journals and has published many books, including Up Against the Corporate Wall (Prentice-Hall), *and* Advocacy Advertising and Large Corporations (D. C. Heath).

JAMES E. POST

James E. Post is Associate Professor of Management Policy at Boston University. He has studied the infant formula industry for several years and testified before the U.S. Senate Subcommittee on Health and Scientific Research when it held hearings on the "Marketing And Promotion Of Infant Formula In Developing Nations" in May 1978.

The activities of multinational corporations (MNCs) in less developed countries (LDCs) have been justified on many grounds. The foremost among the benefits accruing to the less developed countries are the transfer of superior technology and management skills; the creation of jobs and of a broader economic base, and so on, an improved standard of living; and the provision of superior goods at reasonable prices. These benefits are possible because multinational companies operate from a large base of resources, thereby exploiting economies of scale; and because MNC research and development facilities ensure superior products through in-house testing and quality control. The last point is quite critical in the case of a variety of products and services. The consumers in LDCs usually do not have either the information or necessary skills to evaluate the multitude of new products that are introduced by the MNCs. These products are quite often outside their cultural frame of reference, and so evaluation through comparisons with local products is not possible.

The small size of total demand makes it unattractive for more than one or two companies to compete for the market. Thus the role of competition in disciplining the suppliers and providing the consumers with necessary comparative information is limited. The LDCs are generally deficient in institutional mechanisms for inspection and regulation that would ensure the production and sale of products in a manner that serves public interest while also ensuring reasonable profits to the MNCs.

Dimension of the Problem _____

At the aggregate level, the assumption that MNCs serve public interest in host countries through their activities in the private sector is largely supportable. However, at the level of the single company or industry in the single country, this is not necessarily so. Therefore, while a MNC may not have deliberately violated any laws, its normal activities in pursuit of self-interest may have untoward social consequences. All marketing activities of individual firms have second order effects that extend far beyond the boundaries of the parties to the immediate exchange. Quite often, these effects are far more pervasive in their collectivity than visualized by individual firms when making simple transactions. While the users of the product or those indirectly affected by it are unable to seek adequate remedy and relief in the market place, the cumulative effect of their dissatisfactions results in transferring the issue from the private to public domain. The solutions thus arrived at are essentially political in nature; are externally imposed; may be quite inflexible to accommodate specific peculiarities of the individual MNC operations; and, in the long run, may not be the optimal solutions for the MNCs or the LDCs involved.

This article focuses on a study of the infant formula foods by large MNCs in less developed countries to demonstrate the nature of second order effects of primary activities, the promotion and sale of infant formula foods. An analytical framework is presented within which one can compare the activities of different firms at different stages as the issue is gradually converted from private into public domain. Finally, some decision strategies are presented which companies might apply to similar situations. The basic questions raised are:

- To what extent should a firm be responsible for the undirected use of its products? Ought not the demand for a product the marketing of which is legal be the ultimate count in the MNC's decision to undertake its manufacture and sale?
- Under what circumstances should a corporation exercise self-restraint in advertising? Does the corporation have an obligation to promote only those products which it knows will be used correctly? Should a competitor's successful manufacture and promotion of a product influence a company to enter the market and utilize similar tactics?
- The operation of the market economy assures that the second order effects of a firm's activities are in the public domain and so must be handled by government agencies, leaving individual firms to pursue their self-interest unfettered by external considerations. Is it feasible or desirable for a MNC to assume a posture that is primarily market-oriented? What role can the LDC government be expected to play in this area? Should there be a government-directed choice of products a private corporation could manufacture? Finally, once a private market-oriented issue gets into the public domain, what changes should MNCs make to assuage society's demands?

Infant Formula Foods: The Industry _____

Infant formula food was developed in the early 1920s as an alternative to breast-feeding. Sales rose sharply after World War II, and hit a peak in the late 1950s, following the 4.3 million births in 1957.[1] However, birth rates began declining in the 1960s, and by 1974 the annual number of births had declined to 3.1 million. The low birth rate caused a steep downturn in baby formula food sales.

The major U.S. and foreign companies engaged in the manufacture and marketing of infant formulas include Abbott Laboratories, which produces *Similac* and *Isomil* infant formulas through its Ross Laboratories division; American Home Products, which produces *SMA, S26,* and *Nursoy* infant formulas through its Wyeth Laboratories; Bristol-Myers, which produces *Enfamil, Olac,* and *Prosobee* through its Mead Johnson Division; Nestlé Alimentana, S.A., a Swiss multinational; and Unigate, a British firm. In their search for business, these companies began developing markets in third world countries, where population was still expanding, while baby food markets in developed countries were leveling off.

The international market for infant formula grew rapidly during the post-World War II era. Although a number of food companies had sold breast-milk substitutes in western Europe before that time, many of these products, made of evaporated milk or powdered milk, were not nutritionally equivalent to human milk, as are formulas. As prosperity returned to Europe and multinational firms expanded operations in Africa, South America and the Far East, infant formula became the "food of choice" for the children of expatriot Americans and western Europeans.

The large number of wealthy and middle-class persons able to afford infant formula in the U.S. and Europe made mass distribution and promotion of such products a widespread and acceptable phenomenon. In Africa, South America, and the Far East, however, the number of wealthy customers was fewer, and the size of the middle class was notably smaller. Local distributors were often used as a means of distributing the product. In an effort to expand sales, distributors, and sometimes the manufacturers themselves, began to promote the infant formula to broad segments of the population. This promotion reached the poor and those only marginally able to afford the product in less developed nations and produced the infant formula controversy.

Industry Orientation

Producers of infant formula products have two basic orientations which reflect the industry's historical approaches to product development. In the United States, the principal sellers of infant formula were founded after medical researchers produced an infant food substitute for mother's milk. By the late 1920s, Ross Laboratories, Mead Johnson, and Simulated Milk Adaptation (SMA) were in the business of producing and selling humanized infant formula. Through mergers and acquisitions, these firms eventually became part of large integrated pharmaceutical firms. SMA was acquired by Wyeth which in turn was acquired by American Home Products. Ross was merged with Abbott Laboratories, and Mead Johnson was acquired by Bristol-Myers. During the 1960s, a number of special "sick baby" formulas were produced by these companies for children with special dietary and health requirements. While the "sick baby" segment of the market is insignificant in comparison to the "well baby" segment (perhaps 2 percent of total sales volume), the existence of such specialized products is attributable to the pharmaceutical orientation of one segment of the industry and the research emphasis of both segments.

The second orientation in the industry is that of a food processor, and is characteristic of such firms as Nestlé and Borden. Both began in the sweetened and condensed milk business in the 1860s. Through the early decades of the 1900s, new uses were found for the canned milk products which Nestlé sold in Europe and Borden sold in the United States: one use to which they were put was infant feeding. This market segment expanded, but as medical research indicated that humanized infant formulas were nutritionally superior to canned milk for newborns, the food companies sought to retain their share of the infant food market by introducing infant formula products that were either developed internally (Nestlé as early as the 1920s), or whose rights were purchased from others (Borden in 1950s). The approach to the market of these firms was similar to that of other food companies. Sales were generated through heavy advertising, with a special reliance on mass media as newspapers, radio, and television. Brand identification was cultivated through advertising, with price sensitivity the key to preserving brand loyalty.

Business Strategy

After intense competitive battles, Ross Laboratories and Mead Johnson emerged as the winners in the United States market. By the 1960s, the two firms commanded approximately 90 percent of the domestic infant formula business (Ross's *Similac* 55 percent, Mead Johnson's *Enfamil* about 35 percent). So entrenched were these sellers in the domestic market that Nestlé, the acknowledged worldwide industry leader with 50 percent of the market, never attempted to penetrate the U.S. market.

With the leveling off in the U.S. birth rate in the 1960s, both Ross and Mead Johnson began to look outside the U.S. for major growth opportunities. This effort led Ross to industrialized nations with higher disposable income and prospects for market penetration. Canada and Europe became major foreign markets for Ross's *Similac*. Mead Johnson looked primarily to the Caribbean where export was relatively easy. Puerto Rico, Jamaica, and the Bahamas became important Mead Johnson export markets.

Wyeth Laboratories, never a major seller of infant formula in the United States, began to sell internationally before World War II. Following the war, the company's presence as a pharmaceutical manufacturer was the base from which infant formula was marketed by affiliates in Latin America, Europe, and Southeast Asia. Today, Wyeth probably accounts for close to 15 percent of worldwide sales. Table 1 provides a summary of the entry strategies of the five MNC infant formula food manufacturers in the world. These are, however, not the only sellers of infant formula products. Multinational firms from the United Kingdom (e.g., Unigate), Denmark, France, West Germany, and Japan all sell modified infant formula or powdered milks which are used for infant feeding in LDCs. The pharmaceutical and food processor orientations, and the various business strategies discussed above are representative of the basic MNC approaches to the marketing of infant food products in LDCs.

Table 1
PRODUCER ORIENTATION AND BUSINESS STRATEGY

Producer	Industry Orientation	Major Market	Major Area of LDC Markets	Business Strategy
Bristol-Myers (Mead Johnson)	Pharmaceutical	Domestic United States	Caribbean, Central America	Exports excess production from U.S. to nearby countries. Uses distributors. Has plant facilities in Philippines.
Abbott Laboratories (Ross Laboratories)	Pharmaceutical	Domestic United States	Rapidly developing African and Southeast Asian (e.g., Nigeria, Taiwan)	Exports from European plants; aimed at upper income market. Uses own sales force, limited use of distributors.
American Home Products (Wyeth Laboratories)	Pharmaceutical	Selective world markets (e.g., Canada, S. Africa)	Southeast Asia, Latin America, Africa	Exports as complement to drug sales. Uses Wyeth subsidiaries to market. Preference for regional/local production.
Nestlé	Food Processor	Europe, Africa, Latin America, Asia	Worldwide	Sells food products internationally. Established first milk industry in many nations & has full line local food processing plants.
Borden	Food Processor	Worldwide	Latin America, Caribbean	Food product marketed through distributors; participates in some joint ventures.

Growth in Infant Formula Sales in LDCs

Studies point to an increasing trend toward bottle-feeding in LDCs. In developing nations, breast-feeding has declined substantially and the length of the nursing period has shrunk from over a year to a few months.

Three important environmental factors[2] account for the shift toward bottle-feeding in LDCs. These are the sociocultural changes in developing countries, the changing attitudes of health workers and health institutions, and the promotional activities of infant formula manufacturers.

The sociocultural factors influencing change in infant feeding can be understood primarily in terms of urbanization, which has caused the westernization of social mores and the need for mobility in employment. High income groups were the first to use infant formula, in imitation of western practices, and thus bottle-feeding came to represent a high-status modern practice. Low income groups tended to follow suit. Too, the breast has come to be viewed as a sex symbol, which has led to embarrassment in using it for nursing, and fear that nursing will make the appearance of the breast less desirable. Finally, there is the convenience aspect: most places of employment do not provide facilities for a nursing woman, so bottle-feeding of the infant may become a necessity for a working woman.

Health professionals—doctors, nurses, and clinic workers—and the policies of the hospitals and clinics often, wittingly or unwittingly, endorse the use of infant formula. Although much of this activity originates in the promotional efforts by baby food formula manufacturers to the mother, the endorsement may appear to come from the health professionals themselves. Nurses and social workers who staff hospitals and clinics may encourage the use of bottle-feeding. In many hospitals newborn babies are routinely bottle-fed whether or not the mother plans to breast-feed later. Hospitals and clinics receive free samples of infant milk and special plastic milk bottles which nurses distribute to mothers. These nurses may also distribute "vaccination cards" which advertise infant formulas, and baby care booklets which recommend bottle-feeding.

Industry Promotion Practices _____

Many observers claim that the infant formula industry's promotion is overly aggressive and has contributed to the decline of breast-feeding. The industry itself, however, feels that its promotion is generally responsible and performs a valuable function. Individual companies have concentrated on different promotional mixes, based on their orientation, i.e., pharmaceutical vs. processed foods; or depending on their market strategies, i.e., maintaining a dominant market position and protecting market share, or getting entry into new markets and increasing market share. Yet their impact from the public interest point of view is not very dissimilar. These practices can be summarized in the following categories:

Baby Food Booklets

One of the major forms of promotion used by baby food companies is the information booklet. Some typical titles are *The Ostermilk Mother and Baby Book: Caring for Your Baby*, published by Ross Laboratories, and *A Life Begins*, published by Nestlé. These booklets are distributed free in maternity wards of public hospitals, clinics, doctors' offices, and by nurses. They provide information on prenatal and postnatal care, with special emphasis given to how babies should be fed. Many of these books are directed to illiterate or semiliterate women, using pictures to show correct or incorrect feeding methods.

Some baby food booklets, usually pre-1975 versions, describe and illustrate bottle-feeding without mentioning breast-feeding. However, as public concern rose over the possible harmful effects of bottle-feeding, promotional booklets began to discuss breast-feeding and to recommend "mixed feeding," in which the bottle used as a supplement to breast milk. Examples of this type include Nestlé's *Your Baby and You*, which suggests "an occasional bottle-feed . . . if you cannot breast-feed

Baby entirely yourself."[3] A Mead Johnson pamphlet states "More babies have thrived on Mead Johnson formula products than on any other form of supplementary feeding." Cow & Gate recommends its milk to "be used as a substitute for breast-feeding or as a supplement."[4]

In discussing the use of supplements for feeding the baby, these booklets often emphasize reasons to discontinue or diminish breast-feeding. Nestlé, for example, in *A Life Begins*, asserts that bottle-feeding must be substituted for breast-feeding if the mother is ill, if her milk is insufficient for the baby or of "poor quality," or if the mother's nipples crack or become infected. These booklets also suggest that breast-feeding should be diminished to include solid food into the baby's diet. The *Ostermilk Mother and Baby Book* advises introducing solid foods for babies a few weeks old or even earlier, while Cow & Gate suggests feeding its brand of cereal to the baby from two to three months.[5]

Other Media Practices

Companies did promote their baby food products by advertising in magazines, news-papers, radio, television, and through loudspeaker vans. As with the baby care booklets, early advertisements usually did not mention breast-feeding: a magazine advertisement stated that Ostermilk and Farex products were "right from the start—the foods you can trust." Poster advertisements, often exhibited in hospitals and clinics, showed how to prepare baby formula, but gave only minimal attention to breast-feeding. Radio and television ads similarly emphasized bottle-feeding.

Free Samples and Gifts

One of the most widespread promotional techniques is the distribution of free sam-ples, and the offer of free gifts to users or potential users of baby food formula. These usually take the form of samples of formula or free feeding bottles, and may be handed out by nurses and salesmen at hospitals, clinics, or in the home. A survey in Ibadan, Nigeria, found that 9 percent of the mothers surveyed had received samples. These had been given in equal proportion to more affluent mothers and to those who could not afford baby food formula. A spokesman from Nestlé admitted that sampling in the Philippines cost about 4-5 percent of turnover.[6] Free gifts are less often used as an inducement to buy.

Promotion Through the Medical Profession

Hospitals and physicians are a logical focus for promotion and sales-related adver-tising. The users of artificial feeding products are sensitive to the "scientific" quality of infant formula, and physicians were the appropriate counselors to give advice. Also, hospitals are becoming increasingly popular as the site for birth, and the newborns are typically fed at the hospital for the first few days of their lives. The decision a new mother makes before birth to feed her child "Brand X" formula could be changed by the hospital's decision to feed infants "Brand Y" or the physician's recommendation to feed "Brand Z." As a marketing matter, prebirth advertising can create consumer awareness of a product; it cannot create sales. Sales creation occurs in the physician's office or in the hospital. For these reasons, the medical community has become the focal point for infant formula promotion in industrialized and developing nations alike.

In general, all promotional methods such as booklets, free samples, posters, and the use of salespeople are employed in the hospitals and clinics. In addition, the use of "milk nurses" and "milk banks" functions to associate baby food formula with the medical profession. "Mother-craft" or milk nurses are fully or partially trained nurses hired by infant food formula companies, and instructed by them in "product knowledge." Most nurses are paid fixed salaries plus a travel allowance, but some may receive sales-related bonuses. A number of hospitals allow milk nurses to speak to mothers in maternity wards or clinics. Nurses visit mothers in their homes, and in some isolated areas, the milk nurses make formula deliveries. A 1974 study conducted by the Caribbean Food and Nutrition Institute found that Mead Johnson, subsidiaries of Nestlé, Glaxo, Ross Laboratories, and Cow & Gate all employed milk nurses in Jamaica. Mead Johnson employed twelve.[7]

Milk banks, usually set up in the hospitals and clinics that serve the poor, are sales outlets for commercial infant food formula. These banks sell formula at reduced prices to poor mothers. For example, at the milk bank at Robert Reid Cabral hospital in Santo Domingo, a pound tin of Nestlé's *Nido* is sold for 90¢, a 40 percent discount off the regular $1.50 price; Nestlé's *Nan* is sold for $1.35, a 33 percent discount off the regular price of $2.00.

Consumer behavior is directly tied to the influence of these promotional activities. It is generally accepted among marketers of infant products that new mothers are susceptible to advertising. During pregnancy, and immediately after giving birth, the mother is very anxious to use the "correct" product.[8] A number of consumer research surveys, including some proprietary studies by firms in the industry, have indicated that mothers will choose an infant formula based on the implied or actual brand endorsement of the hospital in which the baby was born, and will continue to use that product after discharge.[9] Through detailing, infant formula producers have been able to differentiate their products in the minds of physicians and achieve brand loyalty among the mothers of infants. Given the pharmaceutical orientation of some of the major companies that have developed infant formula in the United States, it is not surprising that the distinctive marketing competence of these firms resides in their ability to deal with health professionals. The success of this promotional strategy is evidenced by its firm entrenchment in the competitive conduct; and by what is more telling, the high priority which new entrants place on improving relations with physicians and hospitals.[10]

Criticism of Industry Promotion Practices _____

All forms of promotion used by infant formula companies have been criticized by different observers. In general, critics claim that most forms of advertising are misleading or use "hard sell" techniques to turn mothers away from breast-feeding.

Baby Care Booklets

The main criticism of baby care booklets is that they ignore or de-emphasize breast-feeding. Critics feel that mothers reading these baby care booklets will be led to believe that bottle-feeding is as good or better than breast-feeding. Even if the booklet directly states "Breast-feeding is best," critics assert that the overall impression is still misleading. The new trend in these books toward promoting "mixed feeding," or the early introduction of solid food is also questioned. The La Leche League International, an organization which promotes breast-feeding, observed that:

> . . . the supplementary formula is one of the greatest deterrents to establishing a good milk supply, and frequent nursing is one of the greatest helps. You see, the milk supply is regulated by what the baby takes. The more he nurses, the more milk there will be. If he's given a bottle as well, he'll gradually take less and less from the breast, and the supply will diminish.[11]

In addition, the use of a bottle and overdiluted formula, even as a supplement, can cause infection and malnutrition in the infant.

Promotion Through Media

The critics' objections to other media promotion is similar to their objections to the baby care booklets. They feel that even with the admission of the superiority of breast milk, media promotion remains essentially misleading in its encouragement of mothers to bottle-feed their children. A survey in infant feeding practices in Ibadan, Nigeria, revealed that of the 38 percent of 400 mothers who remembered having seen ads for formula, the majority recalled statements to the effect that the formula gives infants strength, energy, and power. None remembered having heard that breast milk is better for babies. In Nigeria, when ads for Ovaltine included the picture of a plump smiling baby, observers noted that there was a trend for mothers to feed their babies Ovaltine and water as a supplement.[12] This misinterpretation of ads is an obvious danger in a predominantly illiterate or semiliterate community.

Free Samples and Gifts

Free samples of baby food formula and feeding bottles, as well as gift gimmicks, are considered a direct inducement to bottle-feed infants. The widespread distribution of these items shows an unethical lack of concern for either informing mothers about the superiority of breast-feeding or for determining whether mothers have the economic ability to regularly buy infant formula after the first samples.

Promotion Through the Medical Profession

Critics find the promotion of infant formula through the distribution of free samples and literature of the display of advertising posters in hospitals and clinics especially dangerous. Dr. D. B. Jelliffe, head of the Division of Population, Family, and International Health at UCLA, called these promotional techniques "endorsement by association" and "manipulation by assistance." Jelliffe, along with many other critics, feels that companies providing hospitals and clinics with free samples and information on new developments in infant formula, as well as a barrage of advertisements, influence health care workers to favor and promote bottle-feeding to their patients. It is also argued that because mothers see posters and receive informational booklets and free samples at hospitals and clinics, they come to believe that the health profession endorses bottle-feeding. Thus, this type of promotion works two ways in influencing both the beliefs of professionals and the beliefs of mothers about the value of bottle-feeding.

The use of milk nurses also receives its share of criticism. Observers charge that the nurse uniform conceals the fact that the "nurses" are essentially salespeople who encourage mothers to bottle-feed. They assert that some nurses are paid on a sales-related basis, causing them to be even more eager to push for sales. In support of this belief, critics quote an industry man: "Some nurses will be paid a commission on sales results in their area. Sometimes they will also be given the added stick that if they don't meet those objectives, they will be fired."[13]

Milk Banks

Milk banks are used by companies to expand sales by encouraging bottle-feeding among the poor while still retaining the higher-income market. However, critics assert that the discount prices of the formula are still beyond the economic means of the people at whom the milk banks aim their services. For example, a milk bank in Guatemala City sells Nestlé products for $1.00 per tin, a discount of 80¢ to $1.00 from the regular price. A tin lasts only a few days when properly prepared. However, since the women buying milk there generally have household incomes of between $15 and $45 per month, they commonly buy fewer tins and dilute them. This starts the baby on a cycle of malnutrition and disease.

Business and Social Stress: An Analytical Framework _____

The manner in which all organizations, particularly large corporations, respond to social change is a matter of great public concern. Their economic actions necessarily involve social changes and may have such an impact on established behavioral patterns and underlying cultural values and beliefs as to cause tremendous social stress. This is especially true in the case of LDCs. There is reason to believe that the effect of the modern corporation is even more profound in social and economic settings where there are fewer countervailing influences than exist in industrialized societies. These nations are in the process of becoming modernized and there is tension between the values of the old and the new, the technology of the past and the future, and the aspirations of the present with the traditions of the past. The modern corporation generally represents the new and the future. In such situations, it is not surprising that the impact of the corporation concerns those who care about the pace, the process, and the direction of development and change.

Infant nutrition is one area in which the complex interaction of changing social values, institutions, and technology has produced major changes in social habits.

According to many public health and nutrition experts, there now exists a crisis of monumental proportions in LDCs as mothers abandon traditional breast-feeding practices in favor of bottle-feeding. In the view of some critics, the bottle has become a symbol of the most invidious intrusion of western technology into the lives and welfare of LDC populations. One might fairly conclude that the "great infant formula controversy" is one involving the politics of technology.

The objectives of MNCs and LDCs are not always congruent with each other. Nevertheless, there must be a common ground where the interaction between the two yield net benefits, both tangible and intangible, if any sustained cooperation is to take place. Conventional economic analysis shows direct costs and benefits of individual MNC-LDC cooperation, but usually overlooks social and political costs. These costs are difficult to calculate, as there is no common consensus of what they are or how they might be measured; and there is a fear that if these costs were specified, they could doom MNC projects. The cultural and sociopolitical costs are of critical importance. The long-range social acceptance on the part of the peoples in LDCs of MNC's investments depends on the decisions of MNC and LDC governments to taking these costs into account when developing economic projects.

The analytical framework presented in this section provides one method of examining the nature of the conflict, and also the adequacy of MNC responses, in terms of social relevance, so that comparisons over time and across industries and nations are possible. The framework consists of two components. The first deals with categorization of the types of corporate responses: these are defined not in terms of specific activities, but in terms of types of rationale applied in responding to social pressures. The second component deals with the definition of the external environment, or the context within which the corporate response is being made and evaluated. The emphasis is not on the specifics of a particular social situation or problem, but on the generalized external conditions created by a multitude of acts, by corporations, individuals, and social institutions, that are essentially similar within a given temporal and contextual frame.[14] The issue in terms of social responsiveness is not how corporations should respond to social pressures, but what their long run role in a dynamic social system should be. The corporation here is expected to *anticipate* the changes that are likely to take place. Corporations should initiate policies and programs that will minimize the adverse side effects of their present or future activities. Again, *while the activities relevant to social responsibility are prescriptive in nature, activities related to social responsiveness are proactive, i.e., anticipatory and preventive in nature.*

The External Environment

A distinction must also be made regarding the various external environments—physical, economic, and sociopolitical—within which a given corporate response to a set of social problems must be evaluated. This has been accomplished by describing the time between the emergence of a problem and its solution and ultimate elimination in four stages: the preproblem stage, the identification stage, the remedy and relief stage, and the prevention stage. There is some overlap among these categories because social problems do not fall neatly into discrete groups, nor can they always be solved in distinct successive steps.

The Preproblem Stage

In the process of manufacturing and marketing, business firms are constantly engaged in a series of transactions with individuals and social groups. These transactions have certain direct and indirect adverse effects on the parties involved. The negative side effects may be the normal shortfalls found in any manufacturing activity, or they may pertain to actions by individual firms to cut corners either under competitive pressures or to increase short-run profits. Taken individually, each act or incident is not significant in its impact. However, when similar acts are performed by a large number of companies and continued over a long period of time, their cumulative effect is substantial. When that happens, a problem is born.

The preproblem stage is probably the longest of all the four. Most individuals and institutions respond to the problem passively. The effort is aimed at adaptation, and the problem is treated as given.

The Identification Stage

Once a problem has become large enough, and its impact significant enough, there is a drive among the affected groups to define the problem, identify its causes, and find the source. This is one of the most difficult stages in the whole process. Quite often the business entity could not have known of the problem because the technology for its detection did not exist. In most cases, direct linkages between cause and effect are all but impossible. The best that can be accomplished is to show through inference and weight of evidence that a given source was the major contributor to the problem. The definition of the problem may also involve the vested interest or value orientation of a particular group.

The Remedy and Relief Stage

Once the causal linkage has been established, there arises the question of compensatory and/or punitive damages to the affected parties. This stage is marked by an intense amount of activity by the parties to the conflict. An equally important role is played by courts, legislatures, and executive and administrative agencies of the government.

The Prevention Stage

At this point, the problem has achieved maturity. The causal sources are either well-established or easily identifiable. The attempt is made to develop long-range programs to prevent the recurrence of the problem. These include development of substitute materials, product redesign, the restructuring of organizations and decision-making processes, public education, and the emergence of new special interest groups to bring about necessary political and legislative changes. It should be noted that the prevention stage is not sequential with, but generally overlaps, the problem identification and remedy and relief stages.

This stage is marked by considerable uncertainty and difficulty in making an accurate appraisal of potential costs and benefits. It is not uncommon to find a high degree of self-righteousness in the pronouncements of various groups, which may be long on rhetoric but short on substance. Groups tend to advocate solutions that favor their particular viewpoint, while understating the potential costs to those groups having opposing viewpoints.

Dimensions of Corporate Social Performance

The development of absolute, universal norms of corporate behavior may not be possible or even desirable. Still, there must be some criteria that can serve as a guide for evaluating past and current performance, and for providing useful indicators in future activities. Corporations, like other social institutions, are an integral part of society and depend on it for their existence, continuity, and growth. Corporations constantly strive to pattern their activities—the nature of resources they use, the type of goods they produce, and the manner in which goods are distributed—so that they are in congruence with the goals of the overall social system. The quest for legitimacy by the corporation, and the questioning by its critics of the legitimacy of some of its actions, are the crucial issues in the concept of corporate social responsibility.

An effective way to evaluate corporate social performance is to use the yardstick of legitimacy. Given that both corporations and their critics seek to narrow the gap between corporate performance and its legitimacy, the social relevance and validity of any corporate action depends on one's concept of legitimacy. Legitimization involves not only corporate activities, but also includes the internal processes of decision making; the perception of the external environment; the manipulation of that environment—physical, social, and political—to make it more receptive to corporate activities; and the nature of accountability to other institutions in the system. The corporate behavior thus determined can be defined in three ways: as social obligation, social responsibility, or social responsiveness.

Corporate Behavior as Social Obligation

Corporate behavior in response to market forces or legal constraints is defined as social obligation.

The criteria for legitimacy in this arena are economic and legal only. The corporation satisfies the legitimacy criteria by competing for resources in the marketplace and conducting its operations within the legal constraints imposed by the social system.

This simplistic argument conceals more than it explains. Competition for resources is not by itself an adequate criterion. Corporations constantly strive to free themselves from the discipline of the market through increase in size, diversification, and the generation of consumer loyalty by advertising and other means of persuasion. Even in an ideal situation, the ethics of the marketplace provide only one kind of legitimacy, which has been rejected in times of national crisis or for certain activities deemed vital to the nation's well-being.

Nor can the legality of an act be used alone as the criterion. Norms in a social system are developed from a voluntary consensus among various groups. Under these conditions, laws may codify socially accepted behavior but seldom lead social change. *The traditional economic and legal criteria are necessary but not sufficient conditions of corporate legitimacy.* The corporation that flouts them will not survive, but the mere satisfaction of these criteria does not ensure its continued existence.

Corporate Behavior as Social Responsibility

Most of the conflicts between large corporations and various social institutions during the last two decades, in the United States and in other industrialized nations of the free world, fall into the category of social responsibility. Although few corporations have been accused of violating the laws of their nations, they are increasingly being criticized for failing to meet social expectations and to adapt their behavior to changing social norms. Thus, *social responsibility implies bringing corporate behavior up to a level where it is in congruence with currently prevailing social norms, values, and expectations of performance.*

Social responsibility does not require a radical departure from the usual nature of corporate activities or the normal pattern of corporate behavior. It is simply a step ahead—before the new social expectations are codified into legal requirements. *While the concept of social obligation is proscriptive in nature, the concept of social responsibility is prescriptive.*

Corporate Behavior as Social Responsiveness

The third stage of the adaptation of corporate behavior to social needs is in terms of social responsiveness. The issue in terms of social responsiveness not how corporations should respond to social pressures, but what their long-run role in a dynamic social system should be. Again, while social responsibility-related activities are prescriptive in nature, activities related to social responsiveness are proactive, i.e., anticipatory and preventive in nature.

Applying the Framework _____

The analytical model described above can be used to better understand how social conflicts develop and firms respond. It can also be employed to predict the effectiveness of a particular corporate response at different stages of a conflict's evolution. In this section the framework is applied to the infant formula controversy. In the final section, a number of conclusions are drawn about marketing practices and social conflicts surrounding second-order impacts.

The Infant Formula Controversy

The first criticism of the industry and its promotional activities is traceable to the late 1960s when Dr. Jelliffe, Director of the Caribbean Food and Nutrition Institute in Jamaica, conducted his research. His findings and criticism culminated in an international conference of experts held in Bogata, Colombia, in 1970, under the auspices of the U.N.'s Protein Calorie Advisory Group (PAG). Out of this meeting, and the 1972 follow-up session in Singapore, came increased professional concern about the effects of commercial activity related to infant feeding. The PAG issued an official statement (PAG, Statement #23) in 1973 recommending that breast-feeding be supported and promoted in LDCs and that commercial promotion by industry or LDC governments be restrained.

The first public identification of the issue occurred in 1973 with the appearance of several articles about the problem in *The New Internationalist*.[15] This, in turn, spurred Mike Muller to undertake a series of interviews and observations which were eventually printed as *The Baby Killer*, a pamphlet published in 1974.[16] The popularization of the issue resulted in a German translation of Muller's work published in Switzerland under the title, *Nestle Tötet Kinder* (Nestle Kills Babies); and in a lawsuit by Nestlé against the public action group that published the pamphlet. A period of intense advocacy issued from the trial in the Swiss courts. Thus, between 1974 and mid-1976 when the case was decided, considerable international media coverage was given the issue.

The pressure began in earnest in 1975 when shareholder resolutions were filed for consideration at the annual meetings of the American infant formula companies. This pressure has continued, and several institutional investors such as universities and the Rockefeller and Ford Foundations have taken public positions which sharply question the responsiveness of the firms to the controversy. Church groups have led the fight, and have developed their own institutional mechanism through the National Council of Churches, the Interfaith Council on Corporate Responsibility, to coordinate shareholders' campaigns. At the LDC level, the government of Papua New Guinea recently passed a law declaring that baby bottles, nipples and pacifiers are health hazards, and their sale has been restricted to prescription only. The objective was to discourage indiscriminate promotion, sale and consumption of infant food formulas.[17]

Recently, institutions have acted to broaden their popular base by launching a grass roots campaign to boycott Nestlé products in the United States. By linking public action groups throughout the U.S., the current campaign aspires to heighten First World pressure against the Third World's largest seller of infant formula foods.

Manufacturer Responses

The preproblem stage of the infant formula case existed prior to the 1970s. During this time, the adverse impacts on LDCs were not yet articulated. The MNC's response was of the social obligation type, answering only to prevailing law and market conditions. In effect, MNCs were free to conduct their business in ways most consistent with their own orientations and business strategies.

By the early 1970s the identification stage had been reached, as professional criticism grew and articles and stories began to appear in the mass media. The principal industry response to this professional concern was participation in the conference sponsored by PAG. Abbott (Ross), AHP (Wyeth), and Nestlé each sent representatives to these meetings as did a number of British, European, and Japanese companies. For most companies, this seemed to mark a decision point between *social obligation* and *social responsibility*. Only a few firms, notably Abbott (Ross), took steps to mitigate their negative impact in the LDCs. AHP (Wyeth), Borden, Nestlé and others did not follow suit until 1974, when first plans for the formation of an international trade organization were laid.

The remedy and relief stage seems to have begun in 1975, with the Nestlé trial in Switzerland and the shareholder resolutions filed in the United States. In November 1975, representatives of nine MNC manufacturers met in Zurich and formed the International Council of Infant Food Industries (ICIFI). Nestlé, AHP (Wyeth), and Abbott (Ross) participated in these discussions along with several European and four Japanese companies. Others, such as Borden and Bristol-Myers, sent representatives to the sessions, but chose not to participate actively or to join the council. ICIFI's initial directive was to instruct members to adopt a code of marketing ethics which obliged them to recognize the primacy of breast-feeding in all product information and labelling; to include precise product-use information; and to eliminate in-hospital promotion and solicitation by personnel who were paid on a sales-commission basis. For those companies that joined, the council seemed to mark a passage into *social responsibility* as efforts were undertaken to mitigate negative social impacts.

There was criticism of the ICIFI code from the beginning, and Abbott (Ross) withdrew from the organization, arguing that the code was too weak. The company then adopted its own and more restrictive code, which included a provision prohibiting consumer-oriented mass advertising. For ICIFI, the marketing code has been the most visible manifestation of concern for second-order impacts in LDCs. Additional criticism led to some incremental changes which strengthened the "professional" character of sales activity, but which have not yet proscribed all consumer-oriented mass advertising. Thus, ICIFI, the industry's mechanism for countering criticism and searching for means of addressing problems of product misuse in LDC environments, has been unable to reckon with any but the individual-level secondary impacts. Indeed, the critics continue to charge that the response at the user level has been insufficient.

Borden also moved from the social obligation to social responsibility stage. The company had shareholder resolutions filed with it in 1977. This filing perhaps facilitated a management review of promotional strategies in LDCs. In settling the resolution with the church groups before the meeting, Borden agreed to modify certain advertising and labelling of its powdered milk *Klim*; and to tightly oversee the marketing so as to minimize possible consumer misuse of the powdered milk product as an infant formula food. Separately, the company announced that it was withdrawing its infant formula *New Biolac* from two LDC markets in the Far East because it concluded it could not effectively market this product without extensive consumer advertising which was not permissible in the prevailing social-political environment.

As a public issue matures, companies may adopt actions which operate to prevent further growth in the legitimacy gap by minimizing or eliminating the underlying sources of criticism (the *prevention stage*). This has begun to occur in the infant formula controversy as both ICIFI and individual companies have taken action to prevent some of the secondary impacts discussed above. In 1977, Abbott (Ross) announced its intention to commit nearly $100,000 to a breast-feeding campaign in developing nations, and to budget $175,000 for a task force to conduct research on breast-feeding, infant formula, and LDCs. The company also announced a plan for a continuing cooperative effort with its critics in reviewing the situation. ICIFI has now also gone beyond its marketing code-of-ethics and has begun informally working with international health agencies to prepare educational materials, for use in LDCs, that would encourage breast-feeding and improve maternal and infant health care. The council is also involved in supporting scientific research of breast-feeding, infant formula products, and LDC environments.

Abbott (Ross) Laboratories' attempt to act in a way that will create positive impacts in LDCs signals a shift to a corporate *social responsiveness*. Granting that there is some danger of sending "double signals" to its sales force, the company seems to have adopted a posture that permits the sale of its product in appropriate circumstances, and assists the LDCs in encouraging breast-feeding where that is most appropriate.

Table 2 describes the patterns of responses, from social obligation to social responsiveness, in the evolution of the controversy from the preproblem to the prevention stage.

Table 2

SOCIO-POLITICAL DIMENSIONS OF INFANT FORMULA FOODS CONTROVERSY: PATTERNS OF INDUSTRY RESPONSES (5 MNCs)

Patterns of Industry Response	Stages of Conflict Evolution			
	Preproblem Stage	Identification Stage	Remedy & Relief Stage	Prevention Stage
Social Obligation (Do what is required by law)	Bristol-Myers (Mead Johnson Division) Borden Nestlé American Home Products (Wyeth Laboratories) Abbott (Ross Laboratories)	Bristol-Myers (Mead Johnson Division) Borden Nestlé American Home Products (Wyeth Laboratories)	Bristol-Myers (Mead Johnson Division) Borden	Bristol-Myers (Mead Johnson Division)
Social Responsibility (Mitigate negative impacts)		Abbott (Ross Laboratories)	Nestlé American Home Products (Wyeth Laboratories)	Borden Nestlé American Home Products (Wyeth Laboratories)
Social Responsiveness (Promote positive change)			Abbott (Ross Laboratories)	Abott (Ross Laboratories)

Conclusions _____

The infant formula controversy involves a social conflict of great complexity which illustrates the formidable involvement that can develop between an industry and the society in which it operates. First World products and technologies have consequences in Third World settings that cannot be ignored in the blind search for market opportunities. Artificial feeding, as a technology, and infant formula foods, as a product, have had a strong impact on LDCs in the past twenty years. Some, such as the provision of choices for consumers, have been intended; others have been unintended. Neither type can be ignored. To a number of those involved, the "action question" is now paramount: What is to be done and by whom? Certainly, firms in the industry, LDC governments, professional nutritionists, and public action groups throughout the world are pondering that very question.

There is a second, and perhaps more significant, question to be asked as well. Is it possible for a firm, much less an entire industry, to market its products in an ethically acceptable manner over a long period of time and in different social environments? This is the ultimate marketing question. Because public standards change, the answer lies not in a categorical yes or no. Rather it is to be found in the concerted efforts of a management that is sensitive to the ever changing agenda of public issues, to identify, assess and respond creatively to newly exposed expectations of corporate performance. The breakdown of the marketing concept occurs when managers to whom marketing strategy is entrusted become myopic, focusing on current markets rather than changing societal needs and expectations. The great infant formula controversy is an object lesson in marketing strategies gone awry.

The controversy surrounding infant formula foods is not an isolated case, unrelated to other industries or types of products. It is very likely "opening round" in the public questioning of the underlying legitimacy of marketing activity in societies where public needs are more important than private choice. It is not sufficient to say that any product which offers the consuming public a choice is acceptable in all societies. It is only by matching marketing activities to areas where genuine public needs exist, and by analyzing and assessing the primary and secondary impacts of products in particular social environments, that marketing strategies can remain viable in modern business environments.[18]

A senior executive of one of the infant formula manufacturers discussed above noted that much of the problem of infant malnutrition in LDCs was attributable to "misadventure" by the products' users—that is, a consequence of something the individual initiated. The fatal blow to that argument is the recognition that some actions of the marketer may have contributed to that consumer's misadventure. We believe that the firm must be held responsible for any misadventure that arises as a consequence of the marketing efforts which it initiates. This does not serve to place on managers unlimited responsibility, but puts a premium on their efforts to foresee the public consequences of private action.

It is clear that when a firm or industry ignores the second order effects of its actions, private conflicts between sellers and the customers become public controversies. Managers have the greatest discretion in dealing with conflicts at the earliest stages. But once an issue passes into the remedy and relief stage, and nonusers of the product are drawn into the controversy by proponents of change, the range of responses available to the firm becomes limited. This strongly suggests that managers ought to recognize public issues as quickly as possible, and move from the social obligation and social responsibility patterns of response into the proactive social responsiveness mode.

References

1. Robert J. Ledogar, *U.S. Food and Drug Multinationals in Latin America: Hungry for Profits* (New York: IDOC, North America, Inc., 1975), p. 128.
2. Johanna T. Dwyer, "The Demise of Breast Feeding: Sales, Sloth, or Society?" in *Priorities In Child Nutrition*, report prepared for the UNICEF Executive Board under the direction of Dr. Jean Mayer (E/ICEF/L. 1328, March 28, 1975), vol. II, pp. 332–339.
3. Ledogar, op. cit., pp. 133–134.
4. Ibid.
5. Ibid., p. 142.
6. Frances M. Lappé and Eleanor McCallie, "Infant Formula Promotion and Use in the Philippines: An Informal, On-Site Report," Institute for Food and Development Policy (San Francisco, California, July 1977). Lappé is the author of the new book *Food First*.
7. V. G. James, "Household Expenditures on Food and Drink by Income Groups," paper presented at seminar on Natural Food and Nutrition Policy, Kingston, Jamaica, 1974.
8. *The American Druggist* (May 4, 1970).
9. This has been acknowledged by industry executives and was a key point in a U.S. antitrust action brought by Baker Laboratories against Abbott (Ross) and Bristol-Myers in 1972.
10. James E. Post, "The Infant Formula Industry: Strategy, Structure, and Performance," Working Paper, Management and Public Policy Research Program, Boston University, 1977.
11. *The Womanly Art of Breastfeeding,* 2nd ed. (Franklin Park, Ill.: La Leche League International, 1963), p. 54.
12. "Baby Food Tragedy," *New Internationalist*, p. 10; Mike Muller, *The Baby Killer: War on Want*, 2nd ed. (May 1975), p. 10.
13. Bristol-Myers Co., "The Infant Formula Marketing Practices," p. 13.
14. For a further elaboration, discussion and application of this model, see S. Prakash Sethi, "Dimensions of Corporate Social Performance: An Analytical Framework for Measurement and Evaluation," *California Management Review* (Spring 1975), pp. 58–64; and S. Prakash Sethi, "An Analytical Framework for Making Cross-Cultural Comparisons of Business Responses to Social Pressures," in Lee E. Preston (ed.), *Research in Corporate Social Performance and Policy* (Greenwich, Conn.: JAI Press, 1978), in press.
15. "The Baby Food Controversy," *The New Internationalist*, p. 10.
16. Muller, op. cit.

17. "Baby Bottles Banned in New Guinea," *The Dallas Morning News* (November 3, 1977), p. 8–C.

18. See James E. Post, testimony in *Marketing and Promotion of Infant Formula in the Developing Nations*, Hearings before the Subcommittee on Health and Scientific Research of the Committee on Human Resources, 95th Congress, Second Session, 23 May 1978, pp. 116–125.

III ___ GLOBAL MARKETING STRATEGIES IN PRACTICE _____

6. Do You Really Have a Global Strategy?

GARY HAMEL

Mr. Hamel is a lecturer in business policy at the London Business School.

C. K. PRAHALAD

Mr. Prahalad, associate professor of policy and control at the University of Michigan, has published widely in the area and is coauthoring a book on the work of top managers in MNCs. This is his third article for HBR.

The Japanese competition attacked in the 1970s. U.S. and European companies were caught napping at first, but quickly responded. U.S. auto companies source components, subsystems, and small cars from the low-labor-cost countries like Mexico, South Korea, and Taiwan. Companies are also rationalizing manufacturing operations to meet the new low-cost competitors. Buoyed by these kinds of global strategies, companies firmly believe that they've met the Japanese challenge head on.

They're wrong. According to these authors, the corporate response to Japan's thrust has been half-hearted and without appreciation for its long-term objectives. Many companies have miscalculated both the timing and the workability of their strategies, in part because they don't understand what global strategy really is. So they continually fall behind and lose market share in most of the leading markets of the future. Through a detailed analysis of the tire and television markets, the authors show that only by thinking about strategy in a more analytic light can U.S. companies overtake the competitors.

The threat of foreign competition preoccupies managers in industries from telecommunications to commercial banking and from machine tools to consumer electronics. Corporate response to the threat is often misdirected and ill timed—in part because many executives don't fully understand what global competition is.

They haven't received much help from the latest analysis of this trend. One argument simply emphasizes the scale and learning effects that transcend national boundaries and provide cost advantages to companies selling to the world market.[1] Another holds that world products offer customers the twin benefits of the low-cost and high-quality incentives for foreign customers to lay aside culture-bound product preferences.[2]

According to both of these arguments, U.S. organizations should "go global" when they can no longer get the minimum volume needed for cost efficiency at home and when international markets permit standardized marketing approaches. If, on the other hand, they can fully exploit scale benefits at home and their international export markets are dissimilar, U.S. executives can safely adopt the traditional, country-by-country, multinational approach. So while Caterpillar views its battle with Komatsu in global terms, CPC International and Unilever may safely consider their foreign operations multidomestic.

After studying the experiences of some of the most successful global competitors, we have become convinced that the current perspective on global competition and the globalization of markets is incomplete and misleading. Analysts are long on exhortation—"go international"—but short on practical guidance. Combine these shortcomings with the prevailing notion that global success demands a national industrial policy, a docile work force, debt-heavy financing, and forbearing investors, and you can easily understand why many executives feel they are only treading water in the rising tide of global competition.

World-scale manufacturing may provide the necessary armament, and government support may be a tactical advantage, but winning the war against global competition requires a broader view of global strategy. We will present a new framework for assessing the nature of the worldwide challenge, use it to analyze one particular industry, and offer our own practical guidelines for success.

Thrust & Parry

As a starting point, let's take a look at what drives global competition. It begins with a sequence of competitive action and reaction:

- An aggressive competitor decides to use the cash flow generated in its home market to subsidize an attack on markets of domestically oriented foreign competitors.

- The defensive competitor then retaliates—not in its home market where the attack was staged—but in foreign markets where the aggressor company is most vulnerable.[3]

As an example, consider the contest between Goodyear and Michelin. By today's definitions, the tire industry is not global. Most tire companies manufacture in and distribute for the local market. Yet Michelin, Goodyear, and Firestone are now locked in a fiercely competitive—and very global—battle.

In the early 1970s, Michelin used its strong European profit base to attack Goodyear's American home market. Goodyear could fight back in the United States by reducing prices, increasing advertising, or offering dealers better margins. But because Michelin would expose only a small amount of its worldwide business in the United States, it has little to lose and much to gain. Goodyear, on the other hand, would sacrifice margins in its largest market.

Goodyear ultimately struck back in Europe, throwing a wrench in Michelin's money machine. Goodyear was proposing a hostage trade. Michelin's long-term goals and resources allowed it to push ahead in the United States. But at least Goodyear slowed the pace of Michelin's attack and forced it to recalculate the cost of market share gains in the United States. Goodyear's strategy recognized the international scope of competition and parried Michelin's thrust.

Manufacturers have played out this pattern of cross-subsidization and international retaliation in the chemical, audio, aircraft engine, and computer industries. In each case international cash flows, rather than international product flows, scale economies, or homogeneous markets, finally determined whether competition was global or national. (For a detailed explanation, see the insert entitled "What is cross-subsidization?")

The Goodyear vs. Michelin case helps to distinguish among:

▪ Global competition, which occurs when companies cross-subsidize national market share battles in pursuit of global brand and distribution positions.

▪ Global businesses, in which the minimum volume required for cost efficiency is not available in the company's home market.

▪ Global companies, which have distribution systems in key foreign markets that enable cross-subsidization, international retaliation, and world-scale volume.

Making a distinction between global competition and a global business is important. In traditionally global businesses, protectionism and flexible manufacturing technologies are encouraging a shift back to local manufacturing. Yet competition remains global. Companies must distinguish between the cost effectiveness based on offshore sourcing and world-scale plants and the competitive effectiveness based on the ability to retaliate in competitors' key markets.

Identifying the Target _____

Understanding how the global game is played is only the first step in challenging the foreign competitor. While the pattern of cross-subsidization and retaliation describes the battle, world brand dominance is what the global war is all about. And the Japanese have been winning it.

In less than 20 years, Canon, Hitachi, Seiko, and Honda have established worldwide reputations equal to those of Ford, Kodak, and Nestlé. In consumer electronics alone, the Japanese are present in or dominate most product categories.

Like the novice duck hunter who either aims at the wrong kind of bird or shoots behind his prey, many companies have failed to develop a well-targeted response to the new global competition. Those who define international competitiveness as no more than low-cost manufacturing are aiming at the wrong target. Those who fail to identify the strategic intentions of their global competitors cannot anticipate competitive moves and often shoot behind the target.

To help managers respond more effectively to challenges by foreign companies, we have developed a framework that summarizes the various global competitive strategies (see the *Exhibit*). The competitive advantages to be gained from location, world-scale volume, or global brand distribution are arrayed against the three kinds of strategic intent we have found to be most prevalent among global competitors: (1) building a global presence, (2) defending a domestic position, and (3) overcoming national fragmentation.

Exhibit
A GLOBAL COMPETITIVE FRAMEWORK

	Build global presence	Defend domestic dominance	Overcome national fragmentation
1965	Access volume		
		Response lag	Response lag
1970	Redefine cost-volume relationships		
		Match costs	
1975	Cross-subsidize to win the world		Reduce costs at national subsidiary
		Amortize world-scale investments	
1980	Contiguous segment expansion		Rationalize manufacturing
		Gain retaliatory capability	
1985			Shift locus of strategic responsibility
1990			

Using this framework to analyze the world television industry, we find Japanese competitors building a global presence, RCA, GE, and Zenith of the United States defending domestic dominance, and Philips of the Netherlands and CSF Thomson of France overcoming national framentation. Each one uses a different complement of competitive weapons and pursues its own strategic objectives. As a result, each reaps a different harvest from its international activities.

Loose Bricks

By the late 1960s, Japanese television manufacturers had built up a large U.S. volume base by selling private-label TV sets. They had also established brand and distribution positions in small-screen and portable televisions—a market segment ignored by U.S. producers in favor of higher margin console sets.

In 1967, Japan became the largest producer of black-and-white TVs; by 1970, it had closed the gap in color sets. While the Japanese first used their cost advantages primarily from low labor costs, they then moved quickly to invest in new process technologies, from which came the advantages of scale and quality.

Japanese companies recognized the vulnerability of competitive positions based solely on labor and scale advantages. Labor costs change as economies develop or as exchange rates fluctuate. The world's low-cost manufacturing location is constantly shifting: from Japan to Korea, then to Singapore and Taiwan. Scale-based cost advantages are also vulnerable, particularly to radical changes in manufacturing technology and creeping protectionism in export markets. Throughout the 1970s, Japanese TV makers invested heavily to create the strong distribution positions and brand franchises that would add another layer of competitive advantage.

Making a global distribution investment pay off demands a high level of channel utilization. Japanese companies force-fed distribution channels by rapidly accelerating product life cycles and expanding across contiguous product segments. Predictably, single-line competitors have often been blind-sided, and sleepy product-development departments have been caught short in the face of this onslaught. Global distribution is the new barrier to entry.

By the end of the decade, the Japanese competitive advantage had evolved from low-cost sourcing to world-scale volume and worldwide brand positions across the spectrum of consumer electronic products.

RCA at Home

Most American television producers believed the Japanese did well in their market simply because of their low-cost, high-quality manufacturing systems. When they finally responded, U.S. companies drove down costs, began catching up on the technology front, and lobbied heavily for government protection.[4] They thought that was all they had to do.

Some could not even do that; the massive investment needed to regain cost competitiveness proved too much for them and they left the television industry. Stronger foreign companies purchased others.

Those that remained transferred labor-intensive manufacturing offshore and rationalized manufacturing at home and abroad. Even with costs under control, these companies (RCA, GE, and Zenith) are still vulnerable because they do not understand the changing nature of Japanese competitive advantage. Even as American producers patted themselves on the back for closing the cost gap, the Japanese were cementing future profit foundations through investment in global brand positions. Having conceived of global competition on a product-by-product basis, U.S. companies could not justify a similar investment.

Having conceded non-U.S. markets, American TV manufacturers were powerless to dislodge the Japanese even from the United States.

While Zenith and RCA dominated the color TV business in the United States, neither had a strong presence elsewhere. With no choice of competitive venue, American companies had to fight every market share battle in the United States.

When U.S. companies reduced prices at home, they subjected 100% of their sales volume to margin pressure. Matsushita could force this price action, but only a fraction of it would be similarly exposed.

We do not argue that American TV manufacturers will inevitably succumb to global competition. Trade policy or public opinion may limit foreign penetration. Faced with the threat of more onerous trade sanctions or charges of predatory trade tactics, global competitors may forgo a fight to the finish, especially when the business in question is mature and no longer occupies center stage in the company's product plans. Likewise, domestic manufacturers, despite dwindling margins, may support the threatened business if it has important interdependencies with other businesses (as, for example, in the case of Zenith's TV and data systems business). Or senior management may consider the business important to the company's image (possible motivation for GE) for continuing television production.

The hope that foreign companies may never take over the U.S. market, however, should hardly console Western companies. TVs were no more than one loose brick in the American consumer electronics market. The Japanese wanted to knock down the whole wall. For example, with margins under pressure in the TV business, no American manufacturer had the stomach to develop its own videocassette recorder. Today, VCRs are the profitability mainstay for many Japanese companies. Companies defending domestic positions are often shortsighted about the strategic intentions of their competitors. They will never understand their own vulnerability until they understand the intentions of their rivals and then reason back to potential tactics. With no appreciation of strategic intent, defensive-minded competitors are doomed to a perpetual game of catch-up.

Loose Bricks in Europe, Too

Philips of the Netherlands has become well known virtually everywhere in the world. Like other long-standing MNCs, Philips has always benefited from the kind of international distribution system that U.S. companies lack. Yet our evidence suggests that this advantage alone is not enough. Philips has its own set of problems in responding to the Japanese challenge.

Japanese color TV exports to Europe didn't begin until 1970. Under the terms of their licensing arrangements with European set makers, the Japanese could export only small-screen TVs. No such size limitation existed for Japanese companies willing to manufacture in Europe, but no more than half the output could be exported to the rest of Europe. Furthermore, because laws prohibited Japanese producers from supplying finished sets for private-label sale, they supplied picture tubes. So in 1979, although Europe ran a net trade deficit of only 2 million color televisions, the deficit in color tubes was 2.7 million units. By concentrating on such volume-sensitive manufacturing, Japanese manufacturers skirted protectionist sentiment while exploiting economies of scale gained from U.S. and Japanese experience.

Yet just as they had not been content to remain private-label suppliers in the United States, Japanese companies were not content to remain component suppliers in Europe. They wanted to establish their own brand positions. Sony, Matsushita, and Mitsubishi set up local manufacturing operations in the United Kingdom. When, in response, the British began to fear a Japanese takeover of the local industry, Toshiba and Hitachi simply found U.K. partners. In moving assembly from the Far East to Europe, Japanese manufacturers incurred cost and quality penalties. Yet they regarded such penalties as an acceptable price for establishing strong European distribution and brand positions.

If we contrast Japanese entry strategies in the United States and Europe, it is clear that the tactics and timetables differed. Yet the long-term strategic intentions were the same and the competitive advantage of Japanese producers evolved similarly in both markets. In both Europe and the United States, Japanese companies found a loose brick in the bottom half of the market structure—small-screen portables. And then two other loose bricks were found—the private-label business in the United States and picture tubes in Europe.

From these loose bricks, the Japanese built the sales volume necessary for investment in world-scale manufacturing and state-of-the-art product development; they gained access to local producers, who were an essential source of market knowledge. In Europe, as in the United States, Japanese manufacturers captured a significant share of total industry profitability with a low-risk, low-profile supplier strategy; in so doing, they established a platform from which to launch their drive to global brand dominance.

Regaining Cost Competitiveness

Philips tried to compete on cost but had more difficulties than RCA and Zenith. First, the European TV industry was more fragmented than that of the United States. When the Japanese entered Europe, twice as many European as American TV makers fought for positions in national markets that were smaller than those in the United States.

Second, European governments frustrated the attempts of companies to use offshore sources or to rationalize production through plant closings, lay-offs, and capacity reassignments. European TV makers turned to political solutions to solve competitive difficulties. In theory, the resulting protectionism gave them breathing space as they sought to redress the cost imbalance with Japanese producers. Because they were still confined to marginal, plant-level improvements, however, their cost and quality gap continued to widen. Protectionism reduced the incentive to invest in cost competitiveness; at the same time, the Japanese producers were merging with Europe's smaller manufacturers.

With nearly 3 million units of total European production in 1976, Philips was the only European manufacturer whose volume could fund the automation of manufacturing and the rationalization of product lines and components. Even though its volume was sufficient, however, Philips's tube manufacturing was spread across seven European countries. So it had to demonstrate (country by country, minister by minister, union by union) that the only alternative to protectionism was to support the development of a Pan-European competitor. Philips also had to wrestle with independent subsidiaries not eager to surrender their autonomy over manufacturing, product development, and capital investment. By 1982, it was the world's largest color TV

WHAT IS CROSS-SUBSIDIZATION?

When a global company uses financial resources accumulated in one part of the world to fight a competitive battle in another, it is pursuing a strategy we call "cross-subsidization." Contrary to tried-and-true MNC policy, a subsidiary should not always be required to stand on its own two feet financially. When a company faces a large competitor in a key foreign market, it may make sense for it to funnel global resources into the local market share battle, especially when the competitor lacks the international reach to strike back.

Money does not always move across borders, though this may happen. For a number of reasons (taxation, foreign exchange risk, regulation) the subsidiary may choose to raise funds locally. Looking to the worldwide strength of the parent, local financial institutions may be willing to provide long-term financing in amounts and at rates that would not be justified on the basis of the subsidiary's short-term prospects. One note of caution: if competitors learn of your subsidiary's borrowing needs, you may reveal strategic intentions by raising local

funds and lose an element of competitive surprise.

Cross-subsidization is not dumping. When a company cross-subsidizes it does not sell at less than the domestic market price. Rather than risk trade sanctions, the intelligent global company will squeeze its competitor's margins just enough to dry up its development spending and force corporate officers to reassess their commitment to the business.

With deteriorating margins and no way of retaliating internationally, the company will have little choice but to sell market share. If your competitor uses simple portfolio management techniques, you may even be able to predict how much market share you will have to buy to turn the business into a "dog" and precipitate a sell-off. In one such case a beleaguered business unit manager, facing an aggressive global competitor, lobbied hard for international retaliation. The corporate response: "If you can't make money at home, there's no way we're going to let you go international!" Eventually, the business was sold.

maker and had almost closed the cost gap with Japanese producers. Even so—after ten years—rationalization plans are still incomplete.

Philips remains vulnerable to global competition because of the difficulties inherent in weaving disparate national subsidiaries into a coherent global competitive team. Low-cost manufacturing and international distribution give Philips two of the critical elements needed for global competition. Still needed is the coordination of national business strategies.

Philips's country managers are jealous of their autonomy in marketing and strategy. With their horizon of competition often limited to a single market, country managers are poorly placed to assess their global vulnerability. They can neither understand nor adequately analyze the strategic intentions and market entry tactics of global competitors. Nor can they estimate the total resources available to foreign competitors for local market share battles.

Under such management pressure, companies like Philips risk responding on a local basis to global competition. The Japanese can "cherry pick" attractive national markets with little fear that their multinational rival will retaliate.

The Strategic Imperative _____

International companies like General Motors and Philips prospered in the fragmented and politicized European market by adopting the "local face" of a good multinational citizen. Today Philips and other MNCs need a global strategic perspective and a corresponding shift in the locus of strategic responsibility away from country organizations. That need conflicts with escalating demands by host governments for national responsiveness. The resulting organizational problems are complex.

Nevertheless, companies must move beyond simplistic organizational views that polarize alternatives between world-product divisions and country-based structures. Headquarters will have to take strategic responsibility in some decision areas; subsidiaries must dominate in others. Managers cannot resolve organizational ambiguity simply by rearranging lines and boxes on the organization chart. They must adopt fundamentally new roles.

National subsidiaries can provide headquarters with more competitive intelligence and learn about world competitors from the experiences of other subsidiaries. They must fight retaliatory battles on behalf of a larger strategy and develop information systems, decision protocols, and performance measurement systems to weave global and local perspectives into tactical decisions. Rather than surrender control over manufacturing, national subsidiaries must interact with the organization in new and complex ways.

Such a realignment of strategic responsibility takes three steps:

Analyze precisely the danger of national fragmentation.

Create systems to track global competitive developments and to support effective responses.

Educate national and headquarters executives in the results of analysis and chosen organization design.

This reorientation may take as long as five years. Managing it is the hardest challenge in the drive to compete successfully.

A New Analysis

Managers must cultivate a mind-set based on concepts and tools different from those normally used to assess competitors and competitive advantage.

For example, the television industry case makes clear that the competitive advantage from global distribution is distinct from that due to lower manufacturing costs. Even when they don't have a cost advantage, competitors with a global reach may have the means and motivation for an attack on nationally focused companies. If the global competitor enjoys a high price level at home and suffers no cost disadvantage, it has the means to cross-subsidize the battle for global market share.

Price level differences can exist because of explicit or implicit collusion that limits competitive rivalry, government restrictions barring the entry of new companies to the industry, or differences in the price sensitivity of customers.

The cash flow available to a global competitor is a function of both total costs and realized prices. Cost advantages alone do not indicate whether a company can sustain a global fight. Price level differences, for example, may provide not only the means but also the motivation for cross-subsidization.

If a global competitor sees a more favorable industry growth rate in a foreign market populated by contented and lazy competitors, who are unable or unwilling to fight back, and with customers that are less price sensitive than those at home, it will target that market on its global road. Domestic competitors will be caught unaware.

The implications for these strictly domestic companies are clear. First, they must fight for access to their competitors' market. If such access is unavailable, a fundamental asymmetry results. If no one challenges a global competitor in its home market, the competitor faces a reduced level of rivalry, its profitability rises, and the day when it can attack the home markets of its rivals is hastened. That IBM shares this view is evident from its pitched battle with Fujitsu and Hitachi in Japan.

Global competitors are not battling simply for world volume but also for the cash flow to support new product development, investment in core technologies, and world distribution. Companies that nestle safely in their home beds will be at an increasing resource (if not at a cost) disadvantage. They will be unable to marshal the forces required for a defense of the home market.

Not surprisingly, Japanese MNCs have invested massively in newly industrializing countries (NICs). Only there can European and American companies challenge Japanese rivals on a fairly equal footing without sacrificing domestic profitability or facing market entry restrictions. The failure of Western organizations to compete in the NICs will give the Japanese another uncontested profit source, leaving U.S. and European companies more vulnerable at home.

New Concepts

Usually, a company's decision whether to compete for a market depends on the potential profitability of a particular level of market share in that country. But the new global competition requires novel ways of valuing market share; for example:

■ Worldwide cost competitiveness, which refers to the minimum world market share a company must capture to underwrite the appropriate manufacturing-scale and product-development effort.

■ Retaliation, which refers to the minimum market share the company needs in a particular country to be able to influence the behavior of key global competitors. For example, with only a 2% or 3% share of the foreign market, a company may be too weak to influence the pricing behavior of its foreign rival.

■ Home country vulnerability, which refers to the competitive risks of national market share leadership if not accompanied by international distribution. Market leadership at home can create a false sense of security. Instead of granting invincibility, high market share may have the opposite effect. To the extent that a company uses its market power to support high price levels, foreign competitors—confident that the local company has little freedom for retaliation—may be encouraged to come in under the price umbrella and compete away the organization's profitability.

Critical National Markets

Most MNCs look at foreign markets as strategically important only when they can yield profits in their own right. Yet different markets may offer very different competitive opportunities. As part of its global strategy, an organization must distinguish between objectives of (1) low-cost sourcing, (2) minimum scale, (3) a national profit base, (4) retaliation against a global competitor, and (5) benchmarking products and technology in a state-of-the-art market. At the same time, the company will need to vary the ways in which it measures subsidiary performance, rewards managers, and makes capital appropriations.

Product Families

Global competition requires a broader corporate concept of a product line. In redefining a relevant product family—one that is contiguous in distribution channels and shares a global brand franchise—an organization can, for example, scrutinize all products moving through distribution channels in which its products are sold.

In a corollary effort, all competitors in the channels can be mapped against their product offerings. This effort would include a calculation of the extent of a competitor's investment in the distribution channel, including investment in brand awareness, to understand its motivation to move across segments. Such an analysis would reveal the potential for segment expansion by competitors presently outside the company's strategic horizon.

Scope of Operations

Where extranational-scale economies exist, the risks in establishing world-scale manufacturing will be very different for the company that sells abroad only under license or through private labels, compared with the company that controls its own worldwide distribution network. Cost advantages are less durable than brand and distribution advantages. An investment in world-scale manufacturing, when not linked to an investment in global distribution, presents untenable risks.

In turn, investments in worldwide distribution and global brand franchises are often economical only if the company has a wide range of products that can benefit from the same distribution and brand investment. Only a company that develops a continuous stream of new products can justify the distribution investment.

A company also needs a broad product portfolio to support investments in key technologies that cut across products and businesses. Competitors with global distribution coverage and wide product lines are best able to justify investments in new core technologies. Witness Honda's leadership in engine technology, a capability it exploits in automobiles, motorcycles, power tillers, snowmobiles, lawnmowers, power generators, and so forth.

Power over distribution channels may depend on a full line. In some cases, even access to a channel (other than on a private-label basis) depends on having a "complete" line of products. A full line may also allow the company to cross-subsidize products in order to displace competitors who are weak in some segments.

Investments in world-scale production and distribution, product-line width, new product development, and core technologies are interrelated. A company's ability to fully exploit an investment made in one area may require support of investments in others.

Resource Allocation

Perhaps the most difficult problem a company faces in global competition is how to allocate resources. Typically, large companies allocate capital to strategic business units (SBUs). In that view, an SBU is a self-contained entity encompassing product development, manufacturing, marketing, and technology. Companies as diverse as General Electric, 3M, and Hewlett-Packard embrace the concept. They point to clear channels of management accountability, visibility of business results, and innovation as the main benefits of SBU management. But an SBU does not provide an appropriate frame of reference to deal with the new competitive milieu.

In pursuing complex global strategies, a company will find different ways to evaluate the geographic scope of individual business subsystems—manufacturing, distribution, marketing, and so on. The authority for resource allocation, then, needs to reside at particular points in the organization for different subsystems, applying different criteria and time horizons to investments in those subsystems.

Global competition may threaten the integrity of the SBU organization for several reasons. A strong SBU-type organization may not facilitate investments in international distribution. To justify such investments, especially in country markets new to the company, it may have to gain the commitment of several businesses who may not share the same set of international priorities.

Even if individual SBUs have developed their own foreign distribution capability, the strategic independence of the various businesses at the country level may make it difficult to cross-subsidize business segments or undertake joint promotion. The company loses some of the benefits of a shared brand franchise.

Companies may have to separate manufacturing and marketing subsystems to rationalize manufacturing on a local-for-global or local-for-regional basis. Economic and political factors will determine which subsidiaries produce which components for the system. In such a case, a company may coordinate manufacturing globally even though marketing may still be based locally.

Companies might also separate the responsibility for global competitive strategy from that for local marketing strategy. While national organizations may be charged with developing some aspects of the marketing mix, headquarters will take the lead role in determining the strategic mission for the local operation, the timing of new product launches, the targeted level of market share, and the appropriate level of investment or expected cash flow.

Geography-based Organizations

For the company organized on a national subsidiary basis, there is a corollary problem. It may be difficult to gain commitment to global business initiatives when resource allocation authority lies with the local subsidiary. In this case, the company must ensure that it makes national investments in support of global competitive positions despite spending limits, strategic myopia, or the veto of individual subsidiaries.

Finally, the time limit for investments in global distribution and brand awareness may be quite different from that required for manufacturing-cost take-out investments. Distribution investments usually reflect a long-term commitment and are not susceptible to the same analysis used to justify "brick and mortar" investments.

New Strategic Thought

Global competitors must have the capacity to think and act in complex ways. In other words, they may slice the company in one way for distribution investments, in another for technology, and in still another for manufacturing. In addition, global competitors will develop varied criteria and analytical tools to justify these investments.

In our experience, few companies have distinguished between the intermediate tactics and long-run strategic intentions of global competitors. In a world of forward-thinking competitors that change the rules of the game in support of ultimate strategic goals, historical patterns of competition provide little guidance. Executives must anticipate competitive moves by starting from new strategic intentions rather than from precooked generic strategies.

It is more difficult to respond to the new global competition than we often assume. A company must be sensitive to the potential of global competitive interaction even when its manufacturing is not on a global scale. Executives need to understand the way in which competitors use cross-subsidization to undermine seemingly strong domestic market share positions. To build organizations capable of conceiving and executing complex global strategies, top managers must develop the new analytic approaches and organizational arrangements on which our competitive future rests.

Notes

1. See Thomas Hout, Michael E. Porter, and Eileen Rudden, "How Global Companies Win Out," HBR September-October 1982, p. 98.
2. See Theodore Levitt, "The Globalization of Markets," HBR May-June 1983, p. 92.
3. See Craig M. Watson, "Counter-Competition Abroad to Protect Home Markets," HBR January-February 1982, p. 40.
4. See John J. Nevin, "Can U.S. Business Survive Our Japanese Trade Policy?" HBR September-October 1978, p. 165.

7. MARKET EXPANSION STRATEGIES IN MULTINATIONAL MARKETING

IGAL AYAL

Igal Ayal is Senior Lecturer, Faculty of Management, the Leon Recanati Graduate School of Business Administration, Tel-Aviv University, Tel-Aviv, Israel.

JEHIEL ZIF

Jehiel Zif is Senior Lecturer, Faculty of Management, Tel-Aviv University and Visiting Professor, College of Business Administration, Northeastern University, Boston, MA.

Authors names are listed in alphabetical order. This study was supported by the Israel Institute of Business Research—the project on Export Marketing and International Business Activities. The authors are indebted to their colleagues Yair Aharoni, Seev Hirsch, Dov Izraeli, Yair Orgler, Dov Pekelman and Eli Segev for critical comments and suggestions on drafts of this paper.

This paper presents a framework for planning and evaluation of multinational expansion strategies focusing on the rate of entry into new markets and the allocation of efforts among markets. Two major and opposing strategies are presented and compared: market diversification and market concentration. The factors affecting the choice of strategies are analyzed and illustrated by examples.

Any firm attempting to expand international operations must decide on the number of countries and market segments it will attempt to penetrate at any given period. Given a fixed marketing budget the firm must also decide how to allocate its efforts among different markets served. One can conceive of two major and opposing strategies for making these decisions: market diversification and market concentration. The first strategy implies a fast penetration into a large number of markets and diffusion of efforts among them. The second strategy is based on concentration of resources in a few markets and gradual expansion into new territories.

After a number of years, both strategies may lead the firm to export into the same number of markets. The alternative expansion routes may generate, however, totally different consequences in terms of sales, market shares, and profits over time. In this paper, these two strategies are compared and the factors impinging on the choice between them are analyzed. Within the framework of the two major strategies, a number of more detailed strategic choices are identified, and alternative measurements of market expansion are discussed. Application of the framework for the choice of strategy is discussed and illustrated by a brief case study.

Reprinted from the *Journal of Marketing 43*, No. 2 (Spring 1979), published by the American Marketing Association. "Market Expansion Strategies in Multinational Marketing" by Igal Ayal and Jehiel Zif.

The Research Literature

Questions of market expansion in multinational marketing have received limited attention in the literature. Most of the research has concentrated on questions of national rather than international marketing, and on the allocation of promotional budgets among sales territories. No published attempt for systematic identification and choice of market expansion strategies has been found.

Nordin (1943) applied a basic marginal approach for allocating sales effort between two geographic areas subject to a budget constraint. Zentler and Hyde (1956) considered the allocation of advertising expenditures among a given number of countries. Their model takes into account an S-curve response function to promotion, and time-lag in the effect of promotion. A graphic solution is proposed to solve the complex mathematical problem. Hartung and Fisher (1965) used a model of brand switching and mathematical programming for market expansion in locating new gasoline stations.

Hirsch and Lev (1971; 1973) influenced our research by their empirical study of sales stability and profitability of two alternative penetration strategies into foreign markets. Their findings were supported by data from 200 exporting firms. Their identification of strategies was based on the direction of change in a market concentration index of sales between two periods.

Shakun (1965; 1966) attacked the related problem of promotional effort allocation between products through a game-theoretic approach. Luss and Gupta (1973) concentrated on the mathematical problem of designing an algorithm for solving the sales maximization problem, when marketing effort is allocated between products and sales territories. More recently, Beswick (1977) studied the allocation of selling effort via dynamic programming.

The various research papers mentioned above contribute important points to the analysis of market expansion and resource allocation. None of the papers however, presents a comprehensive framework for identification and analysis of alternative market expansion strategies over time. The purpose of this paper is to help fill this gap.

The Major Strategic Alternatives

The choice of a market expansion policy is a key strategic decision in multinational marketing. To develop such a policy, a firm has to make decisions in the following three areas:

- Identification of potential markets and determination of some order of priorities for entry into these markets.
- Decision on the overall level of marketing effort that the firm is able and willing to commit.
- Selection of the rate of market expansion over time, and determination of the allocation of effort among different markets.

This paper concentrates on the third area, assuming that decisions in the first two areas have already been made. In practice, the process will frequently be iterative; analysis of the third area will be helpful in clarifying and reviewing the first two areas.[1] The major strategic alternatives of market expansion, within the third area, are market concentration versus market diversification.

A strategy of market concentration is characterized by a slow and gradual rate of growth in the number of markets served. On the other hand, a strategy of market diversification is characterized by a fast rate of growth in the number of markets served at the early stages of expansion. It is, therefore, expected that a strategy of concentration will result in a smaller number of markets served, at each point in time, relative to a strategy of diversification. Expected evolution of the number of markets served, for a strategy of concentration versus a strategy of diversification, is presented graphically in Figure 1. The functional forms of the two strategies in Figure 1 represent a family of possible curves, showing the relative changes in the number of markets served over time.

In the long run, a strategy of diversification will frequently lead to a reduction in the number of markets, as a result of consolidation and abandonment of less profitable markets. A fast rate of market expansion is usually accomplished by devoting only limited resources and time to a careful study of each market prior to entry. The firm is, therefore, bound to make a few mistakes and is more likely to enter unprofitable markets and drop them later.[2]

The different patterns of market expansion are likely to cause development of different competitive conditions in different markets over time. The profitability of a late entry into new markets is affected by these competitive conditions and by the length of the product life cycle. As a result, the optimal number of markets served in the long run is not necessarily the same for both strategies.

Figure 1
ALTERNATIVE MARKET EXPANSION STRATEGIES OVER TIME

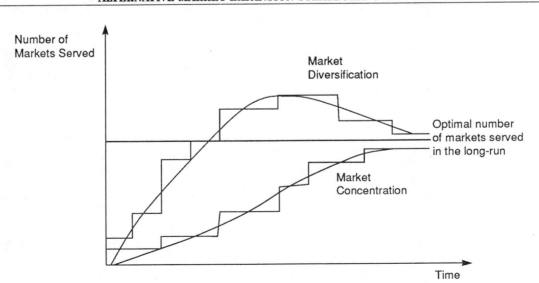

The two strategies of concentration versus diversification lead to the selection of different levels of marketing effort and different marketing mixes in each market. Given fixed financial and managerial resources, the level of resources allocated to each market in a strategy of diversification will be lower than with concentration. The size of the budget gives an indication about possible selection of means or marketing mix. Specifically, a lower level of marketing effort implies less promotional expenditures, more reliance on commission agents, and a stronger tendency for a skimming approach to pricing. A strategy of concentration, on the other hand, involves investment in market share. This implies heavy promotional outlays, a stronger control of the distribution channel and, in some cases, penetration pricing.

Detailed Strategic Options

A strategy of market expansion is characterized not only by the rate of entry into new national markets. Two additional considerations are of particular importance for more detailed identification of optional strategies: (1) market segments within national markets and (2) allocation of effort to different markets (and market segments).

A number of strategic options can be derived based on the consideration of market segments and effort allocation; these are introduced and briefly discussed in this section. The full range of considerations affecting the choice of market concentration versus market diversification is treated in the following section.

Market Segments within National Markets. Four major market expansion alternatives can be identified when market segments are examined. These alternatives are presented in Table 1.

Strategy 1 concentrates on specific market segments in a few countries and a gradual increase in the number of markets served. This dual concentration is particularly appropriate when the product (or service) appeals to a definite group of similar customers in different countries, and the costs of penetration into each national market are substantial in relation to available resources. To be successful with this strategy, the segments served must be sufficiently large and stable.

Strategy 2—characterized by market concentration and segment diversification— requires a product line which can appeal to different segments. The strategy is particularly effective when there are significant economies of scale in promotion (e.g., umbrella advertising) and distribution, and when the sales potential of the home market and other national markets served is large. Under such conditions, a

Table 1
MARKET EXPANSION STRATEGIES BASED ON COUNTRIES AND SEGMENTS

| | | Segments | |
		Concentration	Diversification
Countries	Concentration	1	2
	Diversification	3	4

firm can achieve growth objectives by concentrating on many submarkets within a limited number of national markets.

Strategy 3—characterized by market diversification and segment concentration—is suitable for firms with a specialized product line and potential customers in many countries. With this strategy, a firm frequently can use a similar product and promotion strategy in all markets. The strategy is particularly effective when the cost of entry into different markets is low relative to available resources. For strategy identification, it is important to note that two firms may follow different expansion strategies with respect to countries and segments (strategy 2 versus strategy 3) yet serve the same total number of market segments at each point in time.

Strategy 4 is based on dual diversification in both segments and markets. This aggressive strategy can be employed by firms with a product line appealing to many segments, and sufficient resources to accomplish a fast entry into many markets. Large international firms with sales offices in many countries frequently use this strategy when they introduce a newly developed or acquired product line. A poor-man's version of strategy 4 can sometimes be employed by small firms with limited resources, based on superficial coverage. The commitment of resources in market expansion is the subject of the following paragraphs.

Allocation of Effort to Different Markets. Marketing expansion can be achieved by different means. Even a small firm with limited resources can achieve market diversification quickly by using independent commission agents in each market, with little or no investment. In order to identify a specific strategy of market expansion it is, therefore, necessary to specify the overall marketing effort as well as the allocation of effort to different markets.

Some researchers have defined resource commitments to international markets on the basis of a stepwise expansion of operations (Johanson and Wiedersheim 1975). A sequence of three stages demonstrates successively larger commitments of resources and marketing involvement:

- Export by independent agents
- Sales subsidiary
- Manufacturing subsidiary

The marketing expansion of Volvo into 20 countries between 1929 and 1973 is presented graphically in Figure 2. This figure separates expansion by the three stages above and shows the gradual increase in territorial coverage and resource commitments. Two periods of relatively fast diversification, prior to and after World War II, are indicated.

The first two stages above specify an essential element of distribution strategy in market expansion. Extensive use of independent agents is frequently associated with market diversification; and a resource commitment to sales subsidiaries is a more likely strategic element of market concentration. Many firms like Volvo prefer to employ independent agents in some markets and sales subsidiaries in others. The relative share of each distribution method is an important strategic option of market expansion.

Figure 2

MARKET EXPANSION OF VOLVO INTO TWENTY NATIONAL MARKETS

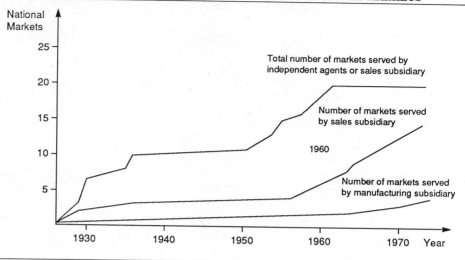

Source of data: Johanson and Wiedersheim (1975).

        Distribution strategies do not always portray a correct picture of effort allocation. A firm may invest the same resources in two markets using a different marketing mix and distribution setup. In one market the firm may employ an independent agent backed by substantial promotional activity. In another market the firm may establish a sales subsidiary with a limited promotional budget. A quantitative measure of effort allocation would be more precise for analytical purposes.

        Managers inside the firm can determine the overall marketing investment in each market, based on internal accounting. With this information, it is possible to calculate a diversification index that takes into account both the number of markets served and the uniformity of effort distribution.[3]

Considerations Affecting The Choice of Market Expansion Strategy _____

The selection of market expansion strategy is influenced by characteristics of the product, characteristics of the market, and decision criteria of the firm. Table 2 summarizes 10 key product/market factors affecting the choice between market concentration and market diversification. The following discussion explains the effect of each factor on the adoption of market expansion strategy.

(1) *Sales Response Function.* Two alternative classes of sales response functions—a concave function and an S-curve function—are common in the literature (Kotler 1971). Graphic examples of these functions are presented in Figure 3.[4] If the firm believes that it faces a concave response function, there will be a strong motivation

Table 2

PRODUCT/MARKET FACTORS AFFECTING CHOICE BETWEEN
DIVERSIFICATION AND CONCENTRATION STRATEGIES

Product/Market Factor	Prefer Diversification if:	Prefer Concentration if:
1. Sales response function	Concave	S-curve
2. Growth rate of each market	low	high
3. Sales stability in each market	low	high
4. Competitive lead-time	short	long
5. Spill over effects	high	low
6. Need for product adaptation	low	high
7. Need for communication adaptation	low	high
8. Economies of scale in distribution	low	high
9. Program control requirements	low	high
10. Extent of constraints	low	high

Figure 3

ALTERNATIVE MARKET SHARE RESPONSE FUNCTIONS

*Effective marketing effort takes into account current marketing effort as well as carry
over effects of previous efforts.

to follow a strategy of market diversification. On the other hand, when the response function is assumed to be an S-curve, a market concentration strategy usually is preferred.

The concave response function implies that the best return of marketing effort (x) is at lower levels of effective effort (see Figure 3). This is based on the assumption that the markets under consideration include a number of clients or submarkets which are particularly interested in the firm's products. Such interest is frequently generated by a unique product or marketing program, possibly the result of substantial investment in R&D. As additional effort is spent, market share increases, but the firm faces stiffer resistance, more skeptical buyers, and increased effort by competitors. Therefore, market response is characterized by diminishing marginal returns and diversification of effort is more productive. It is interesting to note that most empirical studies of advertising effectiveness support the hypothesis of concave market response functions (Simon 1971; Lambin 1976).

The S-curve response function assumes that small-scale efforts of penetration to a new market are beset by various difficulties and buyers' resistance and will not count for much. Increases in market share and profitability will be achieved only after a substantial concentration in marketing effort is made. This type of response function is likely for products that do not enjoy obvious advantages—which is, of course, the case for most products. There are a number of reported cases of geographical market expansion which support the premise of an S-curve response function (Cardwell 1968; Hofer 1975).

A quantitative example of the choice of market expansion under the two sales response assumptions is presented in a footnote below.[5]

(2) Growth Rate of Each Market. When the rate of growth of the industry in each market is low, the firm can frequently achieve a faster growth rate by diversification into many markets. On the other hand, if the rate of market growth in present markets is high, growth objectives can usually be achieved by market concentration.

When the rate of growth of the industry in many markets is high, there are occasional opportunities for diversification with limited resources. Penetration to many markets can be accomplished by relying on marketing efforts of independent sales agents and licensees who are interested in promoting the firm's products in their own growing markets. The case of Miromit, an Israeli producer of unique solar collectors, serves as an example. Following the energy crisis, the firm was flooded by requests for sales representation from interested parties in many countries. In this case, the firm followed a mixed strategy by concentrating its resources in a few markets and diversifying to other markets with little or no investment. By this strategy the number of markets served would increase rapidly, but the effort diversification index would show a slow rate of growth.

(3) Sales Stability in Each Market. When demand in each market is unstable, the firm can spread the risk through judicious diversification. To the extent that markets are independent with respect to demand, an increase in the number of markets is likely to increase sales stability. This was demonstrated empirically by Hirsch and Lev (1971). When sales stability in each market is high, the firm can concentrate its market expansion effort while still satisfying the need for stability.

(4) Competitive Lead-time. The lead-time that an innovative firm has over competitors and potential imitators is an important consideration in selecting a market expansion strategy. When competitive lead-time is short and there is a major advantage to being first in a market with a new innovation, there is a strong motivation to follow the route of diversification. In this situation, the firm faces a favorable response function for a limited period. The urgency to enter many markets quickly is diminished if the innovative firm has a long lead-time, or when there is no innovative advantage. This argument of competitive lead-time was expressed by an executive of a small computer equipment company: "The compelling reason for entering Europe now . . . was to capitalize on our innovative advantage. We consider our products to be well ahead of competitors' . . . but in our fast moving field—data entry systems and input equipment—this could change rapidly" (Sweeney 1970).

(5) Spill-over Effects. Spill-over of marketing effort or goodwill from present to new markets is another factor favoring diversification. This spill-over effect can be the result of geographical proximity, cultural influence, or commercial ties. It is common in TV and radio coverage of close national markets. There is obviously a strong motivation to take advantage of spill-over effects by diversifying into new markets which are influenced by current and past effort in presently-served markets.

(6) Need for Product Adaptation. The experience curve phenomenon of systematic reduction in variable cost with an increase in accumulated production volume has a major impact on international market share strategy (Rapp 1973). Firms that grow faster than their competitors are able to reduce production costs faster and as a result enjoy a major competitive advantage. When the same product is sold in different international markets, market expansion is not only a vehicle for diversification and new profit opportunities, but it also can increase profits by reducing costs in currently-served markets.

Frequently, a company cannot sell the same product in all international markets. There is a need to adapt the product to the standards and regulations of a new country, as well as to the special tastes and preferences of new consumers. The magnitude and nature of the adaptation costs are an important consideration in choosing an expansion strategy. In particular, a firm should assess whether adaptation to new markets requires only a small fixed investment or whether a major change is necessary. If entry into new international markets requires major changes in the production process, the company will not only have to invest a significant amount before entry, but will probably be unable to enjoy the full cost advantage of accumulated experience. In this case there will be a lesser motivation to expand geographically than in the case of an investment that has positive effects on potential economies in production.

(7) Need for Communication Adaptation. Adaptation may be necessary not only for the product, but also for the marketing or communication program. In many situations, the communication program is more important than the technical specifications of the product. In a recent study of international expansion of U.S. franchise systems, 59% of the 80 respondent firms indicated alteration in strategy upon entry into international markets (Hackett 1976). Twenty-five percent of the firms reported a change in product (or service) to fit local tastes, while all other changes were related to communication adaptation. If communication adaptation requires a large investment in consumer and advertising research and in production of new programs, the temptation to follow a diversification strategy is diminished.

(8) *Economies of Scale in Distribution.* When distribution cost is a significant expense and there are economies of scale with increased market share, there is motivation to follow a concentration strategy. A strategy of rapid expansion into many new markets can frequently increase distribution costs substantially as a result of increased transportation distance and a low level of sales over a large territory. Efficient distribution can, however, be achieved in different ways depending on the product and specific channels. For example, it is possible that diversification with respect to countries and concentration with respect to segments (strategy 3 in Table 1) can lead to an efficient distribution system.

(9) *Program Control Requirements.* Extensive requirements for control are typical of custom-made and sophisticated products and services which require close and frequent communication between headquarters (R&D, production, marketing) and clients. The cost of managerial communication with clients and agents, per unit of sales, is likely to increase with the number of markets served. A comparison of average contact costs in concentrated and diversified markets suggests that the difference in favor of a concentrated market is increasing with the number of contacts (Bucklin 1966). We can, therefore, expect that when the program control requirements are extensive, a concentrated strategy of market expansion will have an advantage.

(10) *Constraints.* There are a number of constraints on management action in international markets. External constraints include import and currency barriers created by government authorities in the target markets. There may also be difficulties in finding or developing an effective sales and distribution organization. Internal constraints are based on the availability of resources in order to function in new markets. Trained managers and salesmen may be limited, financial resources may be scarce, and production factors may be in short supply.

In the previously mentioned study of international expansion of franchise systems, respondents were asked to rank problems encountered in international markets (Hackett 1976). The five most important problems were: (1) host government regulations and red tape, (2) high import duties and taxes in foreign environments, (3) monetary uncertainties and royalty retribution to franchisor, (4) logistical problems inherent in operation of international franchise systems, and (5) control of franchisees. The spectacular rate of international market expansion, and the reported plans for further expansion by the respondent firms, indicate that these obstacles were surmountable in most cases. This was partly due to a strategy based on franchisee-owned outlets, which is a form of diversification with limited resources.

External or internal constraints place a limit on the capability or the profitability of market diversification. While some constraints can be overcome, extensive barriers in many markets will lead to market concentration.

Decision Criteria

The expected value and the variance of the net present value of each expansion alternative are common decision criteria. To use these criteria, it is necessary to estimate and express the product/market factor considerations in quantitative terms of sales, prices, costs, and timetable.

Many firms frequently will supplement these profitability estimates with other criteria based on the multiple objectives of the firm. Objectives of international market standing and prestige are frequently stated as major causes for fast diversification with limited regard to profitability consequences. For example, Koor, the largest industrial concern in Israel, established a trading company and decided to enter the European Common Market with a strategy of fast diversification by setting up sales offices in seven European countries within one year (Perry 1977). The major objective was: "to become the largest and most important Israeli commercial organization in Europe." It is interesting to note that profitability results in the short-term quite disappointing.

The criteria used by business firms to select alternatives for action are outside the scope of this study. We merely suggest that these criteria can be another major cause for preference of one market expansion strategy over another.

Application

Selecting a market expansion strategy based on the product/market factors of Table 2 is bound to raise a few application questions. These questions can be clarified by reviewing the case of a leading electronics manufacturer in Israel (name withheld at request of company executives). The firm is a subsidiary of a large and internationally known American firm. Two relatively sophisticated product lines are being exported: communication equipment and control systems. The communication equipment was developed by the parent company while the control systems were developed in Israel. Table 3 and Figures 4 and 5 present, for each product line, a summary analysis of the product/market factors, market expansion graphs, and international sales.

One question of application is illustrated by Table 3. The 10 factors do not point in one direction; some imply market diversification, while others imply market concentration.

Two explanatory remarks can clarify the dilemma: (1) Management must weigh the relative importance of the product/market factors in selecting a strategy. Although some factors such as the sales response function will be important in all cases, the relative importance of other factors such as distribution cost are likely to change from case to case. (2) The concepts of market concentration and market diversification should be viewed in relative terms. Occasionally, the choice between concentration and diversification is not clear-cut in absolute terms and a middle course should be selected. In comparison with extreme alternatives, however, the strategic choice is clear.

In the case of control systems most factors point to a concentrated strategy (Table 3); the firm followed this strategy with respect to both markets and segments. The direction implied by the factors for communication equipment is more mixed, and the firm followed a middle of the road strategy of "prudent" diversification, or

Table 3
CASE STUDY: ANALYSIS OF PRODUCT/MARKET FACTORS BY PRODUCT LINE

Product/Market Factor	Communication Equipment		Control Systems	
	Direction	Implied Strategy	Direction	Implied Strategy
1. Sales response function	Concave	D	S-curve	C
2. Growth rate of each market	High	C	High	C
3. Sales stability in each market	Low	D	High	C
4. Competitive lead-time	Long	C	Long	C
5. Spill-over effects	High	D	Low	C
6. Need for product adaptation	Low	D	High	C
7. Need for communication adaptation	Low	D	High	C
8. Economies of scale in distribution	Low	D	Low	D
9. Program control requirements	High	C	High	C
10. Extent of constraints	High	C	Low	D

Figure 4
CASE STUDY: MARKET EXPANSION GRAPHS BY PRODUCT LINE

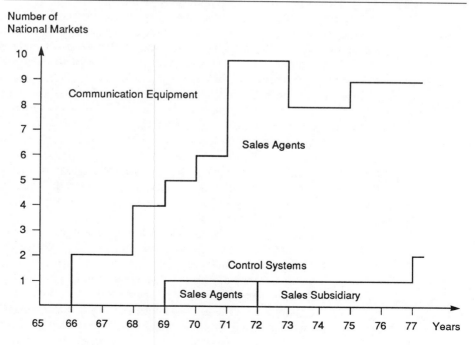

Figure 5

CASE STUDY: INTERNATIONAL SALES BY PRODUCT LINE

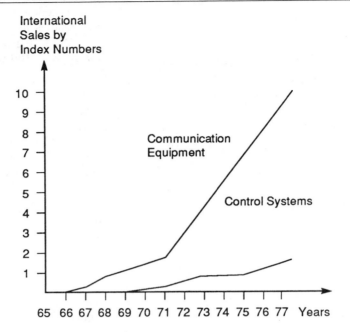

fairly rapid concentrated expansion. The strategy was diversified with respect to segments. Figure 4 demonstrates that the expansion of the communication equipment is much more diversified relative to the concentrated expansion of the control systems.

A second question of application also can be clarified by reference to the case. A summary analysis like Table 3 assumes that the markets under consideration are quite similar and that the effects of the product/market factors can be estimated prior to entry. This is not always the case, as can be seen by the withdrawal from two communication equipment markets in 1973 (Figure 4).

A few points should be made in response to this question:

(1) A summary table, like 3, is applicable to a group of similar markets. When different groups of markets are being considered, it is advantageous to analyze each group separately, since a different expansion strategy may be appropriate for each group.

(2) An investment in market research prior to entry can reduce uncertainty, but not eliminate it. Penetration into international markets which are politically and economically unstable is liable to produce surprises with changing events. This was the case with the communication equipment that was introduced into developing Asian and African markets.

(3) A firm may prefer to acquire information by actual testing in the marketplace, rather than by costly and prolonged market survey prior to entry. This policy is particularly applicable when quick entry is important, or when market

diversification with limited resources is employed. Abandonment of some markets, following testing, is quite likely under this policy.

(4) Market expansion is a discrete process based on a market by market entry. It is therefore possible and desirable to view it as a learning process, and to correct strategic decisions as more information becomes available. This learning process can explain the expansion curve of the control systems (Figures 4 and 5). After three unsatisfactory years in one market, the firm decided to switch from a sales agent to a sales subsidiary, and a second market was penetrated only after eight years of international experience with the product line. It is interesting to note that in spite of necessary corrective action, a different and distinct long-term strategy for each product line was pursued, and that these strategies were consistent with the evaluation of the product **market factors.**

Conclusion

This paper presents a framework for planning and evaluation of market expansion strategies. In particular it focuses on the rate of entry into new markets and the allocation of effort among markets. The framework can be used in national or regional marketing, but has special relevance for international expansion. A careful review of the literature did not reveal any other framework which serves the same purposes.

This framework aids managerial action in multinational marketing in the following ways:

- It helps management specify market expansion alternatives for decision making purposes. In addition to the comparison of the two major and opposing strategies—market concentration and market diversification—the paper aids in defining additional strategic options. By considering market segments within national markets, four viable market expansion strategies are identified (see Table 1). By considering resource commitments to new markets, three strategic options are specified and many more are implied.
- It helps management to systematically analyze the problem of choice among the major alternative strategies. Ten key factors affecting this choice are summarized in Table 2, discussed in some detail in the body of the paper, and illustrated by examples and a case study. In each application it will be necessary to separately assess each factor and its relative importance for comprehensive evaluation of the alternatives.
- It offers guidance for measuring market expansion. Two specific measures suggested are the number of countries and market segments served, and an effort diversification index, both as a function of time. Measuring market diversification can be used not only for evaluating the firm's own expansion policy, but also for evaluating competitive moves. The factors affecting the choice of strategy can be used to interpret competitive assumptions.

A systematic approach to identification of alternatives, analysis of choice, and performance evaluation will clarify managerial planning and help reduce mistakes and disappointments in expansion to new markets.

We hope that this paper will aid in directing research attention to this important and interesting area. Further research can benefit by the following points:

- Comparison of market expansion strategies based on the direction of change between two static measurements—as used in past empirical research (see 4)—may not be sufficient. Figure 1 and the following discussion of dynamic measures point out the complexities of identification and offer some direction.
- Decision making models based on one kind of response function (see 2) are useful in some situations, but can be quite misleading in others. Only by exploring alternative response functions and examining their assumptions and implications, can reliable guidance to action be provided.
- The framework of this paper is useful for planning additional research. Identification of a marketing expansion strategy can be used as an explanatory variable for other marketing decisions. As an example, we have used this framework for studying the related problem of competitive market-choice in multinational marketing (Ayal and Zif 1978). Specific priorities for additional research include further empirical investigation of the relationships among the product/market factors, strategies followed, and business outcomes. There also is room for model building that will offer quantitative analysis of the product/market factors.

References

Ayal, Igal and Jehiel Zif (1978), "Competitive Market Choice Strategies in Multinational Marketing," *Columbia Journal of World Business,* 13 (Fall).

Beswick, C. A. (1977), "Allocating Selling Effort via Dynamic Programming," *Management Science,* 23 (March), 667–678.

Bucklin, L. P. (1966), *A Theory of Distribution Channel Structure,* IBER Special Publications, Berkeley, CA: Graduate School of Business Administration, University of California, 49–50.

Cardwell, John J. (1968), "Marketing and Management Science—A Marriage on the Rocks," *California Management Review,* 10 (Summer), 3–12.

Hackett, D. W. (1976), "The International Expansion of U.S. Franchise Systems: Status and Strategies," *Journal of International Business Studies,* 7 (Spring), 71.

Hartung, P. H. and J. L. Fisher (1965), "Brand Switching and Mathematical Programming in Market Expansion," *Management Science,* 11 (August), 231–243.

Hirsch, Seev and Baruch Lev (1971), "Sales Stabilization Through Export Diversification," *The Review of Economics and Statistics,* 53 (August), 270–279.

_____(1973), "Foreign Marketing Strategies—A Note," *Management International Review,* 13, 81–88.

Hofer, Charles W. (1975). "Toward a Contingency Theory of Business Strategy," *Academy of Management Journal,* 18 (December), 804.

Johanson, J. and Paul F. Wiedersheim (1975), "The Internationalization of the Firm—Four Swedish Cases," *The Journal of Mangement Studies,* 12 (October), 306–307.

Kotler, Philip (1971), *Marketing Decisions Making—A Model Building Approach*, New York: Holt, Rinehart and Winston, 31–37.

Lambin, J. J. (1976), *Advertising, Competition and Market Conduct in Oligopoly Over Time*, Amsterdam: North-Holland Publishing, 95–98.

Luss, Hanan and Shiv K. Gupta (1973), "Allocation of Marketing Effort Among P Substitutional Products in N Territories," *Operational Research Quarterly*, 25 (March), 77–88.

Nordin, J. A. (1943), "Spatial Allocation of Selling Expenses," *Journal of Marketing*, 3 (January), 210–219.

Perry, Michael (1977), Koor-Trade Europe, a Case Study presented in a Management Seminar on International Marketing, Tel-Aviv: Graduate School of Business, Tel-Aviv University.

Rapp, William V. (1973), "Strategy Formulation and International Competition," *Columbia Journal of World Business*, 8 (Summer), 98–112.

Shakun, M. G. (1965), "Advertising Expenditures in Coupled Markets, A Game Theory Approach," *Management Science*, 11 (February), B42-B47.

———(1966), "A Dynamic Model for Competitive Marketing in Coupled Markets," *Management Science*, 12 (August), B525-B530.

Simon, Julian L. (1971), *The Management of Advertising*, Englewood Cliffs, NJ: Prentice-Hall, Inc., 55–76.

Sweeney, James K. (1970), "A Small Company Enters the European Market," *Harvard Business Review*, 48 (Sept.-Oct.), 126–132.

Zentler, A. P. and Dorothy Hyde (1956), "An Optimal Geographical Distribution of Publicity Expenditure in a Private Organization," *Management Science*, 2 (July), 337–352.

Notes

1. Analysis of the third area requires identification of some markets with sufficient potential for entry and a preliminary idea about available budget. The results of the analysis may lead to a reevaluation of the order of entry priorities and provide more definite guidelines for the budget.

2. In their empirical study, Hirsch and Lev (1973) have used the direction of change in a market concentration index of sales between two periods in order to identify the two major strategies. Figure 1 demonstrates, however, that this measure is insufficient for strategy identification. The direction of change for the two strategies is different only during a limited range of time. A more positive identification can rely on the rate or the shape of market expansion over an extended period of time.

3. An effort diversification index for period t, D_{et}, is given by:

$$D_{et} = 1/\sum_{i=1}^{n_t} ME^2_{i,t}$$

where:

$ME_{i,t}$ = Marketing effort in market i and period t, expressed as a fraction of the firm's total marketing effort for period t.

n_t = total number of markets served in period t.

This index is equal to the total number of markets served $D_{et} = n_t$ when efforts are equally distributed; it approaches a lower bound $D_{et} = 1$ when the firm concentrates most of its effort in a single market.

4. For a given initial market size, the sales response function can be separated into a market share response function and a rate of market growth; the first is directly influenced by the firm's marketing efforts while the second is usually more dependent on product life cycles, environmental conditions in the market, and the combined marketing efforts of all competitors.

5. Let us assume that the functional form of Figure 5 is expressed quantitatively, in the following table.

Marketing effort	Concave function. Sales $	S-curve. Sales $
100,000	1,000,000	600,000
200,000	1,800,000	1,200,000
300,000	2,400,000	2,400,000

What is the preferred market expansion strategy for a firm which is planning to invest $300,000 of marketing effort in three identical markets? Under consideration are two strategic alternatives: (1) Concentrate all marketing effort in one market (2) Diversify marketing efforts equally among the three markets (invest $100,000 in each). The outcome of each strategy, depending on the assumed sales response function, will be the following: (preferred strategy indicated by *)

Expansion Strategy	Concave function	S-curve function
1. Concentrate on one market	$2,400,000	$2,400,000*
2. Diversify into three markets	$3,000,000*	$1,800,000

8. STRATEGIC GLOBAL MARKETING: LESSONS FROM THE JAPANESE

SOMKID JATUSRIPITAK

Somkid Jatusripitak teaches at the National Institute of Development Administration in Bangkok, Thailand.

LIAM FAHEY

Liam Fahey is Assistant Professor of Policy and Environment at the Kellogg Graduate School of Management, Northwestern University, Evanston, Illinois.

PHILIP KOTLER

Philip Kotler is the Harold T. Martin Professor of Marketing at the Kellogg Graduate School of Management, Northwestern University, Evanston, Illinois.

As international market opportunities increased, Japan's global marketing strength became evident while American global market shares fell. Having secured its domestic markets, Japan expanded into developing and developed countries. It also pursued a strategy of producing products to sell in selected segments. Concurrent with this expansion was the development of a global marketing network which included the important stage of establishing production facilities around the world. The authors document these two strategies and provide a case example of how Japan's consumer electronics industry became dominant via global marketing. The lessons for US companies are obvious.

Although exporting is of key importance to the success of many firms here and abroad, most US firms still concentrate on domestic selling and ignore foreign market opportunities. The resources and marketing efforts committed to foreign markets are weak and lack marketing depth.[1] This weakness permitted those highly global-oriented Japanese companies to emerge today as the quintessential global marketers at the expense of US firms' global market shares.[2] The US shares in market after market and country after country have fallen victim to the Japanese export invasion.

It is time that American firms shed their international myopia and seek to learn from the Japanese how to capture or recapture leadership in world markets. Reluctance to undertake serious global marketing not only hurts these firms but will also ruin the nation's economy as a whole. The purpose of this article is to draw some lessons on successful global marketing by examining Japan's patterns of global marketing. Two major strategic elements are examined—the strategic global market expansion path and the development of global marketing networks.

The Japanese Global Market Expansion Path

The order in which foreign markets are entered has to be thought through carefully. In general, Japanese business firms followed one of three global expansion paths:

Reprinted from the *Columbia Journal of World Business 20,* No. 1 (Spring 1985), 47–53, by permission of Columbia University.

Global Market Expansion Path: Type I

The most prevalent expansion path among Japanese firms consisted of moving from Japan to developing countries to developed countries. This occurred in steel, autos, petrochemicals, consumer electronics, home appliances, watches, and cameras.

Initially, most Japanese firms relied on building up their home market by seeking to make products that replaced ones imported from the West. By expanding their domestic market share, they managed to gain economies of scale. These firms were assisted and protected by the Japanese government through such means as import restrictions, import duties, and foreign investment restrictions. Because foreign firms faced barriers to entry and did not devote enough resources to the Japanese market, one after the other lost its market position while the Japanese captured almost the whole domestic market. This increased market share helped bring down manufacturing costs and created a competitive advantage permitting Japanese firms to turn their eyes to the overseas markets.

The initial market target of most Japanese companies was the developing countries, especially Southeast Asia and Latin America, since they had less competition and could be used as a base for building volume and sharpening marketing capabilities. For example, Japan used the developing countries to sell surplus production. Although the quality of Japanese consumer electronics, electric appliances, motorcycles, automobiles, and watches that were exported to developing countries was not up to Western standards, the prices were lower and consequently were more in line with the lower purchasing power of these nations.

With the marketing experience gained in overseas markets, the cost improvements realized from volume sold to less developed countries, and the continuous improvement of product quality, Japan reached a point where it was ready to enter its products in more advanced countries. In the 1960s, Japan began to shift its emphasis from less developed countries to highly developed countries, especially the US. As Japan's products became more acceptable to American consumers, Japan's growing reputation made it easier to achieve recognition in other Western countries. The Japanese focused on specific geographical areas and market segments ignored by US producers in order to gain product and customer knowledge from which to build acceptance and to capture market share. Once they gained a foothold, they began to add new products and enter new channels.[3] By the 1970s, nearly 60% of Japanese exports were directed to developed countries, of which more than 30% were sent to the US.

Japan's export invasion spread into Western European countries such as the United Kingdom, West Germany, Italy, and France. Between 1960 and 1979, Japanese exports to European countries increased from 13% to nearly 20%. A flood of imported cars, motorcycles, televisions, watches, cameras, and office equipment entered these countries. A decade ago Europe imported very few Japanese automobiles. Today, Japanese automobiles enjoy a 10% to 12% market share in the United Kingdom and West Germany; a 20% market share in Switzerland, Austria,

Belgium, and the Netherlands; and a 30% share in Denmark, Ireland, and Norway. In motorcycles the Japanese brands dominate the European continent. In watches Japanese brands such as Seiko and Citizen outsell the Swiss brands. In fine cameras Germany was the leader two decades ago. But the Japanese took patient steps to improve their products and adapt them to European tastes and expectations. As a result, German camera makers survive mainly in a very small and expensive market segment while the Japanese dominate the rest of the market.[4]

Although the most prevalent Japanese market expansion path is the movement from its home market to less developed countries and from there to both the US and European countries, the expansion path from the US to European countries is reversed for some Japanese industries. The global expansion path of the Japanese construction machinery and farm machinery industry is a good example.[5] It started in less-developed countries, especially in Asian and African countries. After winning market shares in these markets, developed countries were focused on as the next target. Instead of exporting products to the US, the Japanese first entered European markets and saved the US markets for the last in order to avoid head-on competition with strong US producers such as Caterpillar.

Global Market Expansion Path: Type II

This Japanese expansion path is found in high-technology industries such as computers and semiconductors. After the Japanese had secured their home market for these products, their next targets were developed countries. Developing countries, on the other hand, had market demands which were too small or nonexistent for these products. Later, when developing countries' demand started to grow, the Japanese did not hesitate to make strong inroads into these markets as well.

Let's look at the Japanese computer industry as an example. Computer production in Japan was begun in 1958 by six major companies—NEC, Fujitsu, Hitachi, Toshiba, Mitsubishi Electric, and Oki Electric Industry. Japan allowed IBM to establish a wholly-owned subsidiary in Japan in exchange for IBM granting patent rights to Japanese manufacturers. Once technology was acquired, the Japanese started producing the products. To gain market share in their home market, the Japanese companies aimed their guns at IBM. They fought IBM with a vigorous price-cutting policy. They were also assisted by the Japanese government in several ways, including a "buy Japan" policy and the requirement that Japanese government agencies, universities, and industrial monopolies place their computer orders exclusively with Japanese companies. IBM was not simply competing against Japanese computer

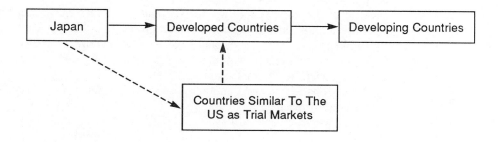

manufacturers but against a powerful partnership that included government and banking interests. As a result, Japanese companies' home market share grew rapidly.

As their home market shares grew, the Japanese turned their eyes to overseas markets. They started an aggressive selling campaign in Australia. The Australian market bore many similarities to the US and could be used as a testing ground. If the company failed, it would not hurt its chances in other markets; if it succeeded, it would be ready to compete in the US. In the US, however, the Japanese product could not compare to IBM's in terms of technology. But the Japanese relied on the key strategies of price and distribution to penetrate the US marketplace. Prices were set 10% to 20% lower than comparable IBM machine prices. The Japanese relied on American manufacturers or distributors to move their products—Fujitsu sold their products through Amdahl's network, Hitachi through Intel, etc. These same strategies were employed to penetrate European markets as well. Fujitsu, for example, made an agreement with Germany's Siemena HG and sold its computers under the Siemena brand in eleven European countries.

As the Japanese penetrated the developed countries, computer demand started to grow in developing countries, particularly Hong Kong, Brazil, Taiwan, etc. In these countries Japan used price cuts as the key strategy. For example, Hitachi offered discounts from 50 to 60% below IBM's list price to Hong Kong banks and government agencies. This marketing approach also worked well in Brazil.[6] In Southeast Asia, each Japanese computer firm targeted a different country. In Thailand, only NEC worked hard to chip away IBM's 80% market share by selling through Datamat Ltd., the sole distributor in the country. Moreover, Hitachi and NEC concentrated on Singapore and Hong Kong, while Fujitsu targeted the Philippines market by selling through Facom Computers.[7] The Japanese sought to build up a strong market position in these developing countries so that they could be there to take advantage of the high rate of economic development expected in these countries.

Global Market Expansion Path: Type III

Although most Japanese exports went through the previous expansion sequences, there were exceptions. Japan produced some products to sell in developed countries instead of the home market. These were products for which home market demand was still not developed or too small to serve. The products included videotape recorders (VTRs), color television sets, and sewing machines.

VTRs, for example, represented a technological breakthrough. They were exported to the US and to other developed countries instead of being sold in Japan because of the huge size of the foreign market. VTRs were later supplied to the Japanese market once the demand began growing.

In the case of color televisions, Japanese manufacturers in 1964 produced mainly for the American market. Not until five years had passed did domestic demand attain a level sufficient to warrant their attention.

Sewing machines were another example. The Japanese makers produced the zigzag sewing machine and exported it to the US almost four years before these machines were available to Japanese consumers.[8]

Development of a Global Marketing Network _____

Japanese ascendancy in global markets could not have been achieved without a highly developed global market network. It took almost three decades for Japanese business interests to develop a strong and efficient global marketing network. Japanese firms passed through the following five stages in the process of becoming internationalized.

Stage I: Relying on Outsiders

Most Japanese firms started their export activities by utilizing the large Japanese trading companies which were familiar with the social atmosphere, business customs, legal procedures, and language of the host countries. More important, the trading companies were able to affect economies through their scale of operation and experience, which helped reduce Japanese firms' distribution costs.

Some Japanese firms started their export activities by directly searching out and signing up local distributors instead of using trading companies. For example, Seiko sold its watches in the US by signing up exclusive regional distributors that were already in the wholesale jewelry business and were able to provide immediate access to jewelers as well as capital sources.[9]

Other Japanese firms entered the US market by working with US producers that had well established sales channels and marketing expertise. In copying machines, for example, Ricoh first sold its machines in the US through the Savin Corporation. After attaining competitiveness and marketing know-how, Ricoh began to sell on its own.

Stage II: Establishing Local Sales Companies

As Japanese companies gained a foothold in the US, many of them started to replace their external agents and distributors with their own overseas sales branches and distribution networks. Through this step they were able to gain managerial experience and strengthened their brand reputation through directly controlling local advertising, promotion, and after-sales service in each market/country.

For example, Toyota and Nissan established their own overseas sales companies and successfully developed their dealer networks in local markets around the world. Nihon Gakki, a highly diversified Japanese manufacturer selling under the Yamaha brand, established Yamaha International Company in the US in 1959 and used it to successfully develop an extensive dealer network.

Stage III: Local Production in Less Developed Countries

In the late 1960s, the Japanese began establishing local manufacturing firms in less developed countries to exploit the cheap, local labor and raw material used in production, as well as to avert the increasing protectionism in these regions. By 1971, the number of manufacturing subsidiaries of large Japanese firms in Asia and Latin America was around 42% of the total.[10]

In consumer electronics, for example, the Japanese began establishing local manufacturing firms in Asian countries such as Korea, Taiwan, and Singapore. Once their products sold well in Asian countries, the next stage was to export to Latin America and the Middle East. In these regions the Japanese also expanded their manufacturing plants. The products produced in these countries not only served the local demand, but were also exported to other countries. Hitachi, for example, exported from its plant in Taiwan to the US; Matsushita exported from Malaysia to nearby countries and the Middle East; and Nippon Electric exported from its plants in Mexico to Panama.[11]

Stave IV: Local Production in Developed Countries

After completing the previous stages, the Japanese firms began to consider establishing local production in developed countries, especially in the US, which was viewed as the most attractive market for volume creation due to its size and high standard of living.

The Japanese began to establish local production either by acquiring companies or starting factories from scratch. By 1980, the Japanese operated 70 plants in machinery manufacturing, 44 plants in electronic products (radio, TV, semiconductors, etc.), and eight plants in precision instruments in the US.

In automobiles, Nissan undertook a huge feasibility study and afterwards established an auto plant in Tennessee, followed by Honda opening an auto plant in Ohio. In Europe, Nissan is contemplating opening a 200,000 cars-a-year assembly plant in Britain.

Stage V: Toward a Global Market

To become a global marketer, one further step is required. The company must establish plants around the world and decide which plants should manufacture which products for which markets to obtain the lowest costs of production and distribution. Today, a number of Japanese firms, especially in automobiles and consumer electronics, have already reached this stage. They are able to distinguish between those production functions that are best left in Japan and those that are advantageously located abroad.

Initially, each overseas subsidiary served only its local market and had no direct ties with subsidiaries in other countries. Beginning in the 1970s, the forging of close multinational links in production began to take place. It was realized that multinational production planning would enable each subsidiary to benefit from economies of scale and to capitalize on factor cost differences in various countries.

Generally, subsidiary manufacturing firms in particular countries produce products to serve local demand and export the surplus to other countries as well as to Japan. Subsidiary manufacturing firms located in low production cost countries also produce and export components to its subsidiaries in high production cost countries. The roles of the manufacturing firms in Japan are to produce high technology components and products, export them to subsidiaries in developing countries and in some developed countries, and send management staffs to subsidiaries all over the world for managerial training, planning, and control[12] (see Chart 1).

Strategic Global Marketing: The Case of the Japanese Consumer Electronic Industry

As an illustration of Japanese global marketing, we will examine in some depth how Japan achieved global market dominance in one major industry—consumer electronics.

Consumer Electronics as a Target Industry

The consumer electronics industry is based on a few technological breakthroughs and is able to lead to the development of a broad range of consumer products—

Chart 1
GLOBAL MARKETING NETWORK

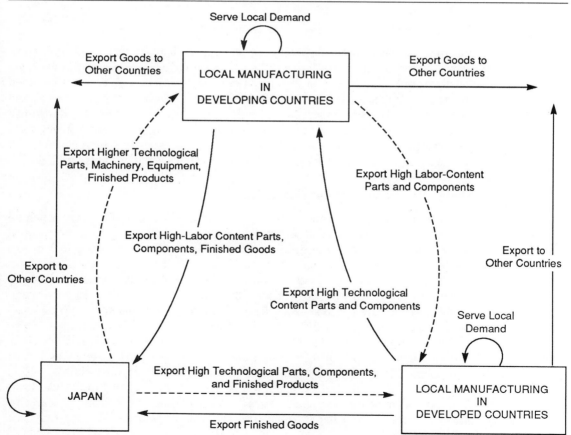

namely, radios, phonographs, tape recorders, TVs, videotape recorders, etc. The worldwide market potential for these products is huge. The Japanese can penetrate any one of those products/markets and use it as a platform to expand to other products/markets that are based on similar technology.

Consumer electronic products rely on technology, highly skilled labor, productivity, and a low requirement for natural resources. These conditions fit Japan's endowments perfectly. The Japanese assessed the consumer electronics industry in the 1950s and knew they could catch up with the West. The high value added by this industry matched the Japanese economic development policy that shifted its interest to higher value-added and heavy industries.

Meanwhile, the US companies, who were the major producers of electronic products in the late 1950s, were more interested in industrial electronics than in consumer electronics. Furthermore, US restrictions against imported electronics products were weak, thus providing the opportunity for the Japanese to enter and compete in global markets much more easily than in other types of industries.

Thus, as early as 1957, Japanese policy makers identified the electronics industry as a priority sector for development, passing into law what was appropriately called Extraordinary Measures for the Promotion of the Electronics Industry.

Building Up Competitiveness at the Home Base

Realizing the need to keep up with the superior technology of foreign producers, especially the US firms, the Japanese began to search for the necessary technology, mostly from US producers, in the early 1950s. The Japanese government provided grants and long term interest loans to stimulate acquisition of foreign technology and underwrite R&D, to set import quotas, and to put restrictions on import and currency exchange licenses in order to encourage the development of an internationally competitive consumer electronics sector. Once their products became highly competitive, the Japanese began to enter overseas markets with carefully planned strategies.

Market Penetration Into Developing Countries

The first strategic move of the Japanese global market expansion path was to penetrate into nonproducer countries such as less developed countries where market competition was not intense. The Japanese spent a number of years patiently developing their export markets in Southeast Asia, Latin America, and the Far Eastern countries. The Asian countries, for decades, have served as Japan's major outlets for consumer electronic products without significant competition from US or European electronic producers. Japanese brand names such as Sony, Sanyo, Toshiba, Hitachi, and National (Panasonic) rapidly replaced American and European brand names in the Far East. In the late 1960s, the Japanese began establishing local manufacturing firms in Asian countries such as Korea, Taiwan, and Singapore to exploit the cheap labor and raw material, as well as to avoid the rising protectionism in those countries. Once their products sold well in Asian countries, the next stage was to export to Latin America and the Middle East. In these regions, the Japanese also expanded their manufacturing plants. At least five Japanese firms entered the Brazilian color TV market compared to two European producers, Philips and Telephunken. Although American brands such as Philco and GE were also sold in countries such as Brazil, they began to lose their leadership to the Japanese because of insufficient willingness to invest in these areas compared to the Japanese. Japanese products manufactured in these developing countries subsequently were exported to other countries as well as back to Japan. Matsushita, for example, began establishing plants in Korea, Taiwan, and Malaysia to manufacture parts and components for subsidiaries in other countries as well as for export to the parent company in Japan.

The Invasion of the US Markets

The Japanese consumer electronic producers started advancing methodically into the US market in the late 1950s. The first strategic step in approaching this market was to carefully research the market, products, and distribution in order to detect the major openings.

The "holes" in the market could be attributed to the strategies chosen by US firms. US firms emphasized higher value products with more "step-up" features for which profit margins were higher. This strategy thus created opportunity gaps for the Japanese to develop. In addition, major US producers tended to promote brand names via extensive national advertising and did not emphasize private label markets. These private label markets were served by weaker firms that were usually divisions of stronger firms, but which did not have high corporate priority. The poorly served private label segment of the market constituted an opening for the Japanese. The private label mass merchandisers provided a mass entry point into distribution. The competitive behavior of US merchandisers further widened the opportunity for the Japanese. In the TV market, the 1964 color TV price war caused a profit squeeze among American firms. RCA's maintenance of high color tube prices to other US manufacturers encouraged US companies, notably Sears, to buy lower priced sets from the Japanese. These circumstances provided the Japanese firms with opportunities to establish themselves in the US market. Not surprisingly, the Japanese never ignored such opportunities. They started making strategic moves into US markets by addressing the markets not effectively served by domestic manufacturers. They focused on a small number of high-volume potential products with high quality, stripped down sizes and features, used aggressive pricing, and marketed them through traditional and nontraditional outlets as well as private label merchandisers that helped them overcome the transportation, servicing, distribution, and brand recognition disadvantages facing them.[13]

After capturing each target segment, the Japanese put heavy emphasis on product innovation by offering to the market new, high quality products at lower prices. The Japanese employed channel integration strategies moving upstream into semiconductor products. Hitachi, Matsushita, Toshiba, etc., gradually turned themselves into major semiconductor suppliers and spent substantial funds to build semiconductor plants and equipment. They also invested heavily in semiconductor R&D in the hope of achieving leadership in this market. With this heavy spending, as well as the competition among the subsidiary and subcontracted semiconductor producers to offer the parent company new innovations of semiconductor products with higher quality and lower prices, the Japanese consumer electronics producers were able to develop innovative products with prices lower than US producers.

In addition, the Japanese also invested heavily in R&D, much of it related to semiconductors with the hope that it would be the leader in a new product market.

Strategic Steps of Market Domination: A Market/Product Evolution

After attaining leadership in a certain market, the Japanese would move into another related product market. Their first success took place in the radio market. After dominating the market, they moved successively into tape recorders, TVs, and video.

The Japanese started their mass production of radios with small, high performance MT tubes in 1952 and began to export them to the US market by the end of the 1950s. The products were viewed as toys and were ignored by US firms. Instead of establishing their own distribution network, the Japanese distributed their products through such nontraditional retailers as catalog outlets, discount chains, drugstores, and mass merchandisers.

As their radios gained a foothold, they lowered the price and began marketing 6-transistor radios with much lower prices than US competitors. The product lines were later extended to include portable multifunction radios. Through these strategies, the Japanese began controlling the radio market in the middle of the 1960s. As they gained control of the radio market, the Japanese took steps to move into the tape recorder industry and started exporting by using strategies similar to those used in the radio market. By the late 1960s, they dominated the tape recorder market, and then moved strongly into the TV market.

Japan's penetration into the US TV market repeated their strategy in marketing radios and tape recorders. To develop a high volume, Japan entered again at the low-price, small-set end of the market while US producers concentrated on the larger, higher-priced, high-margin console business. The Japanese employed a one-step distribution system from manufacturers to retailers to export their products as an economical method of serving a relatively small number of high volume accounts. Mass merchandisers working with the Japanese had extensive warehouses and facilities that eliminated the need for a second step in the distribution chain. In addition, the Japanese promoted their products by spending heavily in advertising and by employing dealer-push strategies to support their brand. These strategies contributed to a great expansion of their market share during the 1960s and 1970s.[14]

From the TV market, the Japanese expanded into the videotape market, and more recently, into the videodisc market. Today, Japanese markets dominate the US video market and account for 90% to 95% of the total output for the world market. Within three decades, the Japanese became the dominant producers of consumer electronics in the US and the world.

Japanese Invasion in Europe

The tremendous successes in the US market provided the Japanese companies with a strong base for further expansion into Europe. The Japanese first entered European markets in the early 1960s by focusing their marketing efforts on major countries such as Germany, the UK, and France. After almost a decade of patiently developing a European distribution network, the Japanese saw their sales on radio, TV, and tape recorders take off in 1969. When Japan's color TV began dominating the US market during the mid-1970s, Japanese exports of color TVs began flooding into Europe. From a negligible level of market penetration in 1974, Japanese exports grew to 6% of Western Europe's color TV market by the end of 1970. These European countries are now facing a new generation of products succeeding color TV, such as videotape recorders and videodiscs, whose sales are rapidly growing.

The swift penetration of Japanese exports produced a protectionist reaction in most European countries, especially in the UK and France. Japan then shifted its pattern of trade from simply exporting to manufacturing in local markets. In the UK, for example, at least six Japanese producers now manufacture their products locally.

At this stage, the majority of Japanese producers are now genuine global marketers with manufacturing plants located in every part of the world as part of a clear strategy of internationalizing production and marketing in order to achieve maximum utilization of labor and capital around the world. Hitachi, for example, has a factory assembling TV sets in the US using chassis imported from subsidiaries located in Taiwan and Singapore, both of which have cheap labor. The tube is made by GE's US plant and other components are either local or from Canada. The only thing imported from Japan is management.

Conclusions _____

Japanese firms today are no longer merely exporting firms but are multinational firms playing for high stakes in the global game of international business. They locate plants and facilities around the world. Japanese exports now consist of goods produced not only in Japan, but also in their overseas factories. Global marketing has greatly benefitted Japan and is the key to its trade success nowadays. Some of these major benefits gained from successful global marketing are summarized below.

Advantage of Experience Curve Effect and Economies of Scale

Research has shown that for many industries, each time the accumulated experience of manufacturing a product doubles, the real unit cost declines at a fairly constant rate.[15] Japan has benefitted from this experience curve effect, as well as from all normal economies of scale made possible by its global marketing strategy. This has enabled Japanese firms to reduce their prices and set them lower than their non-global competitors.

Advantage from Decentralized Production System

The dispersion of Japanese markets, plants, and facilities throughout the world has enabled Japan to achieve the lowest production costs, because many of these countries have cheaper labor or lower costs for raw materials. By establishing decentralized regional production and distribution centers, Japanese firms have reduced their production and transportation costs. This global strategy has helped them maintain their competitiveness in the world market, even in the face of increasing competition and trade protectionism.

Advantage from Profit Transfusions

Japanese firms have frequently used their profits from one market to finance their expensive inroads into new markets. For example, Japan earned a great deal in its home market by keeping prices high and keeping foreign competition low. Zenith claimed that it could sell its TV sets in Japan for less than what Japanese sets were selling for, but it was blocked by invisible trade barriers. It further claimed that Japanese TV manufacturers priced their TVs in the US lower than in Japan . . . an act known as *dumping*. This pattern meant that Japan was using its profits in certain markets to subsidize its attacks elsewhere.

Clearly, the global marketing firm attains distinct advantages in cost and resources not available to its nonglobal competitors. These advantages keep seeding the further growth of the global firm until its containment is no longer possible.

References

1. Somkid Jatursripitak, "Exporting Behavior of the Firm: A Study of Decision Making Processes of U.S. Manufacturing Firms," Ph.D. Dissertation, Northwestern University, Evanston, Illinois, 1984.
2. John E. Roener, *U.S.-Japanese Competition in International Markets* (Berkeley, CA: Institute of International Studies, University of, 1975).
3. Philip Kotler, Liam Fahey and Somkid Jatusripitak, *The New Competition: What Theory Z Didn't Tell You About—Marketing,* (Englewood Cliffs, NJ: Prentice-Hall, forthcoming, 1985).
4. "The Japanese Juggernaut Lands in Europe," *Fortune,* November 20, 1981, pp. 108–22.
5. See details of Japanese strategy in Europe in "Bulldozers Roll In," *Business Europe,* July 28, 1972.
6. "A Worldwide Strategy for the Computer Market," *Business Week,* December 14, 1981, p. 65.
7. "Japan's Lone-Wolf Tactics in Computers," *Business Week,* September 21, 1981, p. 50.
8. Yoshi Tsurumi, *The Japanese Are Coming: A Multinational Interaction of Firms and Politics* (Cambridge, MA: Ballinger Publishing Co., 1976) pp. 31–32.
9. "Seiko's Smash," *Business Week,* June 5, 1978, p. 92.
10. James W. Vaupel and J. P. Curhan, *The World's Multinational Enterprises* (Cambridge, MA: Harvard University Press, 1973), p. 122.
11. Shiro Takeda, "How Japanese Corporations Develop International Markets: Product Diversification and Marketing Efforts," *Wheel Extended,* Vol. X, No. 2, Autumn 1980, p. 6.
12. Ibid., pp. 5–7.
13. *The U.S. Consumer Electronics Industry and Foreign Competition* (Evanston, IL: Northwestern University, Center for Interdisciplinary Study of Science and Technology, May 1980), pp. 52–57.
14. *Ibid.,* Chapter 3.
15. James C. Abegvlen, *Business Strategies for Japan* (Tokyo: C. Sophia University, 1970), p. 67.

9. AN EXAMINATION OF THE INTERNATIONAL PRODUCT LIFE CYCLE AND ITS APPLICATION WITHIN MARKETING

SAK ONKVISIT and JOHN J. SHAW

Sak Onkvisit is Professor of Marketing at the College of Business and Marketing of Northeastern Illinois University, Chicago. John J. Shaw is Associate Professor of Marketing at Bentley College, Waltham, Massachusetts.

The international product life cycle is a relatively unknown and often overlooked concept. The authors argue that it can be a valuable tool for multinational companies to use for marketing new products abroad.

Marketing, as a discipline of study in the United States, is so well developed that it enables American marketers to use the most advanced and highly sophisticated marketing techniques in their own country. Despite these sophisticated marketing theories and techniques, the US market share abroad has been shrinking substantially. The growth of the world's gross national product has been matched with the relative decline of the United States' world market share from 33% to 25%.[1] There are at least two major causes for this decline. First, American marketers appear to function as novices in the international arena, often ignoring or violating sound marketing methods practiced at home. They approach foreign markets with little effort to understand them—something they would never do in the US. Yet, as illustrated by DuPont, Texas Instruments, and Pillsbury, US firms can do very well, even in the tough Japanese market, when they choose to commit themselves to that market.[2] Second, American marketers are hindered by a lack of well-developed theories to serve as a guide in planning their international business strategies. International marketing is probably the least developed field in marketing—at least, in terms of theory. Theories developed exclusively for international marketing are extremely scarce, while theories proven useful domestically have not been extended or refined to become applicable on an international scale. A case in point is the "product life cycle" theory.

The Product Life Cycle is a marketing concept which has been thoroughly discussed in a large number of marketing publications. In contrast, its international counterpart—the international product life cycle (IPLC)—is virtually unknown among either marketing scholars or practitioners. Developed and verified by economists to explain international trade in the context of comparative advantage, the concept is covered rather briefly in international economic textbooks.[3] In spite of the acknowledgment by a few marketing scholars of its potential in providing a valuable framework for marketing planning on a multinational basis, IPLC has never really generated

Reprinted from the *Columbia Journal of World Business 18*, No. 3 (Fall 1983), 73–79, by permission of Columbia University.

serious attention in the marketing world.[4] Consequently, its impact outside its original discipline is practically nil. One reason for this is that its marketing implications are somewhat obscure. In fact, the IPLC phenomenon itself is not well understood. The purpose of this paper is to discuss IPLC in a marketing context. The IPLC has been modified from its original form in international economics in order to make it more relevant for marketing practitioners.

Theory of IPLC

IPLC is concerned with the diffusion process of an innovation across national boundaries. In essence, a developed country, having a new product to satisfy consumer needs, attempts to exploit its technological breakthrough by selling abroad. Other advanced nations soon start up their own production facilities and before long, less developed countries (LDCs) do the same. Finally, advanced nations, having lost their comparative advantage, begin to import products from their former customers. The advanced nation ends up buying its own creation.

Not counting stage 0, there are four distinctive stages in an IPLC. Table 1 shows the major characteristics of such stages in terms of the United States which has developed that particular innovation. Chart 1, on the other hand, shows three life cycle curves for the same innovation; one for the initiating country, one for other advanced nations, and another one for less developed countries. For each curve, net export results when it is above the horizontal line; if under the horizontal line, net imports occur. As the innovation moves through time, the direction of all three curves change. Furthermore, time should be viewed as being relative: the time needed for a cycle to be completed varies from one kind of product to another, and the time interval also varies from one stage to the next.

Table 1
IPLC STAGES AND CHARACTERISTICS (FOR THE INITIATING COUNTRY)

Stage	Import/Export	Target Market	Competitors	Production Costs
0) local innovation	none	USA	few: local firms	initially high
1) overseas innovation	increasing export	USA & advanced nations	few: local firms	decline due to economies of scale
2) maturity	stable export	advanced nations & LDCs	advanced nations	stable
3) worldwide imitation	declining export	LDCs	advanced nations	increase due to lower economies of scale
4) reversal	increasing import	USA	advanced nations & LDCs	increase due to comparative disadvantage

Chart 1
IPLC CURVES

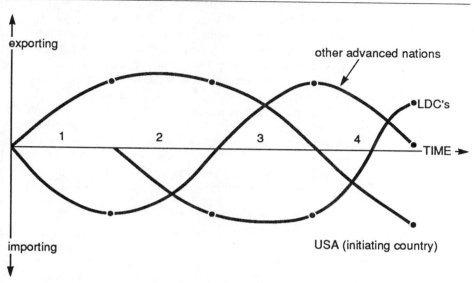

Local Innovation

Stage 0 represents a regular and highly familiar product life cycle in operation. It is a stage through which a new product will go in its development (introduction, growth, maturity, and decline stages) within the original market. For this reason, it is not included in Chart 1 other than as time 0 on the left of the vertical importing/exporting axis.

What are the circumstances that encourage innovation to take place? While innovations can take place anywhere in the world, they are most likely to occur in highly developed countries. On the consumer side, such countries are characterized by affluent consumers with unfulfilled wants. In their demand for a high standard of living, they are receptive to new and better product ideas. On the supply side, firms in advanced nations have both the technological know-how and abundant capital to develop new products. Such countries are likely to be the place of introduction because of the firms' familiarity with domestic market conditions. Firms will also be reluctant to introduce products overseas which may require modification at this early stage.

While any advanced nation can be an innovator, in Chart 1 and Table 1 the country has been assumed to be the United States. As confirmed in one study, US firms accounted for 63.8% of 500 significant innovations.[5] Furthermore, as the United States is the largest market in the world, most innovations are designed to capture this market.

Overseas Innovation

This is the stage when the IPLC begins, and it is known as the "pioneering" or "international introduction" stage. The innovating firm will look to overseas markets because the technological breakthrough creating the new product, in turn creates a corresponding technological gap in other countries. A logical choice is to go to other advanced nations because of their similar needs (cultures) and high income levels. Not surprisingly, countries such as the United Kingdom, Canada, and Australia account for about half of the initial overseas introductions of US innovations.

As the product moves through this stage, there will be increased exports from the US, and correspondingly increased imports by the other developed countries. Production costs reduce substantially because of the economies of scale. This does not necessarily mean a low introductory price overseas, however. Lack of overseas competition coupled with the technological breakthrough permits the company to behave as a monopolist, offering the innovation at a premium.

Maturity

The maturity stage is characterized by "stability." Sales and exports begin to level off, but remain relatively stable. Computers and, perhaps, advanced copying machines are examples of products in this stage. While demands for such products in advanced nations are increasing, the increase is not necessarily translated into greater exports for the US. Firms in other advanced countries, perceiving demand sufficient to create economies of scale, can now justify local production. This justification is bolstered by their governments' protective measures to preserve infant industries: these firms can survive and thrive despite their relative inefficiency. This process may serve to explain the changing national concentrations of high technology exports and the loss of the US share to Japan, France, and perhaps the United Kingdom.[6] As the product moves further into the second stage, the decline in imports by advanced nations tends to accelerate, but is matched by an increase in imports by LDCs.

Worldwide Imitation

All good things must come to an end, and that is how the "worldwide imitation" stage should be handled. At this stage exports from the US decline. Despite stable import demand from the LDCs, the US worldwide export share falls because:

- advanced nations are now self sufficient,
- these countries increasingly replace the United States in exports to LDCs
- consumer demands in LDCs no longer grow to absorb all of the supplies offered by all advanced countries.

Since all advanced nations' target markets are now LDCs, these markets become more finely divided among supplying nations, resulting in a smaller market share for the US. The decline affects economies of scale for the US innovating firm, and its production costs begin to rise. Towards the end of this stage, US exports dwindle to almost nothing and remaining production exists largely for local consumption. The US automobile industry is a good example of this phenomenon.

Reversal

The US, no longer an exporter, may be forced to become an importer instead. The major functional characteristics of this stage are "product standardization" and "comparative disadvantage." The product is no longer a novelty and, with a lack of further modification, it becomes sufficiently standardized for most LDCs to produce simple versions of this product. "Comparative disadvantage" arises because the product is no longer capital-intensive or technology-intensive, but instead becomes labor-intensive. Black and white television sets, for example, are no longer manufactured in the United States because many Asian countries can produce them much less expensively. At this stage, consumers, due to the maturity of the product and the existing price competition, become price sensitive so that domestic manufacturers are now undersold in their own markets.

Validity of IPLC

There are several examples of products which conform to the characteristics described by IPLC. The production of semiconductors started in the United States before diffusing to the United Kingdom, France, Germany, and Japan. Production facilities are now in Hong Kong, Taiwan, and as well as in other Asian countries. Similarly, at one time the United States used to be an exporter of typewriters, adding machines, and cash registers. But, with the passage of time, simple versions of this equipment are now being imported, while US firms export only the sophisticated, electronic models. Other products that have gone through a complete international product life are synthetic fibers, petrochemicals, leather goods, rubber products, and paper.[7]

As explained by Wells, the cycle may be "stretched out" or "shortened," depending on three critical variables.[8] First, high tariffs and freight costs may lengthen the cycle. Harley Davidson, for example, was able to convince the US government to impose high tariffs on Japanese motorcycles. Second, it will take foreign imitators longer to produce products where the economies of scale require substantial volume. Third, a US manufacturer can be partially insulated in the home market if the product is a labor-saving luxury device which may be expensive to purchase, own or operate. Of course, this will not eliminate competition from a standard, economical version of the product desired by the lower-income consumers.

The application of the IPLC is not suitable for all types of products. A product should satisfy basic consumption needs which are essentially homogeneous in other parts of the world. Washers, for example, are much more likely to conform to the IPLC theory than are dryers. Likewise, dishwashing machines are not as useful in countries where labor is very plentiful and inexpensive, and the diffusion of this kind of innovation as described in the IPLC is not likely to take place. Some exceptions are related to climate and natural resources. As a result, manufactured products rather than agricultural or natural resource products are more likely to conform to the described trade cycle.

The IPLC is perhaps most applicable in situations where products are related through some common technology, and these are likely to be products possessing functional utility rather than aesthetic value. If a particular product can render itself to standardization, the trade cycle should be expected to apply. In contrast, a product may be partially or temporarily immune to foreign competition if it is a differentiated product with a unique image. Prestigious, luxury automobiles such as Rolls Royce or Mercedes Benz have their own personalities which are difficult for imitators to duplicate. General Motors, on the other hand, in recent years may have erred in blurring the images among its divisions, by making its Cadillacs almost physically indistinguishable from the model designs offered by the Buick, Oldsmobile, Pontiac, and Chevrolet divisions. This kind of product standardization can speed up the IPLC.

Marketing strategists might object to the IPLC for two reasons: one objection is directed against the IPLC in particular, and the other is concerned with the product life cycle theory in general. The first objection involves the idea that IPLC is a theory which can be refuted and confirmed at the same time. It can be refuted because examples of products can be found which contradict the IPLC phenomenon. But the theory can also be confirmed since many products have actually conformed to the behavior described by IPLC. But it is not the contention of this paper that the IPLC is applicable to all innovations. More work must be done to determine if products applicable to the IPLC are related by function and engineering or by styling and aesthetics. What is the major factor endowment for such products (i.e., is it technological-, research-, capital-, labor-, or land-intensive)? More research is required to determine circumstances which influence new innovations to behave in the manner described in IPLC.

The second objection is somewhat more general because it is directed at the popular and well-known product life cycle itself. Whether the product life cycle is a dependent variable or an independent variable is a subject of much debate. Some market scholars believe that it is a fatal mistake not to adjust the marketing mix to fit a particular stage in the life cycle of a product. Others contradict this view by pointing out that a firm's marketing mix variables should lead, control, and determine a certain life cycle stage for the product.[9] The same controversy, although not yet raised, may eventually extend to the IPLC. The position taken in this paper is that it does not really matter whether the product life cycle (including IPLC) is a causal factor or an effect. The most important fact is that both the product life cycle and marketing mix variables are highly interrelated. It is impractical and unnecessary to separate a cause from an effect in this case. Product life cycle stages require some adjustment in marketing strategy which in turn control those life cycle stages themselves.

While both criticisms are valid, one must remember that no theory can be applicable to all products, and that it is more important to establish the association of product life cycle and marketing variables than to determine a causal relationship between them. The serious problems encountered by many US industries could be reason to consider the IPLC and its implications.

Marketing Strategies and Implications _____

An analysis of the IPLC appears to paint a bleak picture for many US industries. The automobile, for example, is probably near the end of the worldwide imitation stage, implying that the worst is yet to come for Detroit. In contrast, computers, copying machines, and word processors are in the maturity stage as European and Japanese firms begin to challenge the US giants. However, the situation is not hopeless; US firms can adopt marketing strategies to protect themselves. Failure to understand the significance of the IPLC may have led several US industries to take harmful action which has already accelerated the movement of the IPLC for them. US marketers should learn the managerial implications offered by the IPLC and develop strategies for adjusting the marketing mix to their firms' advantage.

Product Policy _____

For an innovating firm in the United States, its most logical market at the beginning is its own local market. As the competition increases at home, the next logical choice is to consider other advanced countries. The firm also must enter LDC markets in order to sustain aggregate sales. Once the maturity stage sets in and its comparative advantage is gone, the firm should switch from producing simple versions of the product to sophisticated models in order to remove itself from cut-throat competition. The implication is that the American marketer must keep on innovating, and one way of doing so is to produce top-quality merchandise during the maturity stage.

Another important strategy consideration is that the firm must keep its production costs competitive. To combat rising costs, it is a wise move for the American firm to start manufacturing in other countries. By doing so, the firm can gain a foothold in those markets, keep transportation costs down, and overcome those countries' resistance to import the firms' product. Another benefit is that those countries can eventually become a springboard for marketing products in other countries within that geographic area. Items produced in other countries can even be imported into the United States; this strategy should enable the American innovator to hold US labor costs down and to hold on to his original market.

A modification of this strategy involves producing various components in different countries in order to take advantage of the most abundant factor of production in each country. Pentax, for example, has its lens for its popular K-1000 cameras made in Taiwan, while bodies for these cameras come from Hong Kong. American firms, however, generally have failed to take advantage of this strategy.

Another defensive strategy is to use patents. A patent granted in the United States, however, does not mean that the firm automatically is protected from product imitation in other countries. Yet, the cost of obtaining foreign patents can run as high as a million dollars. Therefore, the firm must be selective in applying for patent registration in other countries, and potential costs and losses must be considered. Still, under most circumstances, an inventor would find it prudent to get patents in the United States, the United Kingdom, West Germany, and Japan.

Pricing Policy

Due to a lack of initial competition, an innovating firm should price its new product high to recoup research and development costs as soon as possible. A high price also has an indirect effect in terms of consumer perception—the product is perceived as having a high-quality image. As the product enters the second and third stages of the IPLC, it may be wise to lower the price to hold on to market share or to forestall foreign market initiatives by convincing potential competitors that profit margins are too small for market entry. But, once the product is in the last stage of "reversal," the firm should not maintain a low price due to higher production costs and the firm's inability to match the reduced labor costs of its competitors in other countries. Therefore, the firm should go back to a skimming pricing policy (i.e., high price). To support such a policy, only top-quality or sophisticated products should be produced and distributed in the marketplace. This is important because imitators in other countries will then be forced to produce products conforming to the international standard of quality; otherwise, in the long run, they will pay a penalty in the form of lower and lower prices and a reputation for inferior goods. Japan at one time experienced this penalty. It is interesting to note that US automakers have failed to capitalize on this situation. Instead, they allowed their products to decline in quality, and American consumers now perceive Japanese automobiles as superior products.

Promotion Policy

Promotion and pricing strategies in IPLC are highly related. The innovating firm has an initial competitive edge and is in a position to convince the public that it has a superior product due to its technological breakthrough. In effect, it is able to justify its high price at the beginning and the company should not feel obligated to compete with others on a price basis. It may be necessary to cut price, however, in the second and third stages of IPLC as mentioned earlier. But price competition is nothing more than a method to delay the inevitable consequence. A lower price is a tactic that should be used to slow down competitors from capturing a market, but it is not a permanent strategy. Over the long run, higher production costs will not justify a low price strategy indefinitely.

The above discussion should alert the innovating marketer to plan for a non-price promotional policy at the outset of a product diffusion. The implication which can be drawn is that the product should be promoted as a premium product with a high-quality image. This strategy allows the company to trade down later with a simpler version while still holding on to the high-priced, most profitable segment of the market. One thing that the company must never do is to allow its product to become a commodity item with price as the only buying motive, since this process is something that can easily be duplicated by other firms. Marantz, for example, enjoyed a reputation of being a manufacturer of high-quality, top-of-the-line stereo products before making the fatal mistake of deciding to fight it out in the crowded, popular-priced stereo market. A blurred image resulted, and poor profit and sales performance followed. Therefore, product differentiation, not price, is the key concept for insulating the company from the crowded, low-profit market segment. Izod has employed this strategy very successfully by promoting its LaCoste (alligator) shirts as prestigious items. This product is, of course, so standardized as to be easily duplicated, but its image is a much different proposition.

Place (Distribution) Policy

One major strategy that the US innovating firm can employ to protect itself against future competition is to build a strong dealer network. Because of its near-monopoly situation at the beginning, the firm is in a good position to select only the most qualified agents/distributors, and the distribution network should be expanded further as the product becomes more diffused. A strong dealer network will thus make it very difficult for new firms to enter the market. Japanese firms, for instance, were able to break into the US market to sell copy machines by distributing their products through office equipment dealers—a network that was ignored by Xerox.

Once the battle is lost, however, US firms—manufacturing and agents/distributors alike—may have no choice except to adopt a compatible policy. That is, such firms can survive by becoming agents for their former competitors. This tactic involves providing a distribution network and marketing expertise at a profit to competitors who in all likelihood would welcome an easier entry into the marketplace. One reason that it took such a very long time for Japanese automakers as well as manufacturers of audio and video products to capture a significant portion of the US market is because of the lack of a distribution network. American automakers and their dealers at this stage in the process seem to have accepted reality at last and have become partners with their Japanese competitors, as witnessed by General Motors' planned hookup with Toyota, American Motors with Renault, and Chrysler with Mitsubishi.

Conclusion

Competition is a fact of life, and any innovating firm will have to sooner or later face the competitive forces in the marketplace. At the present pace of product diffusion, it is likely to be sooner rather than later.

Japan, not known for innovative behavior, has acquired the reputation of an excellent imitator by refining and improving existing technologies developed by the United States and other advanced nations. Japan's efficiency in manufacturing and distributing enables it to compete on the basis of quantity, price, and distribution. A case in point is the penetration of Japanese printers into the US market. Such printers have no unique features, are reliable, and are produced in high volume on automated production lines.[10] It will not be long in the US before personal and business computers follow the same pattern.

Some scholars claim that Japan has gained superiority over the United States in several basic industries because of "strategic reversals" which have been unfairly gained in part due to protectionism. Japan imports a technology and then nurtures it through very restrictive import policies. Scale economies, experience, cost parity, and momentum, are gained before the technology is exported aggressively, which results in a furthering of Japan's international trade position.[11] Such reversals should not be surprising nor unexpected since they simply confirm the IPLC theory. Furthermore, the importance of such reversals should not be understated or underestimated. US firms should have anticipated the reversals and should have made proper adjustments in production location, advanced production versions, unique product features, specialized services, strong distribution networks, unique brand images and brand loyalty. Apple Computer once dominated the personal computer market in Japan because of the lack of competition, but it has failed to establish a strong distribution network. As a result, its products are perceived as expensive, fragile, and poorly serviced.[12] Apple Computer is now paying the price for ignoring competitive forces as its product moves through its life cycle.

US firms, as innovators, should have exploited their technological lead in order to stretch out the trade cycle and to discourage imitations. For several basic industries, however, it may be too late, and they should either abandon their product line or move into more narrowly defined market niches. US firms would also do well by holding on to carefully selected market segments in which they can distinguish themselves from foreign competitors. In other words, US firms should strive to be specialists, not generalists. There are early warning signals which alert firms can use to determine whether the time has come for them to adopt this strategy. One signal is provided when the product in question becomes so standardized that it can be manufactured in many LDCs. Another warning signal is a decline in US exports due to the loss or narrowing of the US technological lead. By that time, certain forms of market segmentation and product differentiation are highly recommended. Another major weapon for US firms would be to keep innovating to make any imitation strategy adopted by LDCs very risky because the imitated versions would become obsolete rapidly.

Since no country can maintain a monopoly on product knowledge or product production in the long run, it is critical for American marketers to understand the usual stages that an innovation will go through in the international product life cycle arena. Several industries, labor groups, and politicians are advocating the erection of more trade barriers in the name of job protection. This kind of myopic protectionism will result in more harm than good. The real solution depends more on US firms' willingness and ability to apply marketing theories, concepts, and techniques both at home and in international markets.

Notes _____

1. Harold J. Hoy and John J. Shaw, "The United States' Comparative Advantage and Its Relationship to the Product Life Cycle Theory and the World Gross National Product Market Share," *Columbia Journal of World Business* 16 (Spring 1981), pp. 40–50.

2. "The 'Left-Hand-Drive' Barrier to U.S. Sales," *Business Week* February 15, 1982, at p. 60; "Pillsbury Unlocks Japan by Doing As Japanese Do," *Chicago Tribune* February 11, 1982.

3. Raymond Vernon, "International Investment and International Trade in the Product Cycle," *Quarterly Journal of Economics* 80 (May 1966), pp. 190–207.

4. Vern Terpstra, *International Marketing,* 3rd ed. Chicago: Dryden, 1983, pp. 30–31; Warren J. Keegan, *Multinational Marketing Management,* 2nd ed. Englewood Cliffs, N.J.: Prentice-Hall, 1980, pp. 266–68.

5. Alok K. Chakrabarti, Stephen Feinman, and William Fuentivilla, "A Cross-National Comparison of Patterns of Industrial Innovations," *Columbia Journal of World Business* 17 (Fall 1982), 33–39.

6. Robert T. Green, "Changing National Concentration of High Technology Exports, 1974-1979," *Columbia Journal of World Business* 17 (Fall 1982), pp. 72–76.

7. Charles P. Kindleberger, *International Economics,* 5th ed., Homewood, Illinois: Richard D. Irwin, 1973, p. 65.

8. Louis T. Wells, Jr., "A Product Life Cycle For International Trade?" *Journal of Marketing* 32 (July 1968), pp. 1–6.

9. Nariman K. Dhalla and Sonia Yuspeh, "Forget the Product Life Cycle Concept!" *Harvard Business Review* 54 (January-February 1976), pp. 102–12.

10. "Japan's Swift Success in Printers," *Business Week* August 31, 1981, pp. 73–74.

11. William L. Givens, "The U.S. Can No Longer Afford Free Trade," *Business Week* November 22, 1982, p. 15.

12. "Apple Tries a Comeback in Japan," *Business Week* April 11, 1983, pp. 53, 55.

References

Beckman, Harold W., and Ivan R. Vernon, *Contemporary Perspectives In International Business,* Chicago, Illinois, Rand McNally, 1979.

Cateora, Philip R., and John M. Hess, *International Marketing,* 3rd ed., Homewood, Illinois, Richard D. Irwin, Inc., 1975.

International Economic Report of the President, 1976, and 1977, *World Population Data Sheet,* OCED, January, 1978.

Jain, Subhash C., and Lewis R. Tucker, Jr., *International Marketing: Managerial Perspectives,* Boston, Mass., CBI Publishing, Inc., 1979.

"Japan's Swift Success In Printers," *Business Week,* August 31, 1981, pp. 73–74.

Kahler, Ruel, and Roland L. Kramer, *International Marketing,* Cincinnati, Ohio, Southwestern Publishing Co., 1977.

Keesing, Donald B., and Phi Auh Plesch, "Recent Trends in Manufactured and Total Exports From Developing Countries," unpublished working paper, The World Bank, June, 1977.

Kindleberger, Charles P., and Peter H. Lindert, *International Economics,* 6th ed., Homewood, Illinois, Richard D. Irwin, Inc., 1978.

Robinson, Richard D., *International Business Management: A Guide to Decision Making,* 2nd ed., Hinsdale, Illinois, The Dryden Press, 1978.

Robock, Stefan H., Kenneth Simmonds, and Jack Zwick, *International Business and Multinational Enterprises,* Revised ed., Homewood, Illinois, Richard D. Irwin, Inc., 1977.

Root, Franklin R., *International Trade and Investment,* 4th ed., Cincinnati, Ohio, Southwestern Publishing Co., 1978.

Small Business Administration, *Export: Marketing For Smaller Firms,* 3rd ed., Washington, D.C., 1971.

Snider, Delbert A., *Introduction to International Economics,* 6th ed., Homewood, Illinois, Richard D. Irwin, Inc., 1975.

U.N. Yearbook of International Trade Statistics, 1977.

Van Zandt, Howard F. "Learning to Do Business with Japan, Inc.," *Harvard Business Review,* July-August, 1972, pp. 83–92.

Vernon, Raymond, and Louis T. Wells, Jr., *Manager in the International Economy,* 3rd ed., Englewood Cliffs, New Jersey, Prentice-Hall, Inc., 1976.

Wells, Louis T., Jr., "A Product Life Cycle For International Trade?" *Journal of Marketing,* Vol. 32, July 1968, pp. 1–6.

Wexler, Imanuel, *Fundamentals of International Economics,* 2nd ed., New York, Random House, 1972.

Wortzel, Lawrence H., and Heidi Vernon Wortzel, "Export Marketing Strategies for NIC and LDC-Based Firms," *Columbia Journal of World Business,* Vol. 16, No. 1, Spring, 1981, pp. 51–60.

Yoshino, Michael Y., *Japan's Multinational Enterprises,* Cambridge, Mass., Harvard University Press, 1976.

IV ____ SPECIAL TOPICS _____

Relevance of the Marketing Concept and Strategy to Public Enterprises
K. L. K. Rao and Ramesh G. Tagat

10. RELEVANCE OF THE MARKETING CONCEPT AND STRATEGY TO PUBLIC ENTERPRISES

K. L. K. RAO AND RAMESH G. TAGAT

Introduction

The relevance of the marketing concept to the operations of public enterprises still continues to be an elusive area in theory and practice. This is mostly due to certain traditional connotations given to the social objectives of public enterprises which are deemed to be contrary to the Western type of marketing mechanism based on the profit motive. Moreover, the accepted premise that the operations of public enterprises are conditioned more by ministerial directives than market forces has also inhibited clarity of approach in relating marketing to public enterprises. However, a review of the literature on the evolving nature and scope of marketing as well as the organisational dynamics of public enterprises reveals that these two concepts are converging towards points of relevance which are more or less verifiable in practice. This is true in every type of economy—centrally controlled, developing, or developed, as in the Western world, where public enterprises have been accepted as a form of government intervention either on ideological grounds or on the basis of strategic needs, or as an *ad-hoc* instrument to correct market imperfections.

The purpose of this paper is to suggest a tentative conceptual framework which indicates such points of relevance between marketing and public enterprises. The attempt is purely explorative, based on an identification of the changes which have emerged in the perceptions of the two concepts. These changes seem to be moving towards a common focus of objectives and strategies which act as binding links for marketing and public enterprises in a more meaningful and integrative way. A review of the recent literature on marketing as a "discipline" and an "activity" reveals two interesting trends.

Connotative Change

The concept of marketing is being increasingly considered as more comprehensive, to include all transactional activities which are not confined only to profit-seeking objectives. Ever since Kotler advocated the need for broadening the concept of marketing and subsequently enunciated his generic concept of marketing, there has been incessant debate on the nature and coverage of marketing. (See: Kotler and Levy, 1969, pp. 10–15; Kotler, 1972, pp. 46–54). A notable contribution to this discussion is that of Shelby Hunt, who in a more systematic way put across the

Reprinted from *Marketing Perspectives of Public Enterprises in Developing Countries* pp. 14–33, by permission of the International Center for Public Enterprises in Developing Countries.

"three dichotomies model." (See: Hunt, 1976, pp. 17–28; and 1978, pp. 107–110). This model is based on a classification scheme in terms of focus of analysis (positive and negative), level of aggregation (micro and macro) and objectives of organisations or other entities (profit and non-profit). Even though Hunt was able to defend his model against initial critics like Gumacio (1977, p. 8), Robin (1977, pp. 136–138; 1978, p. 6, p. 42), Ross (1977, p. 10, p. 146) and Etgar (1977, p. 4, p. 16, p. 146), some of the inadequacies of the classification scheme pointed out by Arndt (1982, pp. 27–35) continue to be unresolved.

The part of this evaluation which is relevant to our analysis is the dichotomy between profit and non-profit organisations which fails to make a distinction between private and public enterprises. To put it in the words of Arndt (Ibid., p. 34): "Another problem is that the profit/non-profit dichotomy appears to assume a capitalistic or mixed economy. In the socialist world, the profit sector cells would be empty by definition. In the third world, where business often is more a way of life than professional activity, the profit/non-profit categorisation may have less meaning. Hence, this dichotomy is by no means as universal as the positive normative and micro/macro distinctions. An intellectual construction aspiring to become a general paradigm cannot be culture-bound and provincial."

In fact, a great deal of doubt is being raised on the universal applicability of the Western concept of marketing. (See Dholakia, 1980). Most of these viewpoints generally stop at identifying the inadequacies of the concept rather than proposing any suitable alternative. While discarding the theory of convergence, they fail to perceive the impetus given to marketing activity in the centrally-controlled economies as well as the significant role played by the public enterprises in some of the developed Western market-oriented economies.

On the other hand, the convergence theory is highlighted by many marketing analysts who base their findings on empirical evidence. (See: Lauter, 1971, pp. 16–20; Walters and Hart, 1975, pp. 45–51; Samli and Jermankowicz, 1983, pp. 26–33). Samli and Jermankowicz identify the four stages of marketing evolution in East European countries and suggest that this evolution is in the direction of an integrative system of marketing. According to them, "if one looks at the reforms and customs that took place in Europe in general, and in Hungary, Poland and Yugoslavia in particular during the 1960s, it becomes clear that all countries of the region are moving in the direction of the integrative stage. It is also reasonable to observe that non-socialist countries, such as France, Japan and the United Kingdom are moving further away from the *laissez faire* stage in the direction of the integrative stage. As a result, the Eastern and Western macro-economic systems are moving in the direction of the integrative stage (Ibid., p. 32), posing serious challenges to researchers in the application of conventional concepts and models in marketing to either of the systems.

The convergence towards a similarity of marketing operations of the private and public enterprises in international business activities is brought out cogently by several researchers. (See: Mazzolini, 1979; Aharoni, 1980, pp. 14–22; Hafsi, 1982; Collins, 1984; Halfhill et al., 1978, pp. 9–12; Lamont, 1979; Rao and Tagat, 1982; Lauter and Dickie, 1975, pp. 40–46; Walter and Monsen, 1979). The contention is that the public enterprises which enter international business activities may in the earlier stages be directed by governmental policies, but that over a period of time the "distance" between the private and public enterprise operations gradually disappears. This occurs mostly due to the contextual compulsions of the international competitive environment necessitating a change towards a relatively more autonomous organisational structure of such public enterprises. Much of this phenomenon is explained by Mazzolini in terms of two conceptual perspectives: a rational perspective, in which corporate behaviour is explained via postulated goals; and an organisational process perspective, whereby behaviour is explained by the bureaucratic procedures governing corporate decisions.

Interdependence between alternative market structures and public enterprise behaviour has also been lucidly explained by Leroy Jones and Ingo Vogelsang. In their study (1983), based on the dual "markets and ministries" approach, they have set forth a comprehensive conceptual framework of analysis; they deal with the effects of public enterprises on markets in practice; and, finally, they identify the two sets of major general policy implications. The first of these is that appropriate control and incentive systems of public enterprises vary with the markets in which the enterprises operate. The second is that, to improve public enterprises' conduct and performance, explicit attention should be given to devices which improve market signals, given existing control systems. However, their approach considers only one aspect of marketing activity, viz., pricing. It deals only with the economic viewpoint of pricing mechanisms under different market structures in which the public enterprises operate.

Strategic Orientation

The second significant development in the marketing literature is the increasing importance being given to the strategic orientation of marketing activities. Ever since Levitt (1962) cautioned against the myopic view of marketing and highlighted the role of innovation in marketing, researchers have started to recognise the interlinkages of marketing activity with the business and corporate strategies. (See also Anderson, 1982, pp. 15–26). Due to increasing emphasis on strategic planning by corporations, marketing has been repositioned within the firm. This has broadened the scope of marketing so that, instead of being simply a functional area, marketing has gained a corporate orientation. Wiersema (1983, pp. 46–56) defines strategic marketing as having the dual task of providing a market-place perspective to the process of determining corporate direction and guidelines for the development and execution of marketing programmes that assist in attaining corporate objectives. The definition implies that a market-place perspective is an important, but not the only, ingredient in setting a firm's objectives; and further, that objectives place certain constraints on the firm's market-place activities. According to Jain (1981), marketing strategy consists of establishing a match between the firm and its environment in order to seek solutions to the problems of deciding: (a) what business the firm is in and what kinds of business it may enter in the future; and (b) how the chosen field(s) of endeavour may be successfully run in a competitive environment by pursuing products, price, promotion, and distribution perspectives which serve target markets. The marketing strategy has been viewed as the core element for future relationships between the firm and its environment.

Considerable literature has come out on the strategic marketing aspects of private corporations in the Western countries. However, its relevance to public enterprises is still in an exploratory stage of research analysis. Capon (1981, pp. 11–18) has attempted such an exploratory analysis to identify the marketing strategy differences between state and privately-owned corporations. He develops a series of propositions, the major one being that, "only for business portfolio decisions, and matters of government fiat, are state and privately-owned enterprises unambiguously different, solely based on ownership, without consideration of market conditions" (p. 17). Capon's analysis is based on the experiences of public enterprises in the developed Western economies and does not take into account the developing countries in which public enterprises play a more dominant and strategic role. Hence, it is debatable whether his hypothesis in its entirety will hold good for the public enterprises in the developing world.

The foregoing review of marketing as a discipline and activity reveals that even though there has been substantial rethinking on the need for modifying the traditional concept of marketing to suit the dynamics of a changing environment, the relevance of marketing to public enterprises still remains a hazy description with a number of loose ends. The proposed analysis tries to tie up these loose ends and to provide an integrated viewpoint which highlights the relevance of marketing to public sector operations, conceptually and strategically. Section 1 deals with the relevance of strategic marketing to public enterprises.

1. Conceptual Viewpoints

In this paper a "growth-cycle" model of public enterprises is proposed as a basis for analysing points of relevance between marketing and public enterprises. Its implications on policy differentiation, organisational evolution and marketing orientation with an interlinked goal analysis at the macro and micro levels are explored.

The term "public enterprise" is considered in its conceptual definition as having a combination of two dimensions, a "public" dimension and an "enterprise" dimension. (See: Fernandes and Sicherl, 1981). The public dimension includes the elements of public purpose, public ownership and public control in terms of management and accountability. The enterprise dimension includes the field of activity of a business character, investment and returns and marketing of outputs.

The "growth-cycle" model is built on the hypothesis that any public enterprise of the above description generally goes through three phases in its growth pattern over a period of time. These three phases are sequential and represent a combination of a decelerating intensity of the public dimension and an accelerating intensity of the enterprise dimension (see Diagram 1). The three phases are classified as "sheltered", "supportive" and "self-propelling". In exceptional cases, the origin of the curve could be positive anywhere on the Y axis. The intensity of the social and enterprise dimensions influence the shape of the curve.

The sheltered stage is the initial phase, in which the genesis of a public enterprise is mainly conditioned by the nature of public purpose and social goals. The range of

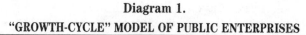

Diagram 1.
"GROWTH-CYCLE" MODEL OF PUBLIC ENTERPRISES

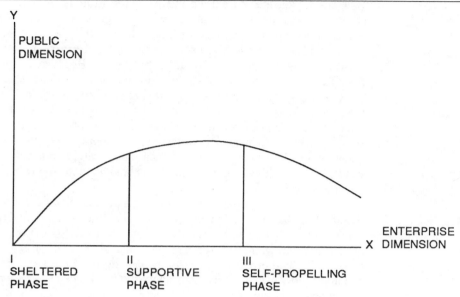

this may extend from long-term socio-economic objectives to short-term achieve-
ment of distributive justice in an imperfect market structure. This is conditioned
mainly by the reasons for and extent of governmental intervention. It can be ideological and hence structural; it can be strategic and sectoral; and it can be adaptive
at the unit level. The distinctive feature of the sheltered phase is that the public
enterprise's immediate concern would be to fulfill the possible range of social goals
expected of it in the initial stages, such as creation of employment opportunities,
setting-up of production capabilities or provision of infrastructural facilities, etc.
Insofar as the public enterprise is successful in achieving all this, its performance is
judged not by purely economic or commercial criteria but by its social effectiveness.
Hence, any shortcoming in the economic performance is always sheltered by direct
or indirect governmental subventions. "The case for the payment of subventions or
direct subsidies rests mainly on the argument that welfare expenditure should be
legitimately borne or shared by the concerned government agencies. Another angle
from which this question can be viewed is that provided by an examination of the
implications of the inter-relationship between the national interest (i.e., macro-goals)
and that of the public enterprise (i.e., micro-goals, whether at the sector or individual
unit level). This generally reveals that the macro-policy decisions must be implemented promptly by the public enterprises concerned, even at the cost of interim
inefficiencies in respect to secondary goals and the operations of the individual
enterprises themselves (Bokhari, 1982, p. 2).

The sheltered phase is generally characterised by the following broad features:

- at the policy level, the national goals and the corporate goals are intermixed, the former playing a dominant role;
- at the organisational level, the public enterprise is rigidly accountable to the concerned ministry for all its policy guidelines and sometimes for its operational details also;
- at the performance level, the criteria for evaluation are terms of fulfilment of macro-objectives rather than micro ones.

The sheltered phase is more or less inevitable for every type of public enterprise. However, the span of this phase depends on the nature of the public purpose for which the individual public enterprise is established, in terms of its exclusiveness and the consequent scope and coverage of the activities of such an enterprise. For instance, for a public enterprise which has the sole purpose of creating mass awareness about socio-economic change in the areas of family planning, sanitation, medical care, etc., the span of the sheltered phase may be longer than for those public enterprises which are created to contribute to the industrial and economic growth of the country over a period of time.

The movement into the "supportive" phase for a public enterprise is conditioned by certain realities of the situation which occur under the sheltered phase. One of the major factors is the tendency of public enterprises to become complacent and, ultimately, inefficient. In such a situation, an exercise is needed to identify the resultant micro-inefficiencies and take steps to reduce or eliminate them. One of the methods resorted to by governments is to motivate the public enterprises to generate a financial surplus through their operations and thereby rely less and less on direct subventions. The purpose of such surplus generation could be to contribute to the mobilisation of resources required by the national plans (as in India), or to serve purely as a success indicator of efficiency (as in the Soviet Union). It is in this sense that the sheltered phase is designated as "supportive".

The policy guidelines for making the public enterprises financially productive through surplus generation would instil the element of "efficiency" as an evaluation criterion. Efficiency can be defined as the ability to carry out activities proficiently by building on strengths and overcoming weaknesses in public enterprise operations. This is achieved through a process of "integration", by narrowing down options and building on the present thrust of the firm's activities. Because of this, during this phase, the public enterprise becomes aware of its separate entity, and the pressure put on it to generate surpluses instils a spirit of competition either amongst the public enterprises themselves or with the private sector units in similar lines of activities.

During the integration process, the public enterprise would become not only cost efficient but also market oriented. Market-imposed pressures on public enterprise efficiency depend on the prevailing market structure in which the concerned public enterprises operate. Even in the extreme case of a monopoly situation, as in the Eastern Bloc, the market-imposed pressures in terms of consumer non-acceptance of the product has led to the adoption of marketing techniques by the individual public enterprises, particularly in the areas of product management and sales promotion methods, including advertising. Marketing orientation during the "integrative" process in the East European countries is characterised by the following features (Samli and Jermankowicz, 1983, p. 29):

- the focal point in the economy is the enterprise;
- competition among the enterprises;
- government influences the behaviour of enterprises indirectly only by the use of economic parameters;
- free market mechanism for all goods and services;
- high autonomy for enterprises to improve their marketing efforts;
- high product differentiation and market segmentation;
- ability to fluctuate prices;
- increased discretionary income and luxury items.

Similar changes are expected to occur in public enterprise operations in the mixed economies of developing countries. Hence, the first point of relevance of marketing to public enterprises is felt at the point of "inflection" from the sheltered phase to the supportive one.

In terms of marketing approaches, the movement is from the "production" concept to the "product" concept and culminates in the "marketing" concept through the "selling" concept. The extent of movement on this vector by the individual public enterprise depends on a host of organisational and managerial factors which are peculiar to its nature and scope of activities.

Movement from the "supportive" to the "self-propelling" phase is an extension of the marketing orientation of the public enterprise, as it comes closer to the environmental dynamics. As efficiency lends internal strength and confidence to the individual enterprise, it strives to become more "effective" in terms of seeking new opportunities in the environment for its growth and stability. Effectiveness is defined as the ability of the public enterprises to relate to their environment by developing opportunities and warding off threats. Just as they become integrative in the "supportive" phases they become adaptive in the "self-propelling" phase. The corporate policy gets its distinct enunciation from the national goals. The corporate image becomes crystallised. Strategic planning of activities of the public enterprises comes into vogue. Organisationally, marketing activities become well delineated laterally and become interwoven vertically with the corporate strategy. The result is the adoption of the elements of strategic marketing postures by the individual enterprises. The marketing orientation looks beyond the traditional concept of a product/market matrix. The public enterprise seeks strategic options which would enable it to become a multi-technology, multi-product and multi-market firm through diversification methods. The point of "inflection" between the supportive and self-propelling phases determines the gradual convergence point of the modern strategic marketing concept and the public enterprise.

The above analysis may sound normative, but the positive aspects are verifiable through case studies. The "growth-cycle" model does not imply that every public enterprise should experience it sequentially. It is possible that there can be one type

Diagram 2

SET OF TRAVERSES

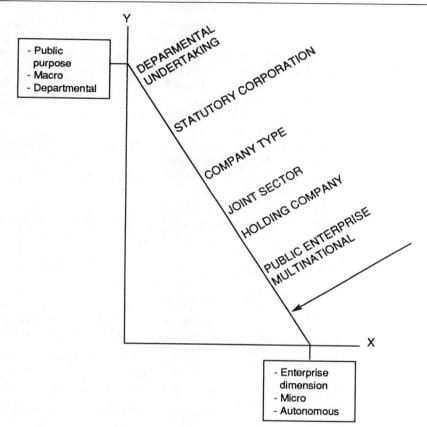

which originates in the first phase and remains in it throughout or whithers off due to cumulative inefficiency; some may only reach the second phase; and some may continue to the end. There is a great potential for research investigation to verify these processes through case studies of public enterprises in the developing countries.

The "growth-cycle" has certain implications on the policy differentiation, organisational evolution and level of performance evaluation (see Diagram 2). It is shown as a traverse downwards from the Y to the X axis; the Y axis indicating the public dimension and the X axis indicating the enterprise dimension. The extremity on the Y axis indicates the starting point of the sheltered phase and the extremity on the X axis indicates the self-propelling phase. In between, there is the supportive phase.

The three sets of traverses are as follows:

- policy-wise, as the public enterprise moves from Y to X, the corporate policy gradually becomes distinct from the national policy;
- organisational-wise, the public enterprise becomes more and more autonomous in structure and operations as it moves towards the X axis. The hypothesis

suggested by some researchers on the phase-wise government-enterprise relationship in terms of cooperative, adversarial and autonomy stages can be aligned with the three phases of the "growth-cycle" model sequentially. (See: Hafsi, 1982; Murthy in Hafsi.) In fact, the pressure of efficiency and effectiveness in the supportive and self-propelling stages leads to adversarial and autonomy types of relationships. The extreme example is the case where the public enterprise becomes global in its operations. The evolution of the organisational structure from the departmental type to the company and corporation type can be traced on this traverse. The holding company is a case in point. Movement on the traverse again can be partial or complete or there can be no movement at all.[1]

■ the performance evaluation increasingly moves towards the micro-level (X axis) from the macro-level (Y axis). Financial performance becomes the ultimate criterion in the self-propelling phase, given the broad social goals.

All three traverses, along with the phases in the growth-cycle, are points of convergence between the modern marketing concept and public enterprise operations.

2. Strategic Marketing Aspects

2.1. Policy-Activity Orientation

The relevance of strategic marketing to public enterprises can be highlighted by redesignating these three phases in terms of "policy-activity" orientation, as follows:

Phase I: Sheltered   → Directive or Imperative
Phase II: Supportive   → Integrative
Phase III: Self-propelling   → Adaptive

The sheltered phase is a "directive" or "imperative" stage because the ministerial pressures to achieve the public purpose will be greater than the market pressures to better economic performance. The supportive phase is effected through either ministerial or market pressure on public enterprises to become efficient. The need for efficiency results in an introspective analysis by the individual public enterprise to assess its internal strengths and weaknesses. Hence, this is the integrative phase. The self-propelling phase arises when a strong public enterprise forges ahead to become stronger by exploiting the opportunities available in the changing environment. It starts adapting its activities to the environmental dynamics and hence this phase is "adaptive".

In this analysis, the relevance of strategic marketing to public enterprises is treated at a general level. The details of each strategy depend on the nature of the normative and legal variables as well as the real variables. However, the analysis is built up on a series of propositions emerging out of the "*ex post* environment → public enterprise intervention → *ex ante* environment" interlinkages, as shown in Diagram 3.

The propositions are sequentially aligned to the phases of the life-cycle concept (see Table 1).

Diagram 3

STRATEGIC MARKETING — SEQUENTIAL FLOW-CHART

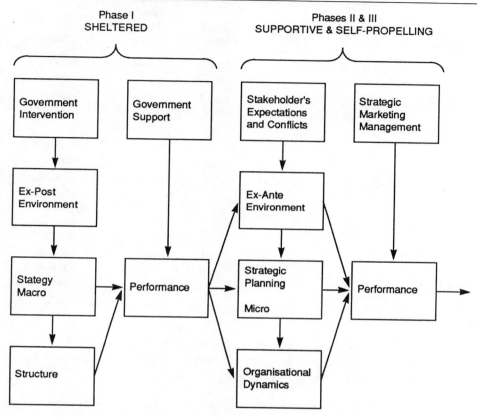

2.1.1 Phase I

Proposition 1: Objective of Governmental Interaction: Ex-post Environment

The nature and scope of governmental intervention depends on the environmental forces prevalent at the given time. Governmental intervention can occur:

- due to ideological necessities;
- as a strategic instrument for economic growth; and
- as a means to correct market imperfections.

Accordingly, the scope of the intervention would be

- structural for ideological;
- sectoral for strategic; and
- unit level for market imperfections.

Table 1
FEATURES OF THE PHASES

Phase	Strategy Posture	Dominant Objective	Level of Analysis	Business/ Government Relation	Mode of Financing	Performance Criteria
I: Sheltered	Directive/ Imperative	National	Macro	Cooperative	Direct Subventions	Public Purpose
II.: Supportive	Integrative	Economic	Micro	Adversarial	Indirect Subventions & Internal Surplus	Efficiency
III: Self-propelling	Adaptive	Commercial	Micro	Autonomous	Institutional Financing/ Capital Market/ Public Deposits/ Internal Cash Generation	Effectiveness

Proposition 2: Strategy Mode: Macro

The nature and scope of intervention determines the nature and type of strategy initially adopted in terms of:

- nature of objectives (regulatory, developmental, promotional);
- weightages of "public" and "enterprise" dimensions;
- area of activities (domestic and foreign);
- nature of strategy (reactive and proactive);
- duration of plan (long-term, medium-term and short-term);
- role of technology, market forces and competitive advantage.

Proposition 3: Initial Organisational Set-up

Adopted strategy indicates the type of initial organisational structure based on:

- legal status (departmental undertakings, statutory corporations, registered companies, joint sector and multi-nationals);
- role and extent of ministerial and market pressures;
- degree of centralisation and decentralisation.

Proposition 4: Evaluation Criteria—Phase I

The nature of governmental intervention, the type of strategy and the organisational structure determine the evaluation criteria of performance of the public enterprise in terms of:

- policy differentiation (national goals and corporate goals);
- success indicator (public purpose, economic contribution and profit management);
- relative strength of the stakeholders (government, customers, employees, suppliers, competitors, social groups and general public).

Positive or negative performance is conditioned by how far the intervention mode, strategy option and structural choices have been matched or mismatched. When they are mismatched, the public enterprise becomes inefficient and inactive.

2.1.2. **Phases II and III**

Proposition 5: Stakeholders' Expectations and Pressures

Both positive and negative performance will have an influence on the emerging environment, which will be largely conditioned by the conflicting aspirations of the stakeholders. A well-matched public enterprise would anticipate conflicts and manipulate to resolve them. This is mainly dependent on the leadership of the Chief Executive Officer and the calibre of top management. At this stage, the successful public enterprise arrives at the threshold of feeling itself a separate corporate entity. The mismatched enterprise becomes a drag, needing governmental support and directives, financially and otherwise.

Proposition 6: Configurations of the *ex-ante* Environment

The emerging environment sets up new aspiration levels and expectations of achievements from the public enterprise. This could be in terms of changed perceptions of the stakeholders as to the role of the public enterprise as a leader to effect changes in:

- market dynamics;
- technological breakthrough;
- international operations.

Proposition 7: Strategic Planning Modes—Micro

The configurations of the emerging environment create the need for clear-cut strategic planning in terms of:

- integrative,
- adaptive and
- international strategy.

The strategic option at this level depends on the competitive strategic position of the public enterprise in the emerging environment. This position could be dominant, strong, favourable, tenable, weak or non-viable. Definitions of these positions are given in Table 2.

Proposition 8: Organisational Dynamics

The nature of the strategic position conditions the change in the organisational structure in terms of its becoming:

- autonomous at the policy level,
- decentralised at the operational level, and
- effective at the control and performance level.

Table 2

CLASSIFICATION OF COMPETITIVE STRATEGIC POSITIONS

1.	Dominant	Controls behaviour of other competitors (performance and/or strategy). Has a wide choice of strategic options (widest choice of options both natural and selected).
2.	Strong	Able to maintain long-term position regardless of competitors' long-term position. Able to maintain long-term position regardless of competitors' actions.
3.	Favourable	Has a strength which is exploitable in particular strategies. Has a more than average opportunity to improve position.
4.	Tenable	Sufficiently satisfactory performance to warrant continuation in business. Has a less than average opportunity to improve position.
5.	Weak	Currently unsatisfactory performance but opportunity exists for improvement. May have most of the characteristics of better position but obvious shortcomings. Inherently short-term condition; must change.
6.	Non-Viable	Currently unsatisfactory performance without opportunity for improvement.

This is the stage where strategic marketing aspects take definite shape in terms of vertical linkages with the corporate policy conditioned by national goals, as well as becoming coordinated laterally with other departments within the organisational structure of the public enterprise.

Proposition 9: Performance Criteria for Phases II and III

Strategic planning necessitates a change in the outlook of the management of public enterprises from conventional to modern concepts of:

- the planning mode in terms of environmental scanning and analysis, which identifies opportunities for breakthrough rather than mere extension of past secular growth;
- the marketing activity focus, from traditional market-mix combinations for product/market options to strategic marketing activities of product portfolio management;
- the conventional two-dimensional product/market strategy, which is gradually replaced by the four-dimensional concept of government, enterprise, customer (stakeholder) and technology; and
- the performance criteria, which gradually changes from social benefits to more financial indicators such as surplus generation and management of profit centers.

These propositions are set out as hypotheses verifiable through case studies of public enterprises in different socio-economic situations. It is highly possible that the chain may have a weak link somewhere or may get disconnected. Such occurrences would indicate a great potential for research investigation to identify the reasons for them from the point of view of strategic management.

The process of strategic marketing can be initiated at any level in the diagram, at the time of initial intervention or at the time of adjustment to the emerging environment. It mainly depends on the intensity of market forces, the extent of technology management and the expectations of the stakeholders. In order to highlight the aspects of the strategic marketing process, a comparison of the perspectives of traditional and strategic connotations of marketing in major planning dimensions is given in Table 3. How far this needs to be related to the operations of public enterprises is an issue worthy of further discussion.

2.2. Portfolio Applications

Using the "life-cycle" model one can also study the implications of the application of portfolio analysis to the financial and profit management of public enterprises at the micro and macro levels. The Boston Consultancy Group related a simple framework of market share and market growth on high-low vectors and identified the product portfolio of an enterprise to fall in the matrix of either potential earners (stars), potential losers (dogs), possible candidates for received (question marks) and current fund formators (cash cows). However, the concept of product portfolio differs from its general connotation when applied to public enterprises. The differences are the following:

- in the Boston Consulting Group (BCG) concept (1972), the analysis is in terms of growth-share matrix, whereas in our analysis it is the "public purpose—enterprise" combination. It is possible that, by virtue of the type of government intervention, the consequent nature of market configurations may not be meaningful in terms of the BCG concept alone. This is so because, in certain cases the public enterprise may act as the initial catalyst to create market situations irrespective of the profit returns. This is the case under the "sheltered" phase. As the public enterprise moves from this phase to the "self-supporting" phase, passing through the "supportive" via the media phase, the BCG concept gains more relevance, as the marketing environment begins to exhibit growth-share trends by that time;
- the BCG concept is purely commercial, based on the profit motive, whereas public enterprise operations are conditioned by social imperatives. It should be noted that social objectives continue to govern the operations of public enterprises even in the "self-supporting" phase. The only difference is in the intensity and scope of the social objectives. Hence, the product portfolio concept when applied to the operations of public enterprises should take into consideration this aspect and the consequent need for a trade-off between social and commercial objectives;
- in terms of cash generation, the public enterprises also have governmental subventions which would help their financially adverse positions. Hence, it is usually contended that most of the interventions and operations of public enterprises would be only in the "dog" quadrant. This may be so initially. But

Table 3
A COMPARISON OF TWO PERSPECTIVES ON MAJOR
PLANNING DIMENSIONS

	Conventional Marketing Management Perspective	Strategic Planning Perspective
Integration Dimension	Individual product-markets as unit of analysis	Strategic business units as unit of analysis
	Optimising product-market performance	Optimising business/corporate performance
	Synergies in marketing mix	Synergies at functional/divisional level
	Competitive advantages based on meeting customer needs	Competitive advantages based on functional capabilities
	Demand orientation	Supply orientation
Adaptation Dimension	Annual planning focus	Long-term planning focus
	Environmental changes are assumed to be steady, predictable	Environmental changes may be turbulent, unpredictable
	Flexibility through marketing mix adjustments	Flexibility through strategic redirections and major changes
	Few constraints perceived on capabilities	Difficult to change
	Product-market definition pretty much a given	Product-market and business definition is a strategic decision
Performance	Market performance focus market share, sales	Comprehensive market and financial performance focus
	Functional plans are driven by sales forecasts	Functional plans require integrated planning
	Cost of goods is (semi) fixed	Cost dynamics, shared activities result in varying cost level
	Assessment of sales potential of marketplace	Assessment of profit potential of marketplace

Source: Wiersema, 1983.

even the public enterprises which intervene to set right the market imperfections or failures have to grow normatively over a period of time. If this is not so, the application of product portfolio loses its meaning. Hence, the concept of the "growth-cycle" is necessary for the application of product-portfolio analysis to public enterprises. The contention is that the public enterprises can even revive the "dogs" given the correct direction and leadership.

Diagram 4

"GROWTH-CYCLE" MODEL OF PUBLIC ENTERPRISES AND PRODUCT
PORTFOLIO ANALYSIS — MICRO AND MACRO

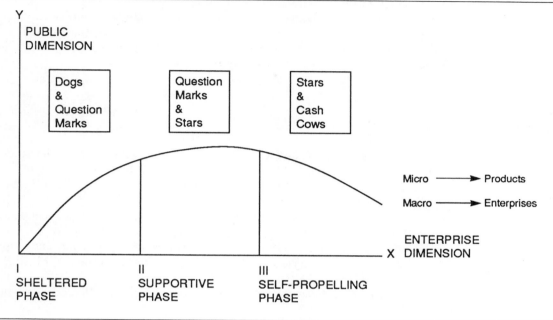

Source: Boston Consulting Group, 1972.

The super-imposition of product-portfolio concepts to the "life-cycle" model is shown in Diagram 4.

It could be deduced that, at the micro level, the individual public enterprises may have clusters of products falling in the sheltered phase which could be "dogs" as well as "question marks"; in the supportive phase, "question marks" and "stars"; and in the self-propelling phase, "cash cows" and "stars". The strategic planning at the unit level has to consider these elements for working out an overall financial management in terms of trade-offs between "public" and "enterprise" dimensions in the product/service offers.

At the macro level, the analysis is in terms of individual public enterprise clustering at the three phases of the life-cycle. Some may be at the "sheltered" phase, needing high cash support from the government; some at the "supportive" phase, needing medium cash support from the government; and some at the "self-propelling" phase, needing less cash support from the government.

3. Conclusion _____

To sum up, the marketing concept need no longer be considered anathema to public enterprise operations. On the contrary, it acts as the dominant instrument to broaden the vision of the public enterprises without surrendering national perspectives. Strategic marketing is the ultimate point of convergence for both public and private enterprises, irrespective of their initial objective variances, organisational differences and end differentials.

Even the new tools and techniques of analysis of strategic performance criteria such as product portfolio can be meaningfully applied once they are modified to accommodate the decelerating intensity of public purpose as the public enterprise enters the "supportive" and "self-propelling" phases.

References

Aharoni, Y., 1980, "The State-Owned Enterprise as a Competitor in International Markets", in: *Columbia Journal of World Business,* New York, Spring

Anderson, Paul F., 1982, "Marketing-Strategic Planning and the Theory of the Firm", in: *Journal of Marketing,* Vol. 46, Spring

Arndt, Johan, 1982, "The Conceptual Domain of Marketing: Evaluation of Shelby Hunt's Three Dichotomies Model", in: *European Journal of Marketing,* Vol. 16, No. 1

Bokhari, Riyaz H., 1982, *Subvention Policy and Practices for Public Enterprises,* International Center for Public Enterprises in Developing Countries, ICPE Monograph Series No. 4, Ljubljana

Boston Consulting Group, 1972, *Perspectives on Experience,* Boston Consulting Group, Boston

Capon, Noel, 1981, "Marketing Strategy Differences between State and Privately Owned Corporations: An Exploratory Analysis", in: *Journal of Marketing,* Vol. 45, Spring

Collins, Paul, 1984, "Strategic and Operational Management Guidelines for SOEs in the International Market Place". Paper submitted to the Second International Seminar on Global Reach of Public Enterprises held at Bangalore; manuscript

Dholakia, Nikhilesh, F. A. Firat and R. P. Bagozzi, 1980, *The De-Americanization of Marketing Thought: In Search of a Universal Basis,* Kansas State University, April

Etgar, M., 1977, "Comment on the Nature and Scope of Marketing", in: *Journal of Marketing,* Vol. 41, October

Fernandes, Praxy J. and Pavle Sicherl, 1981, *Seeking the Personality of Public Enterprise,* International Center for Public Enterprises in Developing Countries, Ljubljana

Gumacio, F. R., 1977, "Comment on the Nature and Scope of Marketing", in: *Journal of Marketing,* Vol. 41, January

Hafsi, Taieb, 1982, "Understanding the International Behaviour of State-Owned Enterprises". Paper submitted to the First International Seminar on Global Reach of Public Enterprises held at the University of Illinois, Urbana, Champaign; manuscript.

Halfhill, D. S., *et al.,* 1978, "Will the USSR Go Multinational?: Some Aspects of Corporate Evolution", in: Management International Review, Vol. 18, No. 1, Wiesbaden

Hunt, Shelby D., 1976, "The Nature and Scope of Marketing", in: *Journal of Marketing*, Vol. 40, January

Hunt, Shelby D., 1978, "A General Paradigm of Marketing", in: *Journal of Marketing*, Vol. 42, April

Iyer, Ramaswamy, R., 1985, "Sectoral Corporations: Some Organisational Experiments in the Public Sector in India", in: *Public Enterprise*, Vol. 5, No. 2, Ljubljana

Jain, S. C., 1981, *Marketing Planning and Strategy*, South Western Publishing Co., Cincinnati, Ohio

Jones, Leroy, P. and Ingo Vogelsang, 1983, *The Effects of Markets on Public Enterprise Conduct; and Vice-Versa*, International Center for Public Enterprises in Developing Countries, ICPE Monograph Series No. 7, Ljubljana

Kotler, Philip and Sidney J. Levy, 1969, "Broadening the Concept of Marketing", in: *Journal of Marketing*, Vol. 33, January

Kotler, Philip, 1972, "A Generic Concept of Marketing", in: *Journal of Marketing*, Vol. 36, April

Lamont, Douglas F., 1979, *Foreign State Enterprises, A Threat to American Business*, Basic Books Inc. Publishers, New York

Lauter, Peter G., 1971, "The Changing Role of Marketing in the Eastern Europe Socialist Economies", in: *Journal of Marketing*, Vol. 35, October

Lauter, Peter G., and Paul M. Dickie, 1975, "Multinational Corporations in East European Socialist Economies", in: *Journal of Marketing*, Vol. 35, October

Levitt, Theodor, 1962, *Innovation in Marketing*, McGraw-Hill Book Company, New York

Mazzolini, R., 1979, *Government Controlled Enterprises*, Wiley and Sons, New York

Rao, K. L. K. and Ramesh G. Tagat, 1982, "Global Reach of Public Enterprises: A Conceptual Framework". Paper submitted to the First International Seminar on Global Reach of Public Enterprises, University of Illinois, Urbana, Champaign; manuscript

Robin, D. P., 1977, "Comment on the Nature and Scope of Marketing", in: *Journal of Marketing*, Vol. 41, January

Robin, D. P., 1978, "Comment on the Nature and Scope of Marketing", in: *Journal of Marketing*, Vol. 42, July

Ross, W. H., 1977, "Comment on the Nature and Scope of Marketing", in: *Journal of Marketing*, Vol. 41, April

Samli, Coskun A. and Wladyslaw Jermankowicz, 1983, "The Stages of Marketing Evolution in East European Countries", in: *European Journal of Marketing*, Vol. 17, No. 2

Walter, K. D. and R. J. Monsen, 1979, "State-Owned Business Abroad: New Competitive Threat", in: *Harvard Business Review*, March–April

Walters Jr. and J. Hart, 1975, "Marketing in Poland in the 1970s: Significant Progress", *Journal of Marketing*, Vol. 39, October

Wiersema, Frederik D., 1983, "Strategic Marketing: Linking Marketing and Corporate Planning", in: *European Journal of Marketing*, Volume 17, No. 6

Notes _____

1. See: Iyer, 1985, pp. 139–153. The author gives an account of some organisational and structural patterns which have been tried out in relation to major public enterprises in certain important sectors of the economy. He presents the logic of the decisions arrived at as seen by those concerned in the decision making and seeks to formulate the issues involved.

ANNOTATED BIBLIOGRAPHY

ANNOTATED BIBLIOGRAPHY

NOTE: The annotated bibliography in this section has been organized into seven major sections to allow a more focused literature search.

I. The Nature and Scope of Multinational Marketing _____

Boddewyn, Jean. "Comparative Marketing: The First Twenty Five Years." *Journal of International Business Studies* (Spring/Summer 1981): 61–79.

This article reviews the field of comparative marketing in terms of scope, types, and depth of studies; methodological issues, conceptual and managerial payoffs, and teaching approaches. After its first quarter of a century as an international business topic, comparative marketing is still relatively green.

Brasch, John T. "Assessing Market Potential for Exports." *Journal of Small Business Management* (April 1979): 13–19.

In this article, Martin Bell's modification of Wroe Alexander's model of market potential shows sales as a function of effort, opportunity, and market resistance. The author discusses the determination of export market potential in terms of the model, and distinguishes it from national market potential. The article concludes with a brief discussion of who actually determines the market potential in typical firms.

Buzzel, Robert D. "Can You Standardize Multinational Marketing." *Harvard Business Review,* 46 (November–December 1968): 102–113.

This article focuses on pros and cons of a standardized vs. a unique approach to multinational marketing. The major thesis advanced by the author is that although there are many obstacles to the application of common marketing policies in different countries, there are also some very tangible potential benefits.

Calvet, A. L. "A Synthesis of Foreign Direct Investment Theories and Theories of Elite Multinational Firms." *Journal of International Business Studies* (Spring/Summer 1981): 43–59.

This paper first presents a taxonomy of foreign direct investment theories following the market imperfections paradigm. It thus focuses on recent developments pertaining to the theory of the multinational firm, specifically the appropriability, internalization, and diversification theories. Subsequently, the multinational phenomenon is seen as the result of an international differentiation of activities and an introfirm integration across national borders—all this within a markets and hierarchies approach. Finally, the paper points to areas for future research.

Cavusgil, S. Tamer. "On the Internationalizations Process of Firms." *European Research,* 8 (November 1980): 273–281.

> *The author develops a conceptual framework of involvement in international marketing activities. A number of stages are identified: domestic marketing, pre-export stage, experimental involvement, active involvement, and committed involvement. The author also discusses those internal and external factors that determine a firm's evolutionary involvement in international marketing.*

Ford, David. "Buyer/Seller Relationships in International Industrial Markets." *Industrial Marketing Management,* 13 (May 1984): 101–112.

> *This article examines the hypothesis that industrial purchasers' assessments of their suppliers are not based on views of suppliers' technical and commercial skills in isolation. Instead they are closely associated with their assessment of suppliers' skills in developing a relationship with them.*

Giddy, Ian H. "The Demise of the Product-Cycle in International Business Theory." *The Columbia Journal of World Business* (Spring 1978): 90–97.

> *This article focuses on the international product life-cycle (IPLC) theory of international business. The author concludes that IPLC, in its original form, is not consistent with much of international trade investment. New approaches discussed in the paper are based on the concept of barriers to entry in international product and factor markets, in which product life cycle is only a subset of a much larger set of barriers to entry.*

Jaffe, E. D. "Are Domestic and International Marketing Dissimilar?" *Management International Review,* 3 (1980): 83–86.

> *This article deals with the subject of comparative marketing. Comparative marketing is defined as the systematic identification and explanation of similarities and differences between two or more marketing systems, with the objective of formulating generalizations, hypotheses, and laws. The author uses a conceptual model developed by Robert Bartels to establish the relationship between the environmental elements and the elements of the marketing system, namely institutions, processes, practices, and structures, and proposes an extension of the model.*

_____."Multinational Marketing Intelligence: An Information Requirements Model." *Management International Review,* no. 2 (1979): 53–60.

> *The purpose of this paper is to present a conceptual framework for determining information needs of a multinational marketing intelligence system. The author first differentiates between marketing research and intelligence. Then an information model is developed with a table showing information needs and sources used by multinational managers. As a result of the applications of the model in the U.S. and Israel, several benefits of the model are brought to light.*

March, R. M. "Some Constraints on Adaptive Marketing by Foreign Consumer Goods Firms in Japan." *European Journal of Marketing* (1977): 491–498.

This article focuses on ways in which firms might adapt their marketing strategies to the Japanese environment.

Meleka, Agia H. "The Changing Role of Multinational Corporations." *Management International Review,* 25 (1985): pp. 36–45.

This article suggests strategies to assist the survival and growth of multinationals, while offsetting some of the threats of international turbulence. These strategies are to "institutionalize" themselves, and to be able to reciprocate to the host government's needs.

Mentzer, John T., and A. Coskun Samili. "A Model for Marketing in Economic Development." *Columbia Journal of World Business* (Fall 1981): 91–101.

The objectives of this article are to (1) explore the role of marketing in economic development, (2) present a model showing the application of marketing technology transfer to economic development goals, (3) develop a procedure for determining stages of economic development and identifying certain kinds of marketing technology transfer, and (4) to discuss practical applications regarding model implementation. The model shows how marketing and production are interdependent and successful growth of a LDC depends not only on increased production, but on improved methods of marketing and distribution.

Walters, Peter G. P. "International Marketing Policy: A Discussion of the Standardization Construct and Its Relevance for Corporate Policy." *Journal of International Business Policy,* 17 (Summer 1986): 55–69.

This paper presents an overview and evaluation of the standardization of marketing programs and procedures debate. The standardization construct is discussed and the evidence regarding corporate implementation of standardization strategies is evaluated.

Wind, Yorum, and Howard Perlmutter. "On the Identification of Frontier Issues in Multinational Marketing." *Columbia Journal of World Business,* 12 (Winter 1977): 131–139.

This paper provides a framework for the identification of gaps in current understanding of multinational marketing. The authors believe multinational marketing has been treated as a "step-child" of the marketing profession because of the difficulty involved in conducting multinational marketing research. The proposed framework centers around the multinational marketing decision-makers and is intended to be used as an aid in identifying frontier issues in multinational marketing.

II. The Environment of Multinational Marketing ——————

Alden, Vernon R. "Who Says You Can't Crack Japanese Markets?" *Harvard Business Review,* 65 (January–February 1987): 52–56.

Some American firms have found out that they can earn market share in Japan by overcoming regulatory and cultural barriers, being prepared, setting long-term goals, and operating in the same sensible fashion in which they would at home.

Bello, Daniel C., and Nicholas C. Williamson. "The American Export Trading Company: Designing a New International Marketing Institution." *Journal of Marketing,* 49 (Fall 1985): 60–69.

To provide guidance to newly-developed trading companies, this article analyzes the relationship between basic operating characteristics and the mix of export services provided by export management companies. The findings suggest that the operating decisions regarding both the type of product exported and the supplier represented have fundamental implications for the export services that American trading companies must be able to provide.

Berkman, Harold W. "Corporate Ethics: Who Cares?" *Journal of the Academy of Marketing Science* (Summer 1977): 154–167.

This article focuses on the ethical problems faced by the U.S. multinational corporations in foreign environments. Particular attention is paid to the issue of bribery as a way of gaining access to foreign markets. The author also addresses the question of whether or not to impose U.S. laws and standards on other countries.

Darling, John R., and Joseph F. Postnikoff. "Strategic Export Information for Small Business." *Journal of Small Business Management,* 23 (October 1985): 28–37.

This article lists several sources of export information from various governmental agencies that can enhance the likelihood of successful foreign marketing.

Dawson, Leslie M. "Marketing to Less Developed Countries." *Journal of Small Business Management,* 23 (October 1985): 13–19.

Smaller companies can capitalize on their unique strengths by marketing to lesser developed countries, which larger firms may have avoided. By being cognizant of host government goals, small firms can take advantage of the profit potential these nations offer.

"Disposable Paper Products in Germany." *Marketing in Europe* (1977): 31–38.

This article provides useful statistics on consumption, production, imports, and exports of paper products in Germany. A major conclusion of the article is that the market for paper products is at saturation level and future growth possibilities are limited.

Douglas, Susan, and Bernard DuBois. "Looking at the Cultural Environment for International Marketing Opportunities." *Columbia Journal of World Business,* 12 (Winter 1977): 102–109.

The purpose of this article is to highlight some of the ways in which cultural factors can influence consumer response patterns, and to illustrate, thereby, the need to consider cultural factors in planning international marketing strategies.

————, C. Samuel Craid, and Warren J. Keegan. "Approaches to Assessing International Marketing Opportunities for Small and Medium-Sized Companies." *Columbia Journal of World Business,* 17 (Fall 1982): 26–32.

This paper examines various approaches to use secondary data to (1) decide which countries or markets merit in-depth investigation, (2) estimate demand potential, and (3) monitor environmental changes. The authors argue that approaches suggested are particularly useful for small and medium-sized companies that may not be able to conduct primary research.

Hester, Susan B. "Export Trading Companies: A Marketing Vehicle for Small Textile and Apparel Firms?" *Journal of Small Business Management,* 23 (October 1985): 20–27.

A study supported the hypothesis that export trading companies can help U.S. textile and apparel manufacturers increase their sales and expand their markets overseas.

Holden, Alfred C. "Small Businesses Can Market in Europe: Results From a Survey of U.S. Exporters." *Journal of Small Business Management,* 24 (January 1986): 22–29.

A survey conducted in 1984 demonstrated that small businesses can export successfully if they are flexible with their in-house marketing-mix fundamentals.

Kennedy, Charles R., Jr. "The External Environment—Strategic Planning Interface: U.S. Multinational Corporate Practices in the 1980s," *Journal of International Business Studies,* 15 (Fall 1984): 99–108.

This paper presents data collected concerning how external environmental analysis and strategic planning are related in major U.S.-based multinational corporations. The research also determined the reasons and the extent to which firms have formally institutionalized the external environmental functions since the Iranian revolution.

es L. Elliott. "U.S. Sale in East-West Trade." *Journal of ness Studies* (Fall/Winter 1977): 5–16.

'e a review of some of the important factors related to U.S. trade. The paper also identifies emerging new forms of trade f East-West trade.

d John W. Zimmerman. "Scanning the International Envi- *ia Management Review,* 22 (Winter 1979): 15–23.

the results of a survey on environmental scanning of mul- both sides of the Atlantic. The authors identify the trouble and explore ways of improving the scanning systems. The the environment for trends, events, and expectations influ- is of businesses.

dener Kaynak. "Marketing Practices in Less-Developed of Business Research,* 12 (1984): 5–18.

historical overview of previously used methods of analyzing pproach consisting of two stages. The first stage consists of ing to their degree of economic development. In the second used to identify the most important research needs of each nore efficient means of development.

itish Market Research Industry." *Journal of the Market 1978): 135–165.*

This paper describes the market research industry in the area of consumer products in Great Britain. The paper analyzes 170 research agencies in terms of services offered, turnover, and number of staff. It also includes a comparison of market research industry in Britain with that in the U.S. and Western Europe. This paper is an excellent reference source.

Van Dam, Andre. "Scarcities, Lifestyles, Waste Management and International Marketing." *European Journal of Marketing,* 12: 306–315.

This article discusses the impact of shortages, the emergence of different lifestyles, and a new international economic order as early warning signals in the business environment. The author stresses the interdependence of scarcities and the market mechanism, and the need for waste management via energy, efficiency and recycling. Modern management is advised to direct their collective advertising campaigns toward the nonwasteful living and consumption styles of the new international and economic order.

Wang, Chih-Kang, and Charles W. Lamb, Jr. "Foreign Environmental Factors Influencing American Consumers' Predispositions Toward European Products." *Journal of the Academy of Marketing Science,* 8 (Fall 1980): 345–356.

This study examines the relationship between U.S. consumers' perceptions regarding (1) the products' country of origin, (2) level of economic development of that country, and (3) the political environment of that country, and their willingness to buy products from these countries. The results of the study reinforce previous studies that show some Americans exhibit a product bias toward products from some foreign countries. Furthermore, Americans' willingness to purchase European-made products can be partially attributed to their varied perceptions of the economic and political environments of the products' country of origin.

"When Free Trade Means Higher Consumer Prices." *Business Week* (September 5, 1977): 61–62.

This article reports the results of a study conducted on the apparel industry, concerning the benefits of free trade. The study concludes that consumers do not necessarily benefit from low-cost imports because retailers, in the absence of price controls, tend to mark up prices to the domestic level, and thus provide support for the protectionist position of domestic textile and apparel producers.

Wind, Yoram, and Susan Douglas. "Some Issues in International Consumer Research." *European Journal of Marketing,* 8: 209–217.

The article focuses on the importance of precise and appropriate investigation of international consumers' needs and wants. The authors suggest that the design of strategies for international marketing operations should be based on this kind of study. The paper suggests that other variables besides the cultural elements (such as social class, group influence, and attitudes) and their interaction with cultural patterns in affecting consumer responses, should also be considered in advancing the quality and utility of international consumer research.

"Wines and Spirits in Austria, Industrial Bread in France, Aperitifs in Italy. Flowers and Plants in Belgium, Blankets and Bedspreads in Italy. Office Furniture in the Netherlands; The Pharmaceutical Market in France, Skin and Face Care Products in the Netherlands." *Marketing in Europe* (July, 1978; August, 1978; September, 1978).

The reports published in July, August, and September, 1978, issues of Marketing in Europe include detailed data on production, consumption, foreign trade, manufacturers and brands, distributions, prices and margins, advertising and promotion, and a trend analysis for each industry. These should be of special interest to exporters and researchers interested in a specific industry abroad.

III. Global Strategic Marketing ——————

Berlew, F. Kingston. "The Joint Venture—A Way Into Foreign Markets." *Harvard Business Review* (July/August 1984): 48, 50, 54.

> *Berlew briefly examines the advantages and disadvantages of entering into a joint venture with a majority or 50-50 foreign partner in an effort to participate in foreign market development. He then offers a few suggestions on how to locate and negotiate with that potential partner.*

Dawson, Leslie M. "Setting Multinational Industrial Marketing Strategies." *Industrial Marketing Management,* 9 (1980): 179–186.

> *This article offers five new models of industrial development as alternatives to the "stages of growth" theory. It also gives several marketing strategies for Multinational Corporations that wish to operate in Less Developed Countries. Finally, an appendix of the Marketing Strategy Profile of each of the five models lists examples of countries, characteristics/development emphasis, an analysis of market opportunities, possible product/service opportunities, and key marketing mix adjustments.*

Holt, John B. "Industrial Corporations in Eastern Europe: Strategies of U.S. Agricultural and Construction Equipment Companies." *Columbia Journal of World Business* (Spring 1977): 80–89.

> *This article focuses on host country pressures faced by U.S. manufacturers of farm and construction equipment in East European markets. The author describes the strategies used by U.S. firms to maintain or expand their markets in these countries.*

Marrell, Gilbert D., and Richard O. Kiefer. "Multinational Strategic Market Portfolios." *MSU Business Topics* (Fall 1981): 5–15.

> *The objective of this article is to present a logical approach to strategic planning for sorting international market environments in such a way that market portfolios rather than product portfolios are emphasized. Ford Motor Company's International Tractor Operations division is used to illustrate key points. Several matrices are developed, showing market portfolios, country attractiveness scale development, competitive strength scale development, and strategic situations in an effort to provide an objective tool to aid in analysis of international markets.*

Shanklin, William L., and John K. Ryans, Jr. "Is the International Cash Cow Really a Prize Heifer?" *Business Horizons,* 24 (March–April 1981): 10–16.

> *This article suggests that the traditional product portfolio analysis, if adopted to take account of the domestic/international dichotomy, can help to insure that the international side of a multinational corporation gets the necessary input and attention to make it a major contributor in the long run.*

Thorelli, Hans B., and Helmut Becker. "The Information Seekers: Multinational Strategy Target." *California Management Review*, 23 (Fall 1980): 46–52.

The authors explore a new concept; the use of the search behavior of consumers in market segmentation strategy in order to segment consumers across national borders of Western industrialized countries. In contrast to the average consumer, the cosmopolitan information seeker actively searches for product information so as to make a wise purchase. This article examines this small but influential group and offers strategic marketing implications for the MNC seeking influence with this market.

Vernon, Raymond. "Gone Are the Cash Cows of Yesteryear." *Harvard Business Review* (November/December 1980): 150–155.

In a climate of pessimism concerning American industry, Vernon offers an optimistic appraisal of the position of U.S. companies in the world market today. Despite America's apparent declining position in industry, their foreign subsidiaries offer them great untapped strength in developing innovations and sharing information. Furthermore, their scientific and technological resources are unsurpassed by any other country. Finally, if Americans will realize and accept that they are faced with a new climate of competition, they will stop trying to produce the newest, most unusual products, and concentrate on having the best price, quality, and after-sales service.

Wortzel, Lawrence H. "Marketing to Firms in Developing Asian Countries." *Industrial Marketing Management*, 12 (1983): 113–123.

The objective of this article is to show potential sellers what strategies they might use to market to Asian Newly Industrialized Countries and, in the future, to Asian LDCs. Information is presented from firms in three Asian NICs and two Asian developing countries. First, the general technological background of these firms is explored in order to show the nature of products demanded. Second, a buyer behavior analysis contains decision processes, choice criteria, and buying center organization. Finally, these firms are compared with firms in advanced, industrialized countries, and marketing strategy implications are discussed.

IV. Cross Cultural Consumer Behavior _____

Becker, Helmut, and David J. Fritzsche. "Energy Consumption and Marketing: A Comparison of German and American Life Style." *Proceedings/AMA 1776–1976:* 527–532.

This article explores the marketing opportunities and responsibilities to contribute to and stimulate energy conservation as a means to help alleviate energy shortages. The authors compare the energy consumption patterns in the residential sectors of Germany and the United States. Exploring the areas of potential energy savings will present the marketer with a formidable challenge to contribute to and stimulate energy conservation in the consumer sector.

Douglas, Susan P., and Christine D. Urban. "Life-Style Analysis to Profile Women in International Markets." *Journal of Marketing* (July 1977): 46–54.

The article attempts to determine whether standardized marketing strategies can be used throughout the world, and how far they need to be adapted to specific countries or market segments. The question of standardizing versus adapting strategies is discussed. It focuses on the studies of women in the U.S., the U.K. and France, in order to illustrate how life-style research can be used in examining strategic issues in international marketing.

Ehrenberg, A. S. C., and G. J. Goodhart. "A Comparison of American and British Repeat-Buying Habits." *Journal of Marketing Research* 5 (February 1968): 29–33.

The repeat-buying habits for branded non-durable consumer goods in America are compared with those in Great Britain. The NBD/LSD theory of stationary purchasing behavior, based on the Negative Binomial and Logarithmic Series Distributions is used to summarize the repeat-buying patterns in this study.

Hempel, Donald J. "Family Buying Decisions: A Cross-Cultural Perspective." *Journal of Marketing Research,* 11 (August 1974): 295–302.

The cross-cultural comparisons of husband-wife interaction in specific house-buying decisions were studied through a series of questions about the relative importance of each spouse in specific decisions at different steps in the house-buying process. The results indicated that perceived roles vary more by sex and stage in the decision process than by the cultural context of the purchase.

Partanen, Juha. "On National Consumption Profiles." *European Research* (January 1979): 27–39.

This article examines the issue of globalization versus uniqueness of consumption by utilizing data on possession and use of a wide range of products and services across sixteen Western European countries. Factorial structure of consumption pattern is examined. The results indicate that three factors explain much of the variation in consumption level of various items. The first two factors are seen as explaining consumption phenomenon along sociocultural dimensions.

Plummer, Joseph T. "Consumer Focus In Cross-National Research." *Journal of Advertising,* 6 (Spring 1977): 5–15.

The author points out the importance of cross-national research and marketing to multi-national marketers in developing relevant strategies and executions for each market. Two major constructs, "Life-style" research and "three analytic models," are explored. The "Life style" construct measures the activities, interests, opinions, and basic characteristics which comprise the everyday living patterns of people. The second construct discusses three models for analyzing life style data crossnationally.

Schaninger, Charles M., Jacques C. Bourgeois, and W. Christian Buss. "French-English Canadian Subcultural Consumption Differences." *Journal of Marketing,* 49 (Spring 1985): 82–92.

Consumption differences were examined between French-speaking, bilingual, and English-speaking Canadian families from the greater Ottawa/Hull metropolitan area. Significant differences were found for a wide variety of consumption behaviors, media usage, and durable goods ownership. These differences remained, even after the removal of social class and income.

Urban, Christine D. "Life-Style Patterns of Women: United States and United Kingdom," paper presented at the American Academy of Advertising Conference Knoxville, Tennessee, April 20,1975.

The article describes the importance of life-style analysis, combining demographic, psychographic, media usage, and product usage data into descriptive consumer profiles for effective and realistic multinational marketing.

V. Global Product Policies _____

Anderson, Ronald D., and Jack L. Engledow. "Perceived Importance of Selected Product Information Sources in Two Time Periods by United States and West German Consumers." *Journal of Business Research,* 9 (December 1981): 339–351.

This article focuses on the perceived use of various types of information sources in the purchase of a major durable good in the U.S. and West Germany. The authors used time (two different time periods), country and age as explanatory variables; they used type of information source as response variables. Using a logit model, the authors concluded that product testing in combination with peer group as an information source had the highest probability of use and that its importance has increased over time. Also, it was found that advertising had a higher probability of use in the U.S. than in Germany.

Ayal, Igal. "International Product Life Cycle: A Reassessment and Product Policy Implications." *Journal of Marketing,* 45 (Fall 1981): 91–96.

This study focuses on certain aspects of the IPLC theory from the perspective of Israeli export performance. The data show the best overall performance occurs in the early stages of IPLC while the worst performance occurs in the middle stage, exactly opposite the predictions of the first hypothesis. The findings did, however, support the second hypothesis, which states that early stage success can only take place through narrow specialization of projects.

Cattirs, Philippe J., Alain Jolibert, and Colleen Lohnes. "A Cross-Cultural Study of 'Made In' Concepts." *Journal of International Business Studies,* 13 (Winter 1982): 131–141.

This article replicates and extends previous investigations of the "made-in" concept.

Chadraba, Peter, and Robert O'Keefe. "Cross-National Product Value Perceptions." *Journal of Business Research,* 9 (December 1981): 329–337.

The authors used a psychographic variable—value perceptions of a product—to examine similarities and differences across national boundaries. Using student respondents in four countries (the U.S., Switzerland, France, and Austria), the authors found similarities in value perception bridging national boundaries.

Friedmann, Roberto. "Psychological Meaning of Products: A Simplification of the Standardization vs. Adoptation Debate." *Columbia Journal of World Business,* 21 (Summer 1986): 97–104.

The psychological meaning that consumers derive from and ascribe to products can simplify the debate over whether or not one ought to standardize or adopt international marketing strategies. With theoretical support from a variety of disciplines, the psychological meaning of products is argued to provide decision makers with a diagnostic tool from which strategic marketing choices can be derived.

Narayana, Chem L. "Aggregate Images of American and Japanese Products: Implications on International Marketing." *Columbia Journal of World Business* (Summer 1981): 31–35.

This article presents the results of a study which used semantic differential responses to set of attitudinal variables in order to identify a composite "made-in" image for U.S. and Japanese products as perceived by U.S. and Japanese consumers. Clearly, an understanding of the relationship between advertising and perceptions in an intercultural context would greatly enhance our ability to position U.S. products in a desired manner.

Niffeneger, Phillip, John White, and Guy Marmet. "How European Retailers View American Imported Products: Results of a Product Image Survey." *Journal of the Academy of Marketing Science,* 10 (Summer 1982): 281–282.

The authors surveyed 163 retail store managers in Britain and France to study their attitudes toward American products. Each respondent was asked to rate American products in six consumer product categories on a number of image dimensions. Impli-

cations of the findings for U.S. firms interested in British and French markets are also discussed.

Terpstra, Vern. "International Product Policy: The Role of Foreign R & D." *The Columbia Journal of World Business* (Winter 1977): 24–32.

This article discusses basic reasons for centralizing the R & D function domestically. About 10% of U.S multinational firms' R & D is foreign-based. The main reasons for localization of R & D are also discussed in this paper.

_____. "On Marketing Appropriate Products in Developing Countries." *Journal of International Marketing,* 1 (1981): 3–15.

The author suggests that "product appropriateness" is a key factor from the perspective of LDC governments to allow MNCs to participate in LDC markets. On the other hand, MNCs must strike a balance between "product appropriateness" and "corporate appropriateness." The author suggests a number of recommendations for multinational product policy.

Ting, Wenlee. "The Product Development Process in NIC Multinationals." *Columbia Journal of World Business,* 17 (Spring 1982): 76–81.

This article investigates the product development practices in the multinationals based in newly industrialized countries and points to the fact that American firms should understand the nature of competition in these "mini-Japans" in the future.

VI. Global Promotion Policies _____

Boddewyn, J. J. "Advertising Regulations in the 1980s: The Underlying Global Forces." *Journal of Marketing,* 46 (Winter 1982): 27–35.

The central theme of this paper is that consumer protection, as the major rationale for the regulations of advertising, will take novel forms and emphases in the 1980s. The author discusses these new forms in terms of 12 major regulatory forces that must be closely monitored.

Colvin, Michael, Roger Heeler, and Jim Thorpe. "Developing International Advertising Strategy." *Journal of Marketing,* 44 (Fall 1980): 73–79.

This article describes how Ford of Europe implemented a "pattern standardization" approach to new car advertising in Europe. This system employs comparisons of consumer preferences (measured by tradeoff analysis) with consumer perceptions of new and existing products. Thus, it will provide an effective means of segmenting promotional strategies for international markets, by allowing for cross-country differences in product perceptions and product attribute preferences. The results appear to be of reasonable validity, and the costs appear to be in proportion to the benefits derived.

Hornik, Jacob. "Comparative Evaluation of International vs. National Advertising Strategies." *Columbia Journal of World Business,* 15 (Spring 1980): 36–48.

This paper investigates the standardization dilemma by focusing on (1) the theoretical discussion on the controversy, (2) a pilot study comparing American-made ads and Israeli-made ads for the same American products promoted in Israel, and (3) differences in strategy and creativity approaches and forces that might create disparity.

————, and Steven C. Rubinow. "Expert-Respondents' Synthesis for International Advertising Research." *Journal of Advertising Research,* 21 (June 1981): 9–17.

The objective of this article is to show that cross-national research must be approached differently from domestic research. A discussion of the advantages of Experts/ Small Sample Size (ESSS) is followed by an analysis of the Bayesian Algorithm for decision making. An illustrative study shows the use of ESSS in an international advertising-decision process. ESSS can be considered an economical and reliable method for decision making.

Killough, James. "Improved Payoffs from Transnational Advertising." *Harvard Business Review* (July/August 1978): 102–110.

This paper reports the result of in-depth interviews with senior managers of multinational companies, concerning the transferability of advertising resources from one country to another. The author makes a strong case for an international advertising strategy that is geared to global markets rather than a domestic approach that requires constant adjustment for each foreign market. In a global approach, the idea content can normally be retained, but, due to cultural, competitive, legislative, and other unique factors, the creative aspect needs adaptations.

Kaynak, Erdener, and Lionel A. Mitchell. "Analysis of Marketing Strategies Used in Diverse Cultures." *Journal of Advertising Research,* 21 (June 1981): 25–32.

The purpose of this paper is to discuss Canadian, British, and Turkish communication practices, and the probable problems international companies may encounter in communicating with consumers in the respective countries. It is given in an effort to gain more insight and understanding of the facets of international communications practices. It is hoped that international marketers will recognize the advantages of tailoring their communications messages to local needs.

Leff, Nathaniel H., and John V. Farley. "Advertising Expenditures in the Developing World." *Journal of International Business Studies,* 11 (Fall 1980): pp. 64–79.

This paper discusses the attributes of developing countries' marketing character-
istics as they relate to advertising optimizations and public policy decisions in LDCs.
In addition, the authors provide an international comparison of levels of advertising
expenditures in both developing and LDCs.

Peebles, D. M., J. K. Ryans, and I. R. Vernon. "A New Perspective on Advertising
    Standardizations." *European Journal of Marketing* (1977): 566–576.

This paper focuses on the well-known problem of standardized versus unique
approach to advertising in multinational markets. The authors suggest a compromise
solution and discuss a number of factors that affect the implementation of the proposed
approach.

Rich, Tom, David Owens, and Irving Ellenbogen. "What Canadians Dislike About
    TV Commercials." *Journal of Advertising Research,* 18 (December 1978): 37–
    44.

This article reports the results of a survey concerning the attitudes of Canadians
with respect to Canadian TV broadcasting. The result indicated that commercial ad-
vertising is viewed negatively.

Robinson, Deanna Campbell. "Changing Functions of Mass Media in the People's
    Republic of China." *Journal of Communications,* 31 (Autumn 1981): 58–73.

The author focuses on the role of media in China, comparing the traditional role
with that of an emerging pattern which may one day be indistinguishable from the role
played by media in Western societies.

Still, Richard Ralph. "Sales Management: Some Cross-Cultural Aspects." *Journal of*
    Personal Selling & Sales Management (Summer 1981): 6–9.

The purpose of this article is to examine several aspects of sales management
from a cross-cultural perspective. These are ethnocentrism and polycentrism, developing
a sales force cross-culturally, sales job descriptions for internal use, and sales training
in a cross-cultural context. Dr. Still then offers four suggestions which should facilitate
a general broadening of sales management, both cross-culturally and micro-culturally.

Wills, James R., Jr., and John K. Ryans, Jr. "Attitudes Toward Advertising: A Mul-
    tinational Study." *Journal of International Business Studies,* 13 (Winter 1982):
    121–129.

This paper reports the results of a study concerning advertising's role in society.
An international sample of managers, academicians, students, and consumerists re-
vealed contrasting views on the subject, particularly on the value of advertising as an
information source. The authors suggest that more research regarding the role of ad-
vertising on a multi-national basis is needed.

VII. Global Distribution Policies _____

Anderson, Erin, and Anne T. Coughlan. "International Market Entry and Expansion via Independent or Integrated Channels of Distribution." *Journal of Marketing*, 51 (1987): 71–82.

This article examines the issue of downstream vertical integration through an empirical investigation of distribution channel choice in foreign markets by U.S. semiconductor companies. The results of the study and implications for managers faced with a channel choice are discussed.

Delagneau, Bernard. "Some Influences of EEC Competition Policy Upon Marketing and Distribution Service Requirements." *European Journal of Marketing* (1977): 390–405.

Recent EEC legislation on marketing policy within EEC countries is the focus of this paper. The author discusses the impact on firms which try to set up exclusive or selective distribution networks in EEC market areas.

Goldman, Arieh. "Adoption of Supermarket Shopping in a Developing Country: The Selective Adoption Phenomenon." *European Journal of Marketing*, 16 (1982): 17–26.

This study analyzes issues involved in the introduction of the supermarket into Israel, a developing country. Tables show the adoption patterns and group differences in adoption of supermarket shopping. Results show the existence of both "joint" and "dual" patterns in Jerusalem. About 51.1% of the respondents use both supermarkets and traditional food retail outlets, 35.7% use only the traditional stores, and 13.2% use only supermarkets for their food needs.

Kaynak, Erdener, and S. Tamer Carusgil. "The Evaluation of Food Retailing Systems: Contrasting the Experience of Developed and Developing Countries." *Journal of the Academy of Marketing Science*, 10 (Summer 1982): 249–268.

This article reviews and contrasts the evolution of food retailing systems in urban parts of developed and developing economies. It examines the relationship between these systems and prevailing shopping patterns, as well as economic, social, and cultural factors. Discussion of food retailing trends, origins of the modern food store, self-service stores, and supermarkets are also included. The authors conclude by giving implications for public policy and future research.

Rosson, Philip J., and I. David Ford. "Stake, Conflict, and Performance in Export Marketing Channels." *Management International Review*, 20 (1980): 31–37.

The major concern of this paper is to examine conflict in export manufacturer-distributor relationships and the degree of association between conflict and (1) the stake of the manufacturer in the relationship, and (2) the performance of the channel in question. Several hypotheses are tested, using a sample of Canadian manufacturing companies exporting industrial goods to the U.K.

Shimaguchi, Mitsuaki, and William Lazer. "Japanese Distribution Channels; Invisible Barriers to Market Entry." *MVS Business Topics,* 27 (Winter 1979): 49–60.

The authors examine sociocultural characteristics of the Japanese distribution system. The authors view the system as inefficient and a barrier to entry into the Japanese market. Implications for American businesses are discussed.

Takeuchi, Nirotaka, and Louis Bucklin. "Productivity in Retailing: Retail Structure and Public Policy." *Journal of Retailing,* 53 (Spring 1977): 35–46.

This article focuses on the structure of retailing in the U.S. and Japan and the factors that affect retail productivity in the two countries. The authors suggest that three sets of factors play a major role in determining the retail structure: (1) the personal wealth of the society, (2) the level of technology employed by the retail sector, and (3) the degree of competition among retailers.

The above forces were operationalized and used as independent variables in a regression analysis to examine their effect on retail structure in each couuntry separately. Differences between the two countries are discussed and implications for public policy are suggested.

Yavas, Ugur, Erdener Kaynak, and Eser Borak. "Retailing Institutions in Developing Countries: Determinants of Supermarket Patronage in Istanbul, Turkey." *Journal of Business Research,* 9 (December 1981): 367–379.

The purpose of this study was to identify the determinants of supermarket patronage in Istanbul, Turkey. The study utilized a random sample of 200 female shoppers, evenly divided between supermarket and nonsupermarket shoppers. The authors compared supermarket and nonsupermarket shoppers in terms of socioeconomic and demographic characteristics, shopping habits, and life style patterns.